Olympiad Champs

LOGICAL REASONING

Class 2

with **Chapter-wise Previous**
5 Year (2018 - 2022) Questions

DISHA™
Publication Inc

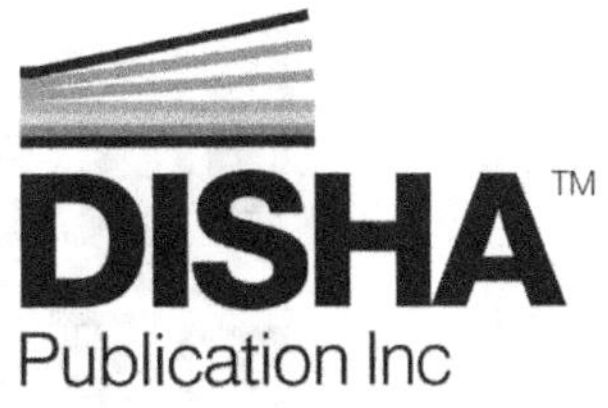

DISHA Publications Inc.

45, 2nd Floor, Maharishi Dayanand Marg,
Corner Market, Malviya Nagar, new Delhi -110017
Tel: 49842349/ 49842350

Typeset By

DISHA DTP Team

Preface

We are pleased to launch the 2nd edition of **Olympiad Champs Logical Reasoning Class 2** which is the first of its kind book on Olympiad in many ways.

The Unique Selling Proposition of this new edition is the inclusion of past year questions till 2022 of different Olympiad exams held in schools.

The book is aimed at achieving not only success but deep rooted learning in children. It is prepared on content based on National Curriculum Framework prescribed by NCERT. All the text books, syllabi and teaching practices within the education programme in India must follow NCF. Hence, Olympiad Champs become an ideal book not only for the Olympiad Exams but also for strengthening the concepts for Class 2.

There is an exhaustive range of thought provoking questions in MCQ format to test the student's knowledge thoroughly. The questions are designed so as to test the knowledge, comprehension, evaluation, analytical and application skills. Solutions and explanations are provided for all questions. The questions are divided into two levels - Level 1 and Level 2. The first level, Level 1, is the beginner's level which comprises of questions like fillers, analogy and odd one out. When the child covers Level 1, it means his basic knowledge about the subject is clear and now it is ready for Level 2. The second level is the advanced level. Level 2 comprises of techniques like matching, chronological sequencing, picture, passage and feature based, statement correct/ incorrect, integer based, puzzle, grid based, crossword, venn diagram, table/ chart based and much more.

The first concern which each parent faces is how to make their children read a book especially when it is based on academics. Keeping this in mind interesting facts, real life examples, historical preview, short cut to problem solving, charts, diagrams, illustrations and poems are added. In addition to this, we have introduced comic strip which increases the readability quotient and make the reading experience for the children more exciting.

With the vision to remove all the misconception a child may have pertaining to the subject, to relate his knowledge to the real world and to develop a deeper understanding of the subject this book will cater all the requirements of the students who are going to appear in Olympiads.

While preparing this book, some errors might have crept in. We request our readers to identify those errors and send it across on **feedback_disha@aiets.co.in.**

We wish you all the best for your Olympiads and happy reading.......

Team Disha

For feedback : feedback_disha@aiets.co.in.

CONTENTS

10 Principles to CRACK ANY EXAM

1. Chase consistency, not intensity.

Doing intensive study makes your day. But it also exhausts you in the long run, leading to lesser output and added pressure. Toppers always focus on doing consistent work daily, for consistency is far more valuable than intensity.

Remember consistent study of 4 hours every day is more important and powerful than studying 12 hours a day and then not studying at all for next 2 days.

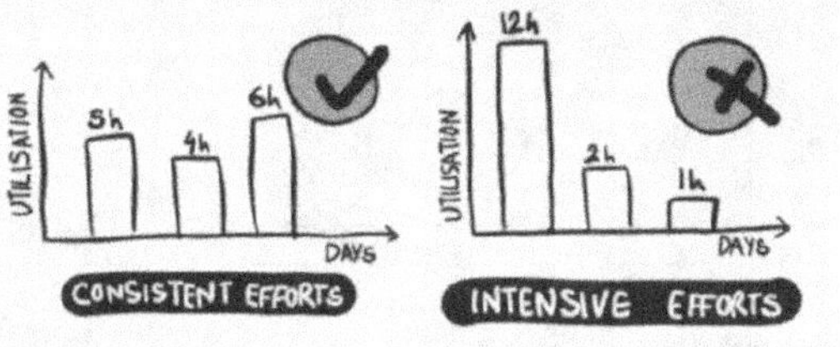

2. Go beyond the surface.

Most students only see a few reasons (teacher, coaching, books, etc) behind Toppers' success, which is only the tip of the iceberg. What they donot see is Toppers Mindset, self belief, habits and discipline and that is where the real problem is.

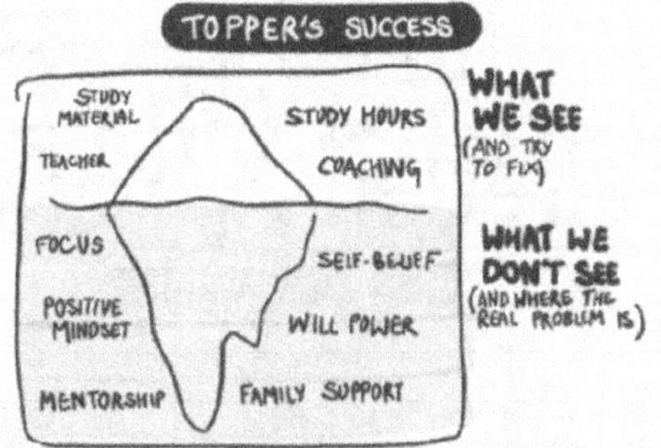

3. Focus on giving your best, not chasing the best.

We want the best coaching, the best teacher, best batch and the best books but we are not ready to give our BEST. Success comes only when we are ready to give our best. We must focus on giving our best than chasing excuses to cover up our failures.

4. Clarity of concept is the key

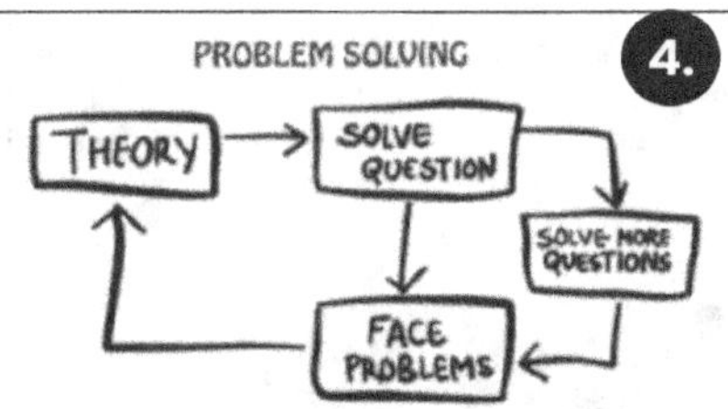

Concept clarity is critical. If you cannot solve a question, you must go back to the theory and thoroughly examine the concept instead of referring to the solutions. Remember question is one of the chehra(face) of the concept. When toppers get stuck in a problem, they go back and refer the theory(read the concept again and again on which the question is based)

5. Every failure should be a lesson learned.

Most students do not learn from their failures and repeat their mistakes. Toppers also face failures, but they learn from mistakes and elevate themselves. Making mistakes and learning from them is the key to success.

6 Choosing the quality of resources is more important than quantity.

More than 90% of the questions in most books are the same as their substitutes. Instead of practicing from four books and failing to complete them, it is best to prepare from two books and complete them with thorough revisions.

7

Difficult things become easy by taking it one day at a time.

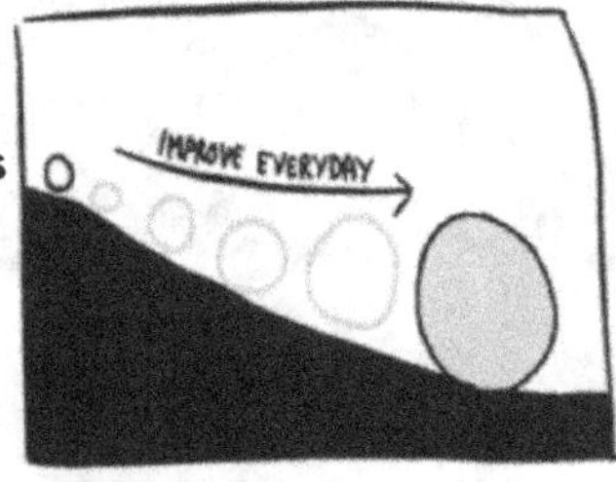

The best way to take any preparation forward is by taking it one day at a time. It makes the impossible possible by taking small steps every day.

Starting a difficult subject. No worries. Keep on working session by session, day by day and week by week and one day you will become unstoppable force.

8. Everything is easy

Before starting everything looks difficult. Once you take a first step, it slowly starts looking easy and over a period of time you become master in the activity. This is toppers secret to become master in any subject.

9. Nobody is gifted

We think toppers are god gifted. We think toppers have high IQ. We think toppers are special/lucky. But the truth is every topper was once an average student(no body is born topper). What makes them different is their consistent and focused efforts

10. Believe in your journey and success will come to you.

There is never a straight path to success; hard work & patience is required for the results to show up. Keep on working hard without thinking too much about the results and success will come to you eventually.

Past Year Olympiad Questions (2018-2022)

Chapter-1 : Analogy

Level-1

1. Which of the following is exactly same as the given figure? (2021)

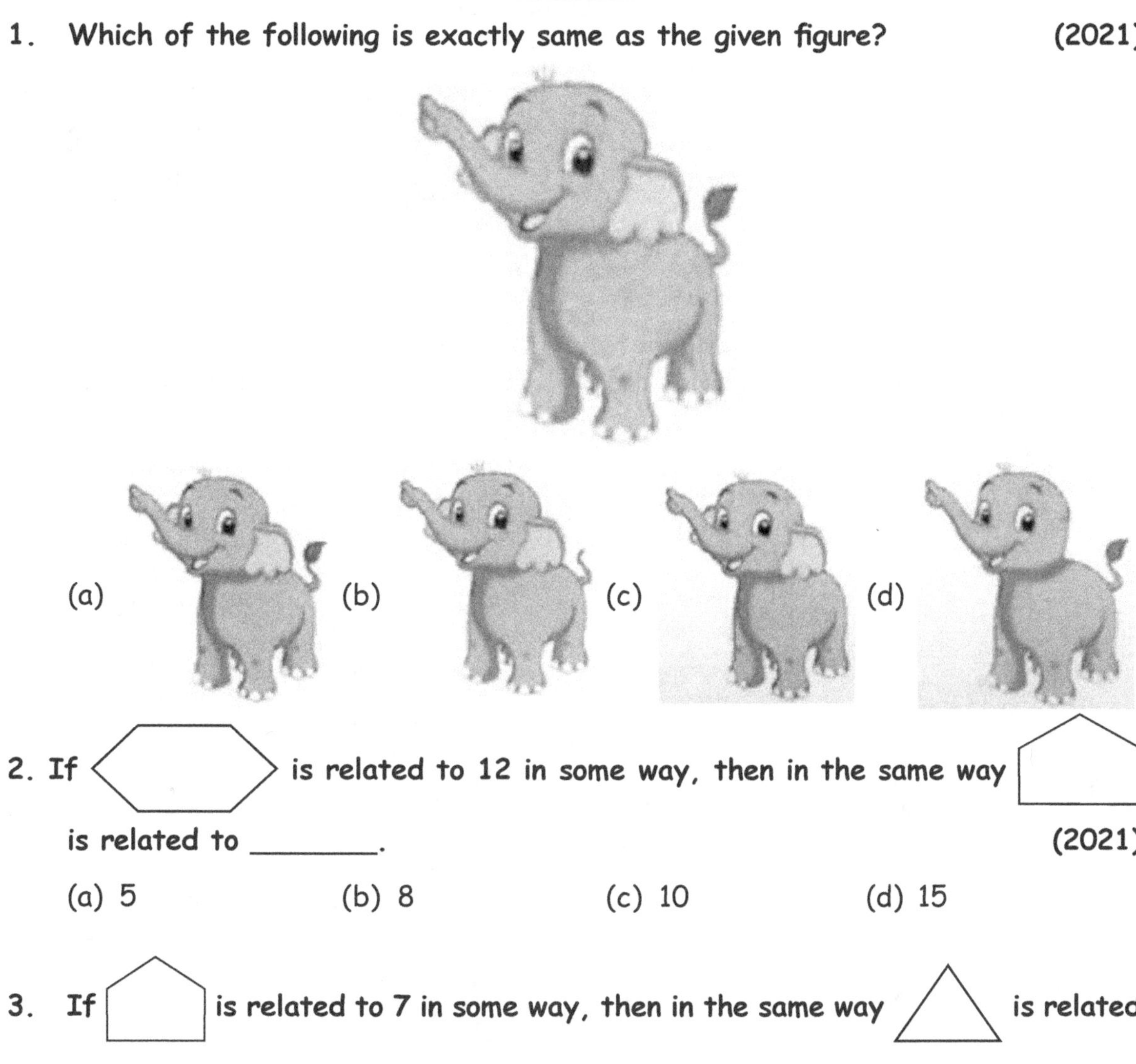

(a) (b) (c) (d)

2. If [figure] is related to 12 in some way, then in the same way [figure] is related to ________. (2021)

(a) 5 (b) 8 (c) 10 (d) 15

3. If [figure] is related to 7 in some way, then in the same way [figure] is related to ____________. (2022)

(a) 5 (b) 3 (c) 7 (d) 6

4. Which of the following figures is exactly same as the given figure? (2022)

(a) (b) (c) (d)

Level-2

5. There is a certain relationship between the pair of figures on either side of ::. Identify the relationship between the left pair and find the missing figure.

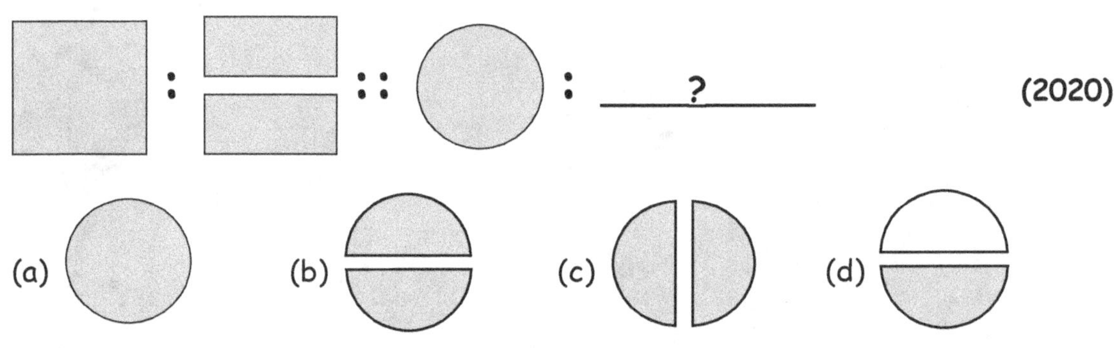

(2020)

Chapter-2: Patterns

Level-1

6. Study the patterns 1, 2 and 3. Using the same pattern, tell the number of ball in Pattern 6. (2018)

Pattern 1 Pattern 2 Pattern 3

(a) 16 (b) 10 (c) 14 (d) 19

7. Study the pattern 1, 2 and 3. Using the same pattern, tell the number of mice in Pattern 6. (2019)

Pattern 1  Pattern 2  Pattern 3

(a) 15 (b) 12 (c) 13 (d) 20

8. 5 groups of - bottles each can be formed from the given bottles. (2019)

(a) 4 (b) 5 (c) 6 (d) 8

9. ______________ groups of three mangoes each can be formed from the given mangoes. (2020)

(a) 4 (b) 5 (c) 6 (d) 8

10. Which of the following figures will complete the given figure pattern? (2020)

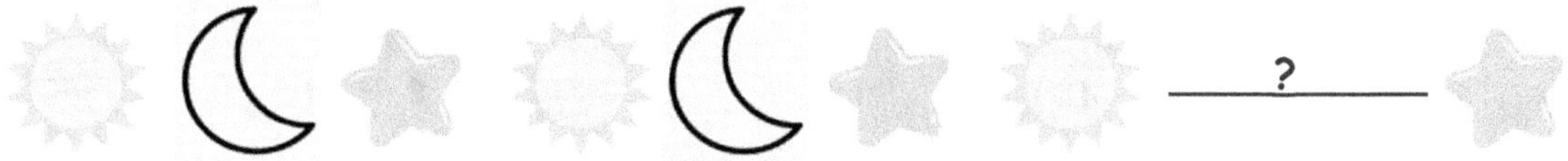

_____?_____

(a)  (b) (c)  (d) Can't say

11. How many groups of 5 necklaces each can be formed from the given necklaces?

(2021)

(a) 5 (b) 4 (c) 6 (d) 3

12. Find the missing figure to complete the given figure pattern. (2021)

13. Find the missing number, if same rule is followed in all the three figures.

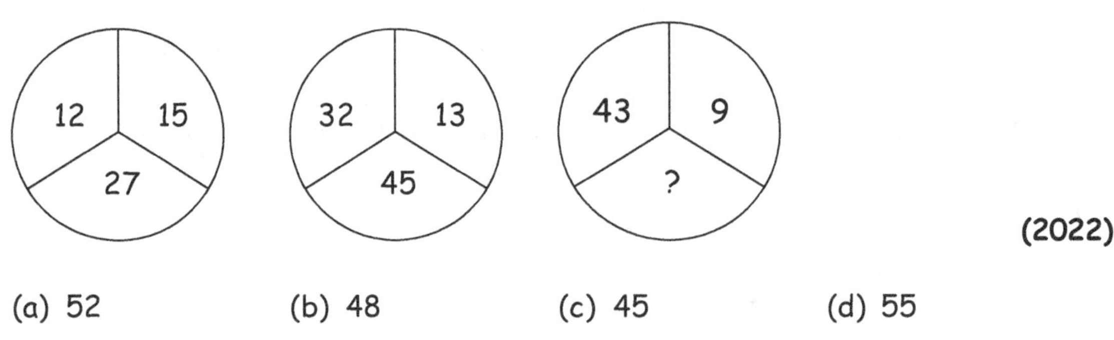

(2022)

(a) 52 (b) 48 (c) 45 (d) 55

14. 3 groups of ____________ crayons each can be formed from the given crayons.

(2022)

(a) 3 (b) 4 (c) 5 (d) 6

Level-2

15. Study the given pattern and tell the number of balloons in Pattern 5. (2020)

Pattern 1 Pattern 2 Pattern 3

(a) 12 (b) 15 (c) 10 (d) 16

Chapter-3: Sequence

Level-1

16. How many burgers are there in each group, if 4 groups of equal number of burgers are formed from the given burgers? (2018)

(a) 4 (b) 5 (c) 6 (d) 8

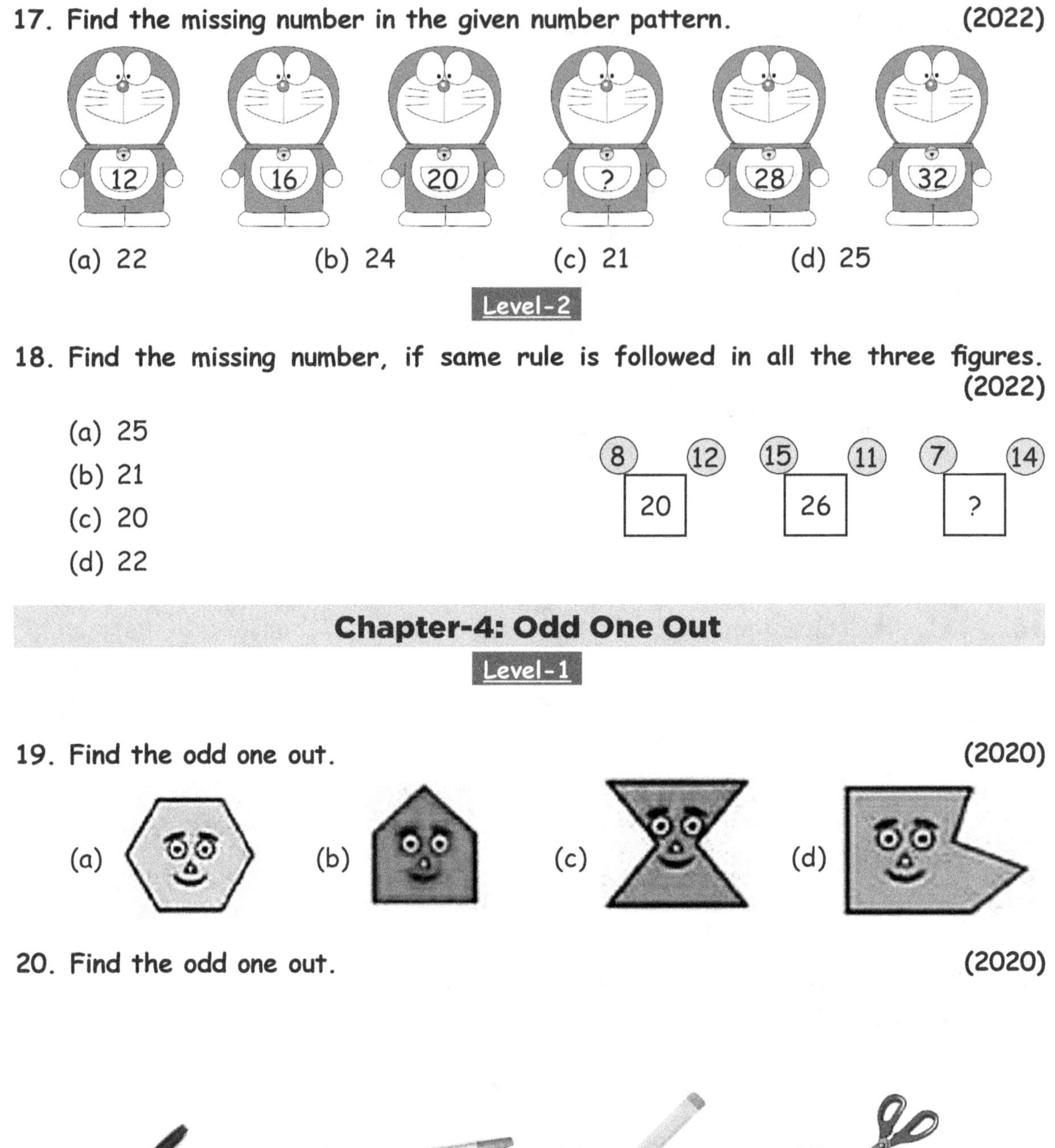

17. Find the missing number in the given number pattern. (2022)

(a) 22 (b) 24 (c) 21 (d) 25

Level-2

18. Find the missing number, if same rule is followed in all the three figures. (2022)

(a) 25
(b) 21
(c) 20
(d) 22

Chapter-4: Odd One Out

Level-1

19. Find the odd one out. (2020)

(a) (b) (c) (d)

20. Find the odd one out. (2020)

(a) (b) (c) (d)

21. Select the odd one out. (2022)

(a) 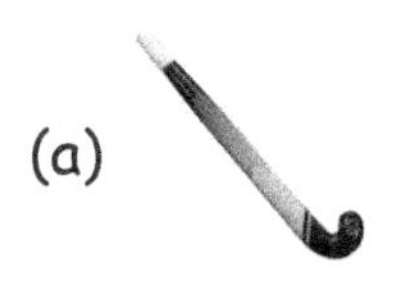 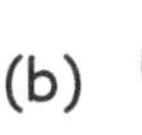 (b)  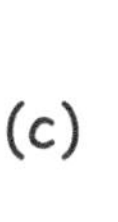 (c)  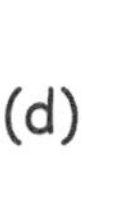 (d) 

22. Select the odd one out. (2022)

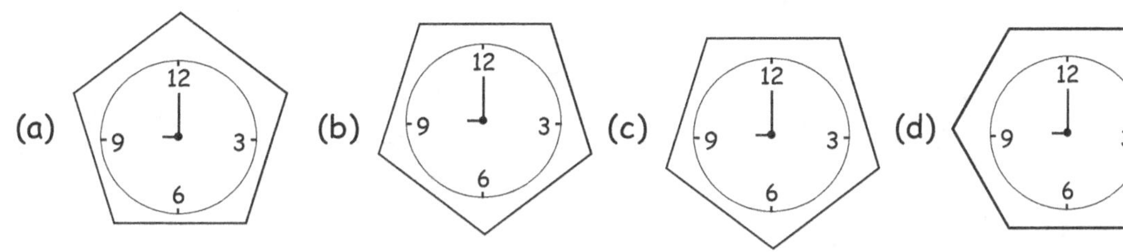

Chapter-5: Position / Ranking Test

Level-1

23. Which of the following is 4th to the left of T? (2018)

(left) P Q R S T U V W (Right)

(a) P (b) W (c) Q (d) V

24. If [comb] is called [mirrors] is called [hairband] and [hairband] is called [ring] then we can see our face in ___________. (2019)

(a)  (b)  (c)  (d) 

25. If toy duck K and M are removed from the given arrangement, then toy duck - is third from the left end. (2020)

P Q K S J T M O R (Right)

(a)  J (b)  S (c)  K (d)  M

26. Monkey ________ is third to the left of second monkey from the right end.

(Left) K M T U P S L J

(2020)

(a) S (b) P (c) U (d) M

27. Toy horse __________ is fourth from the right end in the given arrangement.

(Right) P Q R S M U T V W (Left)

(2021)

(a) U (b) S (c) M (d) T

28. Which of the following boats is second to the right of fourth boat from the left end? (2022)

P Q R S T U V (Right)

(a) S (b) U (c) T (d) Q

29. Hen __________ is third to the left of fourth hen from the right end in the given arrangement. (2022)

(a) L (b) M (c) O (d) K

30. Ribbon badge _________ is fourth from the right end. (2022)

(a) R (b) S (c) O (d) I

Chapter-6: Coding Decoding

Level-1

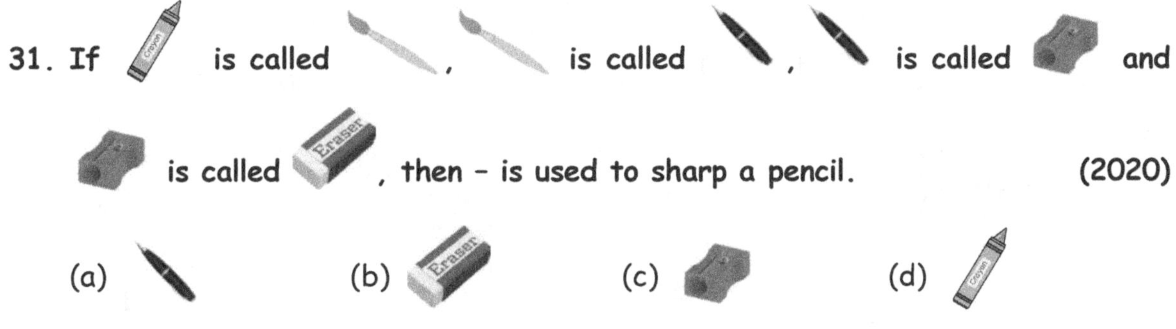

31. If [crayon] is called [brush], [brush] is called [pen], [pen] is called [sharpener] and [sharpener] is called [eraser], then – is used to sharp a pencil. (2020)

(a) [pen] (b) [eraser] (c) [sharpener] (d) [crayon]

32. If 'Doctor' is called 'Teacher', 'Teacher' is called 'Chef' and 'Chef' is called 'Barber', then _______ cooks food for us. (2022)

(a) Doctor (b) Chef (c) Barber (d) Teacher

33. If [envelope] is called [nail cutter], [nail cutter] is called [lipstick] and [lipstick] is called [bulb], then ________ is used to cut nails. (2022)

(a) (b) (c) (d)

Chapter-7: Spatial Understanding

Level-2

34. In how many different ways the dog can reach the dog house? (2021)

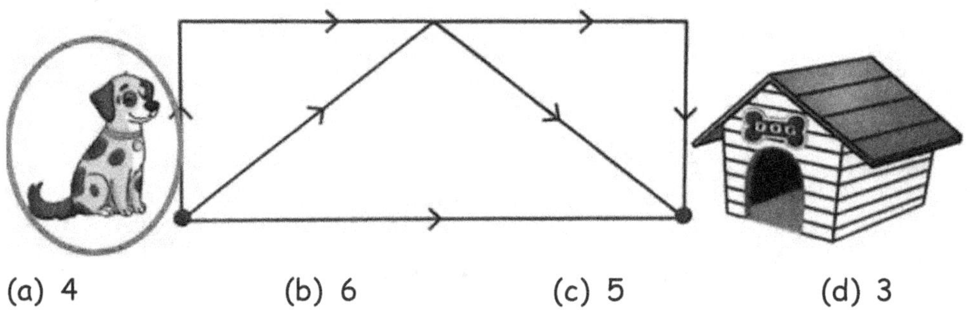

(a) 4 (b) 6 (c) 5 (d) 3

Chapter-8: Geometrical Shapes

Level-1

35. Which of the following figures does not have any curved line? (2019)

(a) (b) (c) (d)

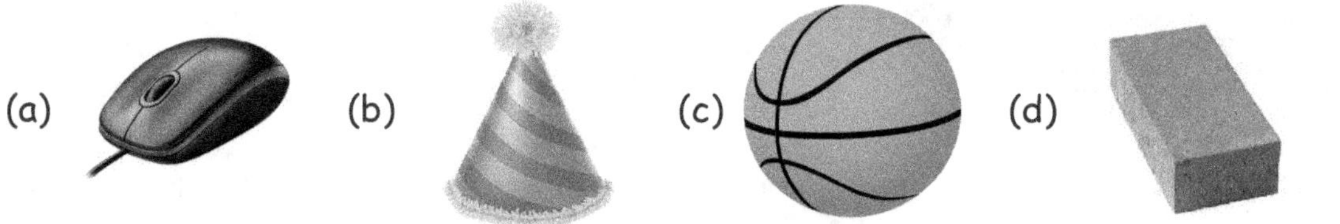

36. How many triangles are there in the given box? (2020)

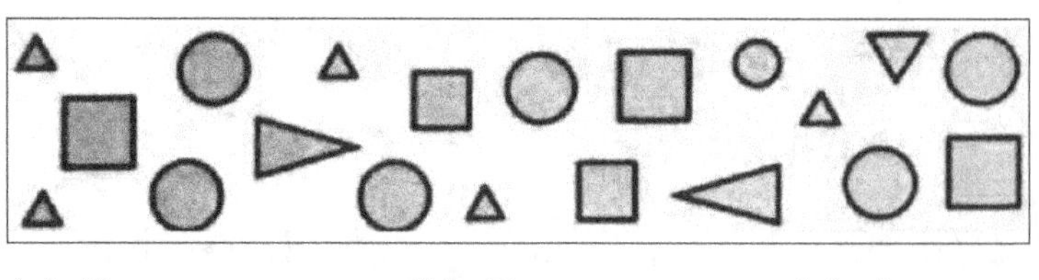

(a) 5 (b) 7 (c) 6 (d) 8

37. Select a figure from the options in which the given figure is exactly embedded as one of its parts. **(2021)**

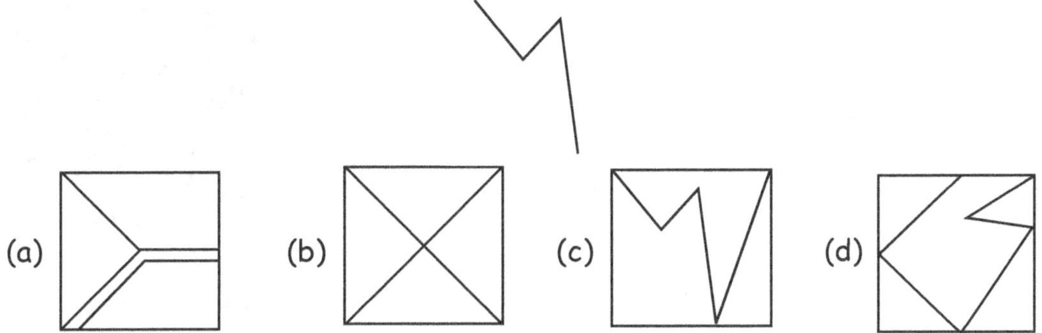

38. If 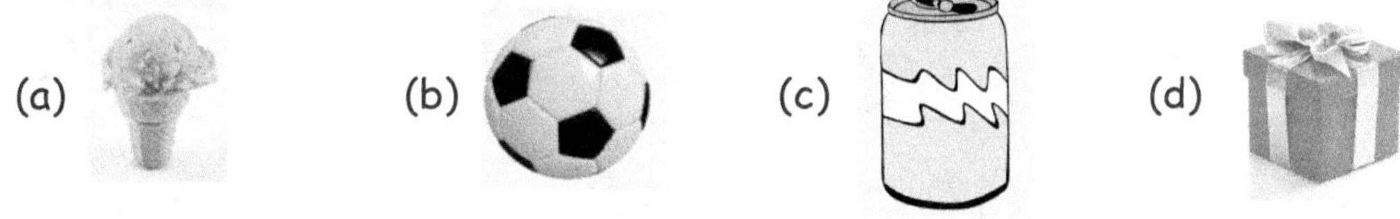 **is related to ____.** **(2022)**

(a) (b) (c) (d)

Level-2

39. How many circles are there in the given figure? **(2018)**

(a) 30 (b) 20 (c) 16 (d) 28

40. Find the number of triangles in the given figure. (2020)

(a) 8

(b) 10

(c) 9

(d) 11

41. There are __________ triangles and __________ squares in the given figures.

(2021)

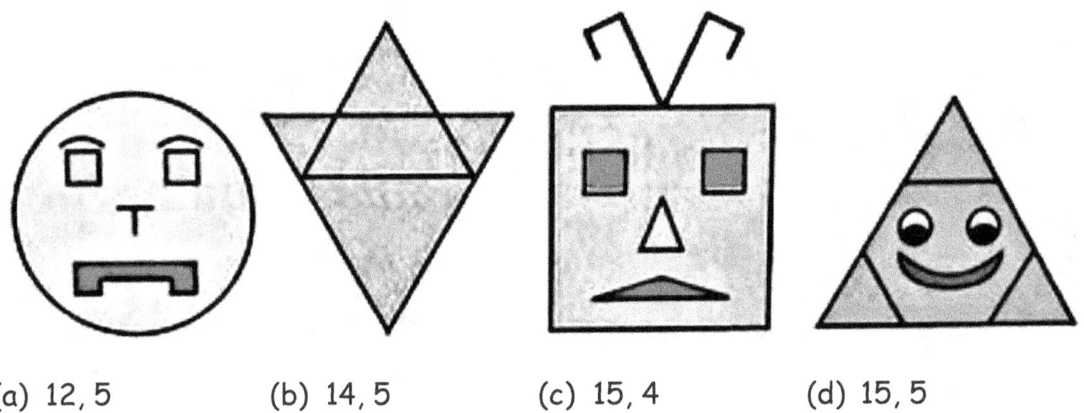

(a) 12, 5 (b) 14, 5 (c) 15, 4 (d) 15, 5

42. Which of the following shapes is NOT present in the given figure? (2022)

(a) Circle

(b) Triangle

(c) Square

(d) Rectangle

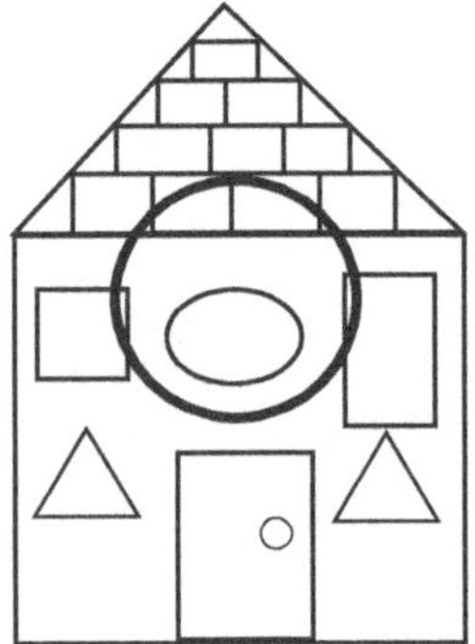

Chapter-9: Embedded Figure

Level-1

43. In which of the following figures, given figure is exactly embedded as one of its parts? (2022)

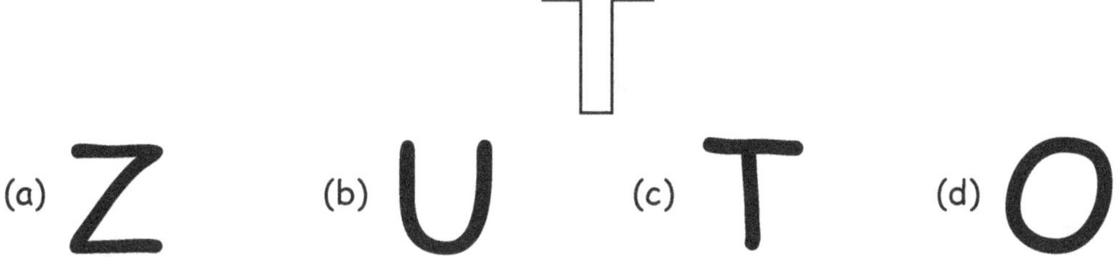

44. Select a figure from the options in which the given figure is exactly embedded as one of its parts. (2022)

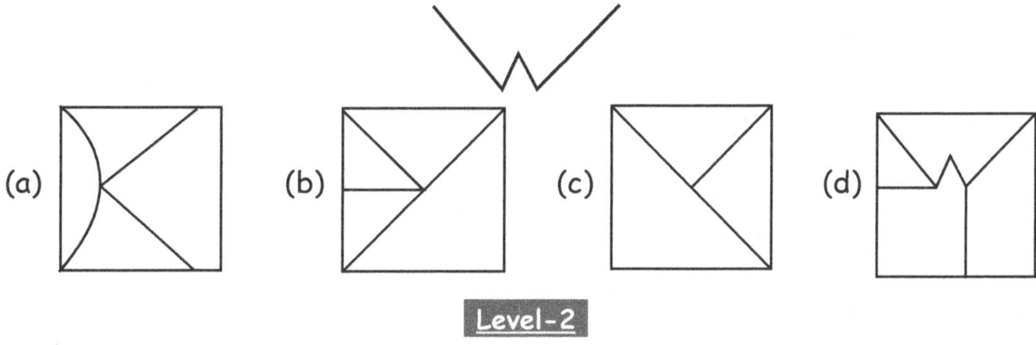

Level-2

45. Which of the following figures is exactly embedded in the given figure as one of its parts? (2020)

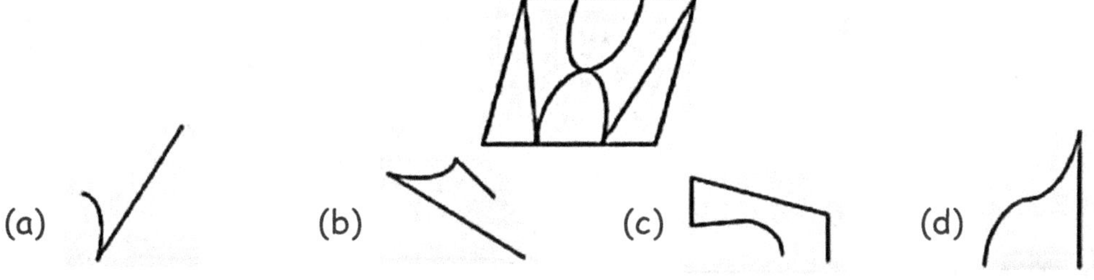

Chapter-10: Estimation

Level-1

46. Which of the following is the lightest? (2020)

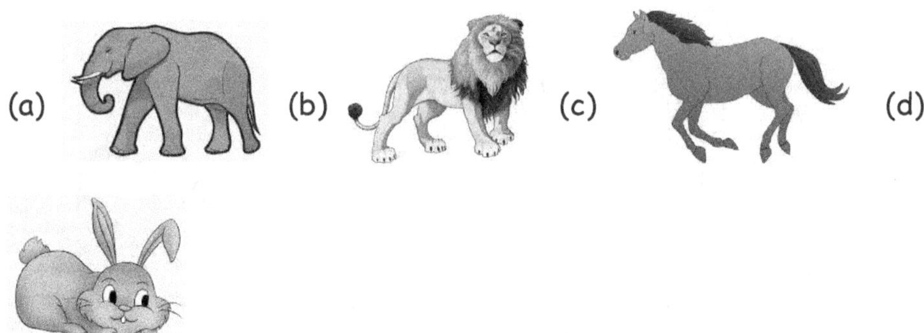

47. Train P is ____________ m shorter than Train Q. (2021)

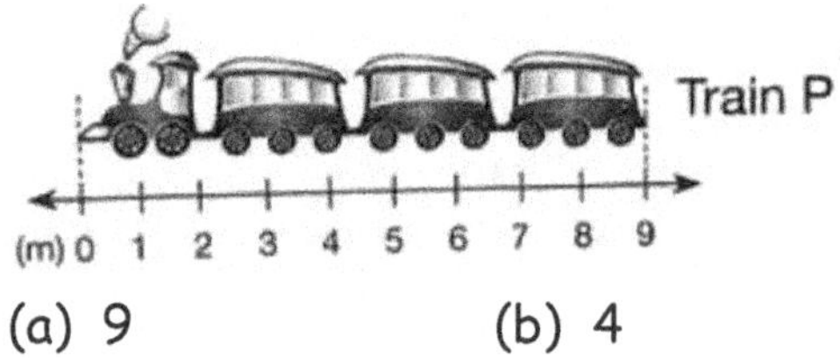

(a) 9 (b) 4 (c) 5 (d) 13

48. Who is the heaviest? (2022)

(a) Karan (b) Sumit (c) Puneet (d) Tarun

49. Which of the following items can be bought with the given amount of money?

(2022)

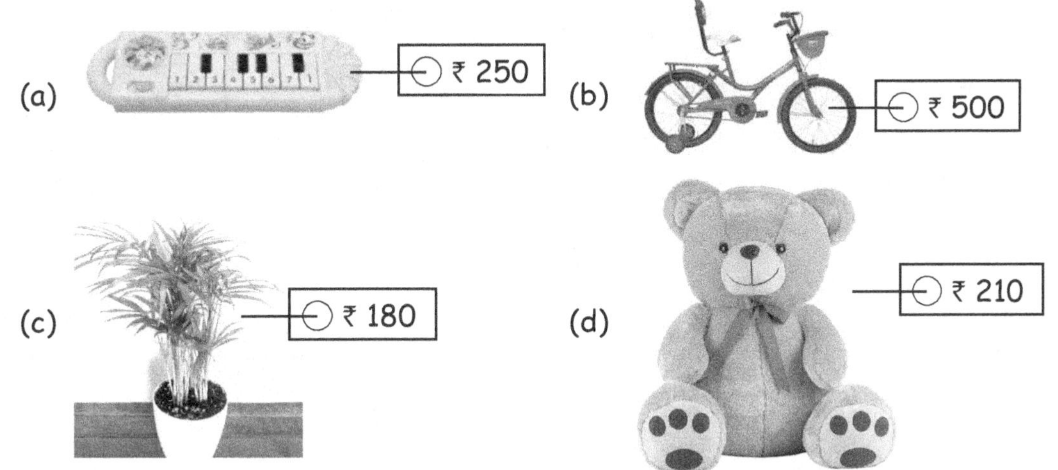

50. Which of the following is the lightest? (2022)

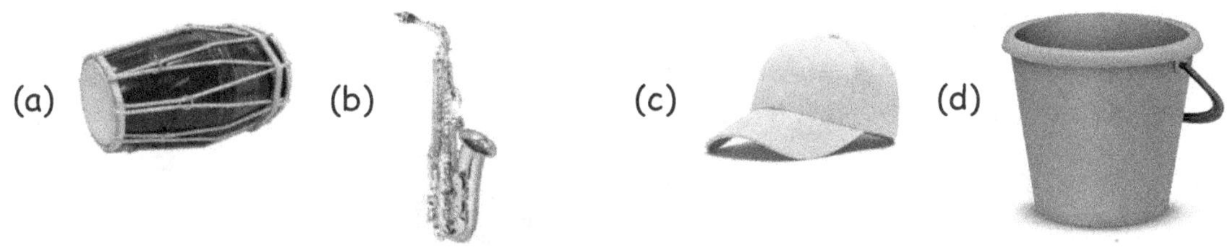

Chapter-11: Problem Solving

Level-1

51. Which of the following clocks shows 20 minutes past the time shown in the given clock? (2019)

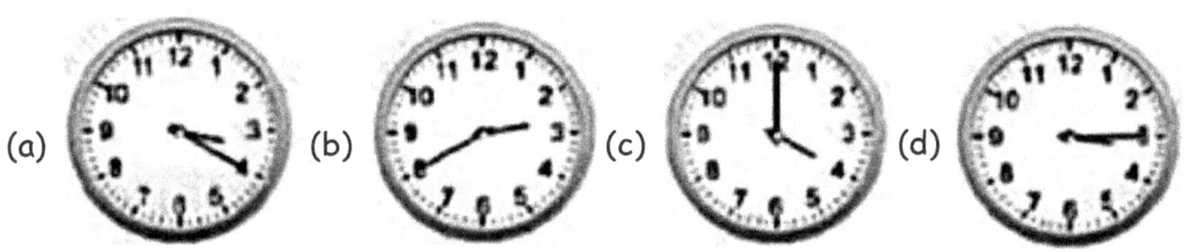

Level-2

52. ________ walks the longest distance and ________ walks the shortest distance respectively. (2018)

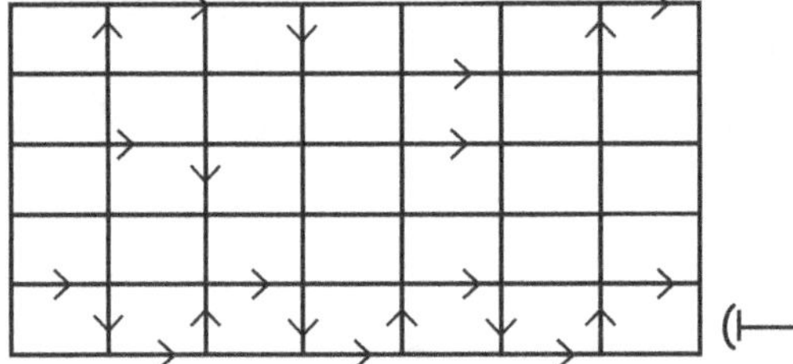

(a) Nisha, Sanchi (b) Sanchi, Jyoti (c) Jyoti, Sanchi (d) Jyoti, Nisha

53. If Sneha's skating competition is on second Thursday of October 20XX, then on which date will be her competition held? (2020)

OCTOBER 20XX						
Sun	**Mon**	**Tue**	**Wed**	**Thu**	**Fri**	**Sat**
			1	2	3	4
5	6	7	8	9	10	11
12	13	14	15	16	17	18
19	20	21	22	23	24	25
26	27	28	29	30	31	

(a) 10th October

(b) 9th October

(c) 8th October

(d) 18th October

54. Sneha's karate classes will start on the next day of third Friday of April 20XX. On which date will her classes start? (2020)

April 20XX						
Sun	Mon	Tue	Wed	Thu	Fri	Sat
	1	2	3	4	5	6
7	8	9	10	11	12	13
14	15	16	17	18	19	20
21	22	23	24	25	26	27
28	29	30				

(a) 18th April (b) 19th April (c) 20th April (d) 13th April

55. Find the missing number, if a certain rule is followed either row-wise or column-wise. (2021)

17	5	22
20	?	30
15	11	26

(a) 10

(b) 12

(c) 18

(d) 15

Hints & Solutions

Chapter-1: Analogy

Level-1

1. (a)

2. (c)

No. of side × 2 = 12

(6) × 2 = 12.

Similarly,

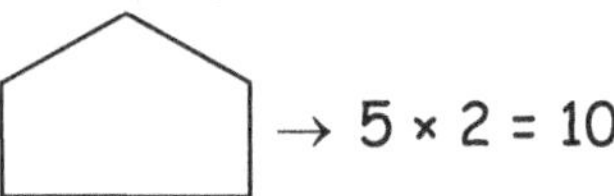

→ 5 × 2 = 10

3. (a) "No of sides + 2"

So, 3 + 2 = 9

4. (c)

Level-2

5. (b) First figure is divided into two parts from the middle.

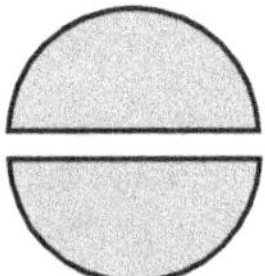

Chapter-2: Patterns

Level-1

6. (a)

Number of balls in pattern 1 = (3 × number of pattern) – 2 = (3 × 1) – 2 = 1

Number of balls in pattern 2 = (3 × number of pattern) – 2 = (3 × 2) – 2 = 6 – 2 = 4

Number of balls in pattern 3 = (3 × number of pattern) – 2 = (3 × 3) – 2 = 9 – 2 = 7

Similarly,

Number of balls in pattern 6 = (3 × number of pattern) – 2 = (3 ×6) – 2 = 18 – 2 = 16.

7. **(c)** Pattern followed :-

2 × (Pattern number) + %

Therefore, 2 × (6) + 1 =13

8. **(a)** 4 bottle each.

9. **(d)** 8 groups 3 mangoes each, can be formed.

10. **(c)**

11. **(b)** 4 groups of 5 necklaces each.

12. **(a)** Pattern is repeating after every 4th figure.

13. **(a)** 12 + 15 = 27

32 + 13 = 45

Similarly

43 + 9 = 52

14. **(a)** 3 groups of 3 crayons each.

Level-2

15. **(b)** (Pattern No.) × 3

i.e.

Pattern 1 → (Pattern No.) × 3.

→ 1 × 3 = 6

Pattern 2 → 2 × 3 = 6.

Pattern 3 → 3 × 3 = 9.

Similarly

Pattern 5 = 5 × 3 = 15.

Chapter-3: Sequence

Level-1

16. **(a)** Number of burgers in each group = $\frac{\text{Totalburgers}}{\text{Number of groups}}$

Number of burgers in each group = $\frac{16}{4} = 4$

17. **(b)** 12 16 20 [24] 28 32

(+4) (+4) (+4) (+4) (+4)

Level-2

18. **(b)** 8 + 12 → 20
15 + 11 → 26
7 + 14 → 21.

Chapter-4: Odd One Out

Level-1

19. **(b)** Option 'b' is made of by 5 straight lines only where as other options 6 straight lines are used.
20. **(d)** All other options are used for writing.
21. **(d)** Except (d), all are sports items.
22. **(d)** Quter figure contains 6 sides whereas in all other options qouter figure in made by 5 sides.

Chapter-5: Position / Ranking Test

Level-1

23. **(a)** 4th to the left of T is P.
24. **(b)** We can see our face in "Mirror" and mirror is called "hairband".

25. **(b)** P W ~~K~~ S J T ~~M~~ O R
S duck is 3rd from the left.
26. **(c)** U is third to the left of second monkey from the right end.
27. **(b)** S in the fourth from the right end.
28. **(b)** Fourth boat from left end is S and second.
The right of boat S in boat U.
29. **(a)** Then ∠ in the third to the left of hen O from right end.
30. **(b)** S in 4th from the right end.

Chapter-6: Coding Decoding

Level-1

31. **(b)** Eraser is used to shop a pencil.
32. **(c)** "Chef" cooks food in reality, but in question chef 5in called Barber, So option (c) in answer.
33. **(a)** Nail cutter is used to cut the neals and in our question Nail cutter in called lipstick.

Chapter-7: Spatial Understanding

Level-2

34. (c) 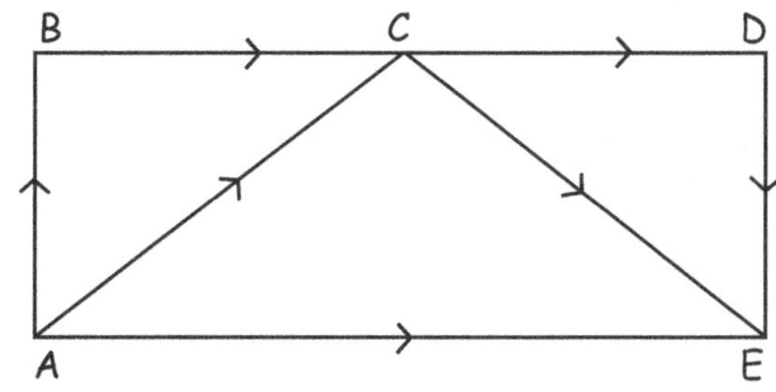

5 ways i.e.,
AE, ABCDE, ABCE, ACDE, ACE.

Chapter-8: Geometrical Shapes

Level-1

35. (d) Brick does not have any curve.
36. (d) 8

37. (c) 

38. (c) 

Level-2

39. (d) 28
40. (b) 10 triangles.
41. (a) 12 triangles and 5 squares.
42. (c) Square in not present.

Chapter-9: Embedded Figure

Level-1

43. (c)

44. (d) 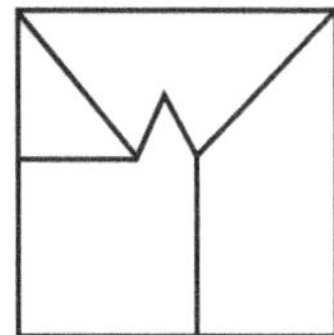

Level-2

45. (a) 

Chapter-10: Estimation

Level-1

46. (d) Rabbit is the lightest among. The given options.

47. (b) 13 - 9 = 4m

48. (b) From figures, Sumit in the heaviest.

49. (c) Flowerpot can be bought with 200 rs note.

50. (c) Cap in the lightest

Chapter-11: Problem Solving

Level-1

51. (a) It show 3 : 20

Level-2

52. (c) Jyoti, Sanchi

53. (b) 9th October 20XX is 2nd Thursday.

54. (c) Next day of third friday will be 20th April.

55. (a) $17 + 5 \rightarrow 22$

$15 + 11 \rightarrow 26$

$20 + ? = 30$

$? = 30 - 20$

$? = 10$

ANALOGY

OBJECTIVES

- Students will be able to explore relationships between like and unlike things.
- They will understand the more obscure things by picturing the more common things.
- Students will visualize characters and places.
- They begin to relate analogies with real life.

INTRODUCTION

An analogy is a comparison between things which are basically not alike but which share some kind of striking similarity.

HOW TO "READ" ANALOGIES

The symbol (:) means "is to" and the symbol (: :) means "as." Thus, the analogy, "apple : fruit : : carrot : vegetable," should be read "apple is to fruit as carrot is to vegetable." Stated another way, the relationship between apple and fruit is the same as the relationship between carrot and vegetable.

Steps to Solve

Step 1: Look carefully at the first pair of examples.

Step 2: How are these two pairs connected?

Step 3: Complete the second pair in the same way as the first pair.

Step 4: Make sure that all the necessary changes are made.

Types of Analogy

(i) Picture-based Analogy

Directions (Examples 1-2): Choose the correct matching pair.

1.  : :: : ?

(a)  (b) 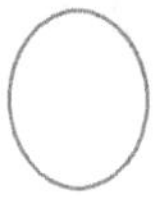 (c)  (d)

Ans. (b)

Explanation:

The first figure is a part of second figure and the second image is the complete figure.

So, the correct answer is (b).

2.

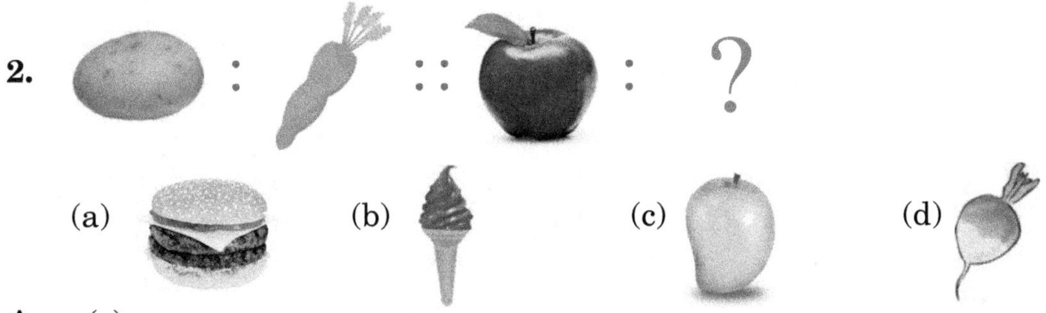

Ans. (c)

Explanation:

Pair of figures on the left side of : : are vegetables. Pair of figures on the right side of : : are fruits.

(ii) Number-based Analogy

Direction (Example 3): Choose the correct matching pair.

3. (2) : (4) : : (3) : (?)

(a) 4 (b) 1 (c) 6 (d) 7

Ans. (c)

Explanation:

As, $2 \times 2 = 4$

Similarly,

$3 \times 2 = 6$

So, the correct answer is (c).

(iii) Alphabet-based Analogy

Direction (Example 4): Choose the correct matching pair.

4. B : D : : X : ?

(a) D (b) Z (c) Y (d) U

Ans. (b)

Explanation:

Letter B of first pair is moved two steps forward i.e., B $\xrightarrow{+2}$ D

Similarly,

Letter X of second pair is moved two steps forward i.e., X $\xrightarrow{+2}$ Z

(iv) Word-based Analogy

Direction (Example 5): Choose the correct matching pair.

5. Birds : Fly : : Men : ?

(a) Fly (b) Walk (c) Swim (d) Hop

Ans. (b)

Explanation:

As birds fly to move, similarly, men walk to move.

LEVEL-1

Direction (Qs. 1-21): There is a certain relationship between the pair of figures/number/letters/words on the either side of : :. Identify relation between the pair and find the missing term.

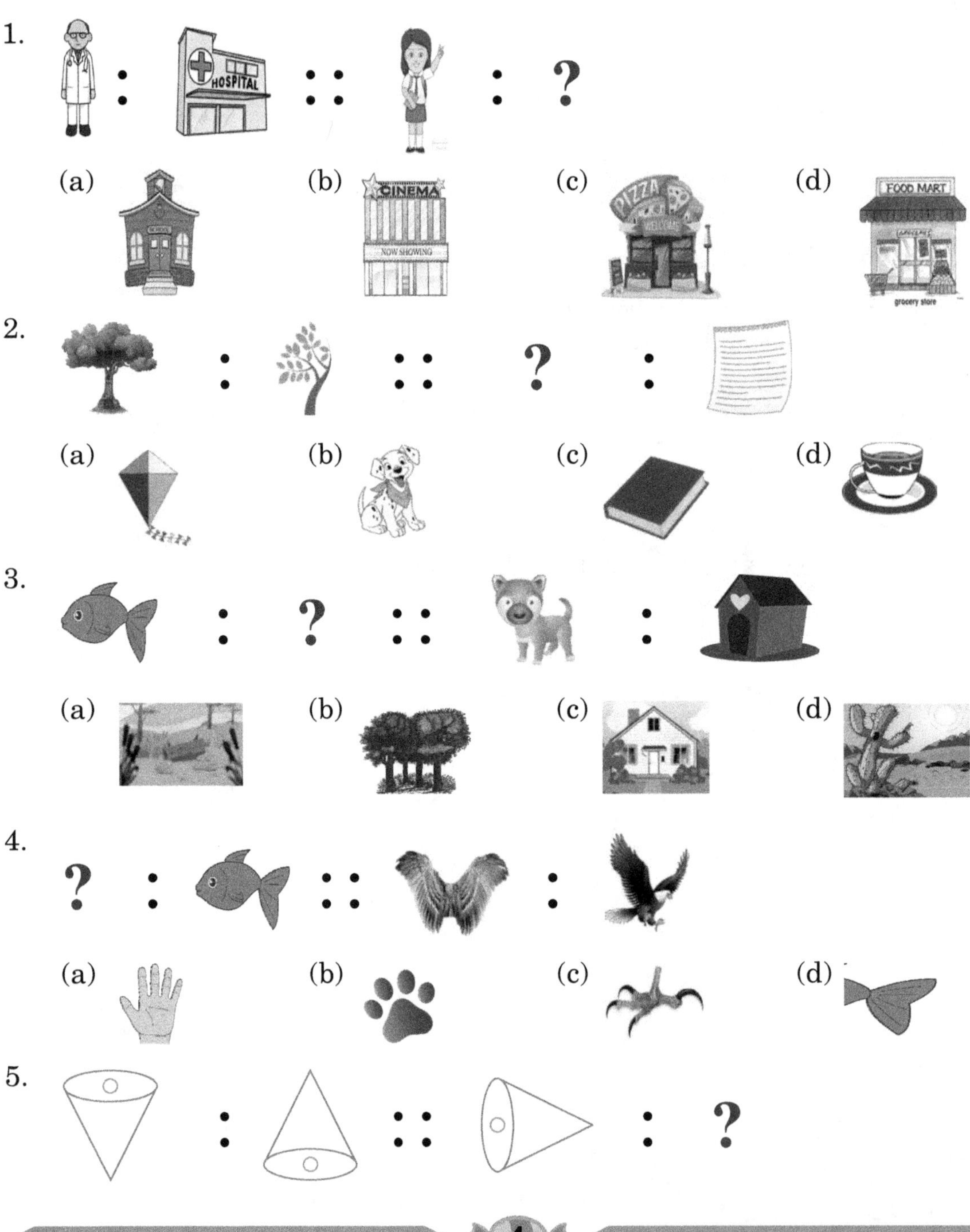

(a) (b) (c) (d)

6.

(a) (b) (c) (d)

7.

(a) (b) (c) (d)

8.

(a) (b) (c) (d)

9.

(a) (b) (c) (d)

10.

(a) (b) (c) (d)

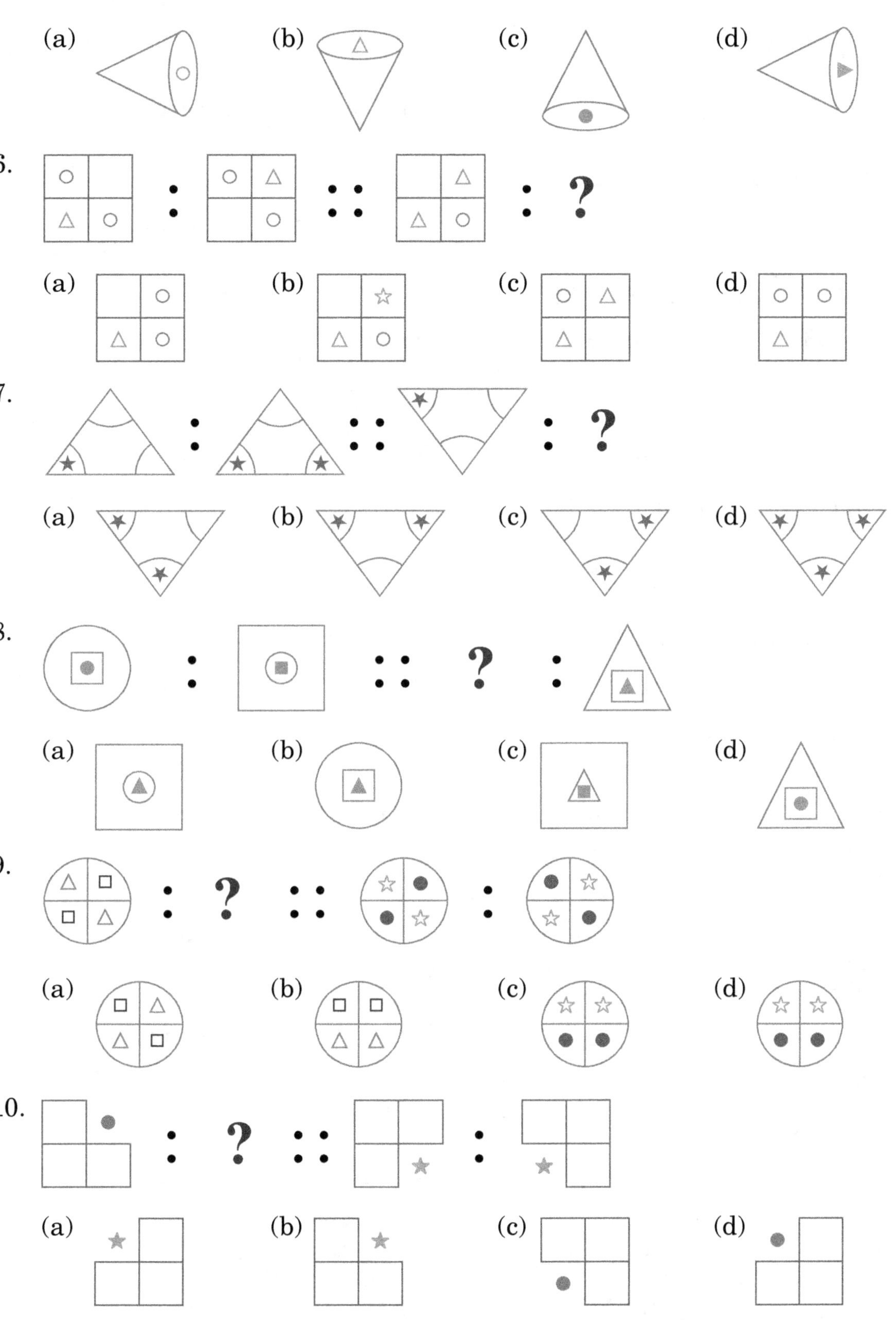

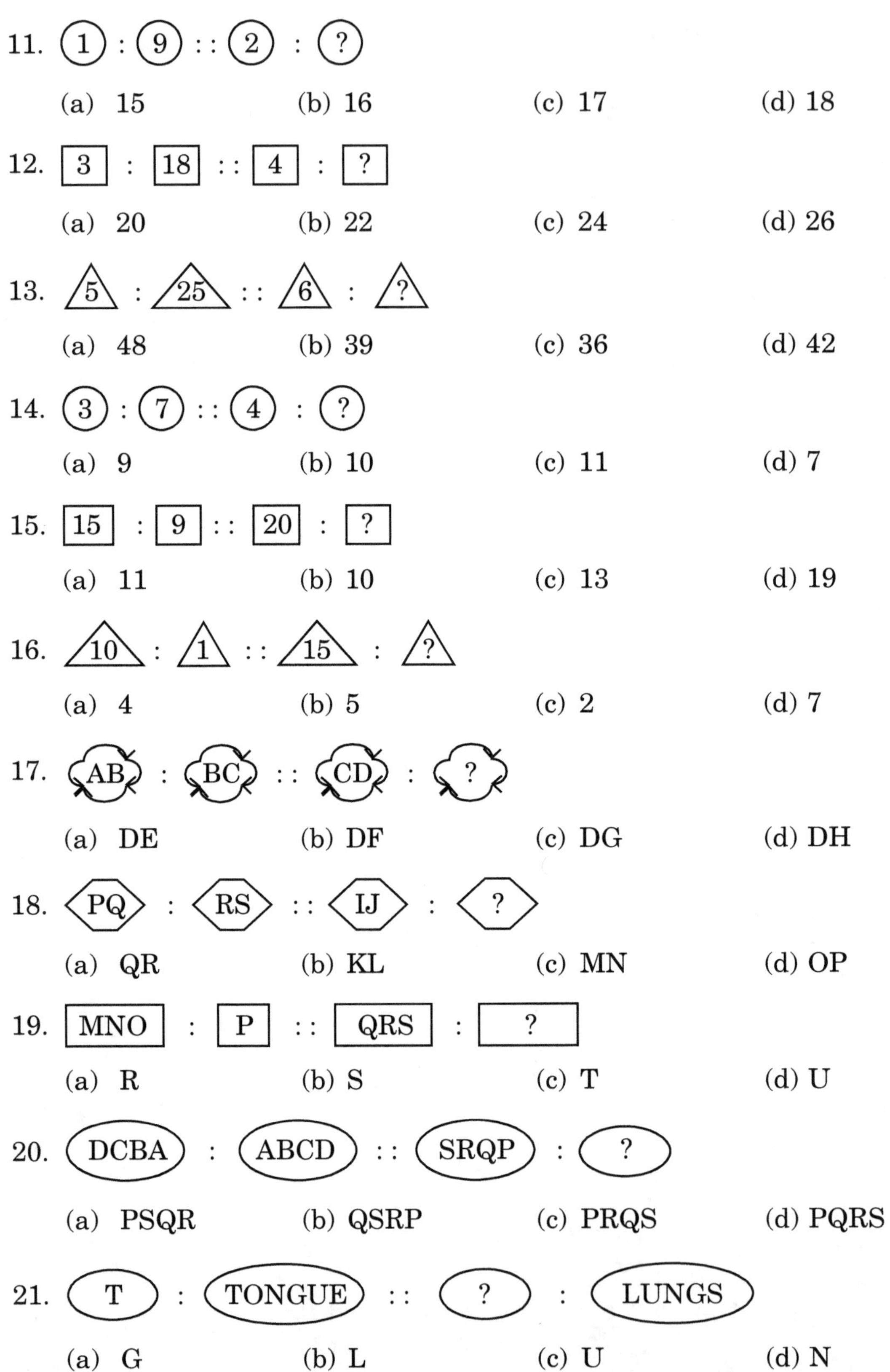

11. 1 : 9 : : 2 : ?

(a) 15 (b) 16 (c) 17 (d) 18

12. 3 : 18 : : 4 : ?

(a) 20 (b) 22 (c) 24 (d) 26

13. 5 : 25 : : 6 : ?

(a) 48 (b) 39 (c) 36 (d) 42

14. 3 : 7 : : 4 : ?

(a) 9 (b) 10 (c) 11 (d) 7

15. 15 : 9 : : 20 : ?

(a) 11 (b) 10 (c) 13 (d) 19

16. 10 : 1 : : 15 : ?

(a) 4 (b) 5 (c) 2 (d) 7

17. AB : BC : : CD : ?

(a) DE (b) DF (c) DG (d) DH

18. PQ : RS : : IJ : ?

(a) QR (b) KL (c) MN (d) OP

19. MNO : P : : QRS : ?

(a) R (b) S (c) T (d) U

20. DCBA : ABCD : : SRQP : ?

(a) PSQR (b) QSRP (c) PRQS (d) PQRS

21. T : TONGUE : : ? : LUNGS

(a) G (b) L (c) U (d) N

Direction (Qs. 22-30): Find out the missing word.

22. Cat : Kitten :: Dog : ?

(a) Puppy (b) Baby (c) Chick (d) Cub

23. Honey : Sweet :: Lemon : ?

(a) Hot (b) Sour (c) Salty (d) Bitter

24. Fish : Pond :: Dog : ?

(a) House (b) Hut (c) Kennel (d) Tree

25. Big : Tall :: Small : ?

(a) Low (b) Great (c) Large (d) Short

26. Car : Road :: ? : Water

(a) Boat (b) Train (c) Plain (d) Cycle

27. Mother : Daughter :: Father : ?

(a) Aunty (b) Son

(c) Grandma (d) Great grandma.

28. Blue : Water :: Green : ?

(a) Trunk (b) Hair (c) Clouds (d) Grass

29. Scissors : Cloth :: Knife : ?

(a) Fruits (b) Paper (c) Leather (d) Hair

30. Difficult : Easy :: Strong : ?

(a) Stout (b) Lazy (c) Angry (d) Weak

LEVEL-2

Direction (Qs. 1-27): Find the matching pair.

1. ? :  ::  : 

(a)  (b)  (c)  (d) 

2. 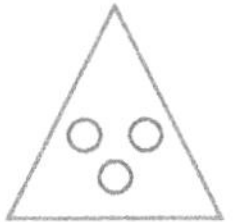 : ? ::  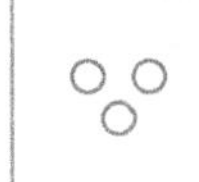 : 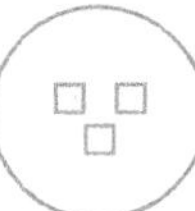

(a)  (b)  (c) 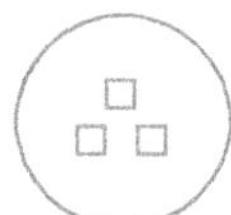 (d) 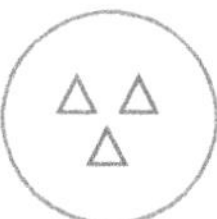

3. 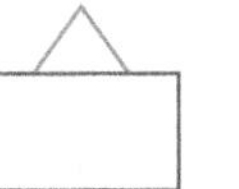 : 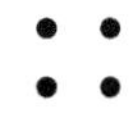 :: 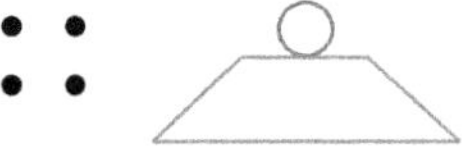 : ?

(a) (b) (c)  (d) 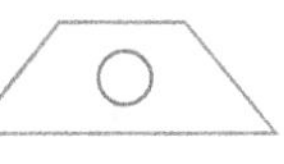

4. 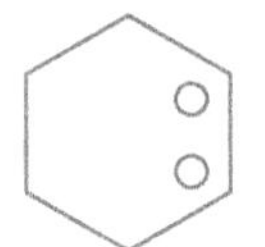 : 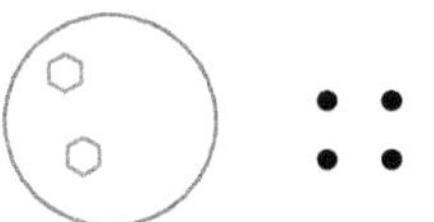 :: ? : 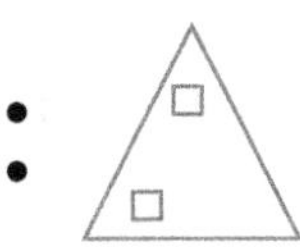

(a) 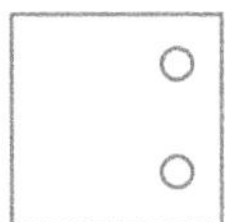 (b) 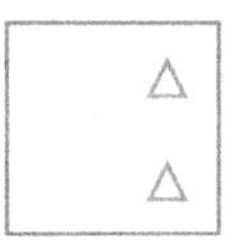 (c) 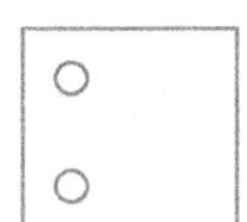 (d) 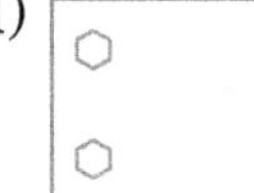

5.  : ? :: 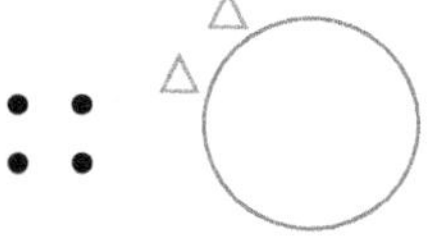 : 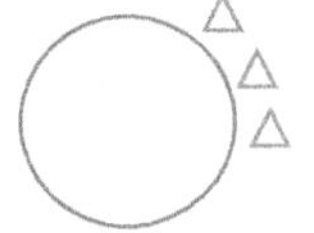

(a) 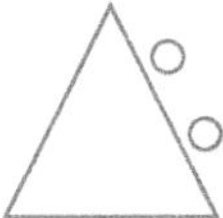 (b) 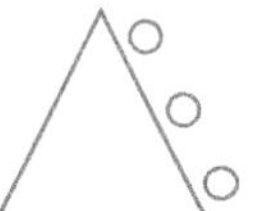 (c)  (d) 

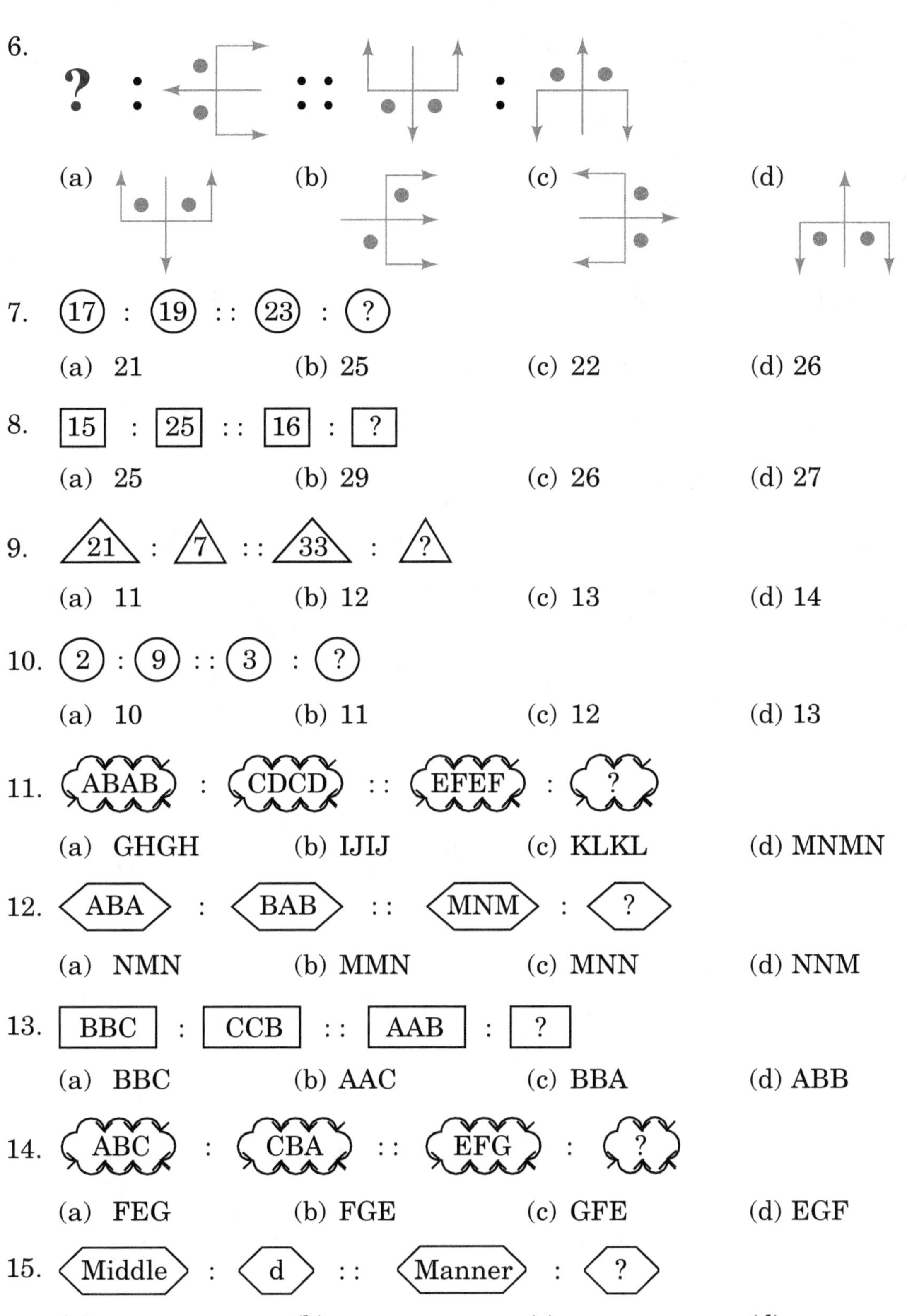
6.
?
(a)
(b)
(c)
(d)
7. 17 : 19 :: 23 : ?
(a) 21
(b) 25
(c) 22
(d) 26
8. 15 : 25 :: 16 : ?
(a) 25
(b) 29
(c) 26
(d) 27
9. 21 : 7 :: 33 : ?
(a) 11
(b) 12
(c) 13
(d) 14
10. 2 : 9 :: 3 : ?
(a) 10
(b) 11
(c) 12
(d) 13
11. ABAB : CDCD :: EFEF : ?
(a) GHGH
(b) IJIJ
(c) KLKL
(d) MNMN
12. ABA : BAB :: MNM : ?
(a) NMN
(b) MMN
(c) MNN
(d) NNM
13. BBC : CCB :: AAB : ?
(a) BBC
(b) AAC
(c) BBA
(d) ABB
14. ABC : CBA :: EFG : ?
(a) FEG
(b) FGE
(c) GFE
(d) EGF
15. Middle : d :: Manner : ?
(a) a
(b) e
(c) r
(d) n

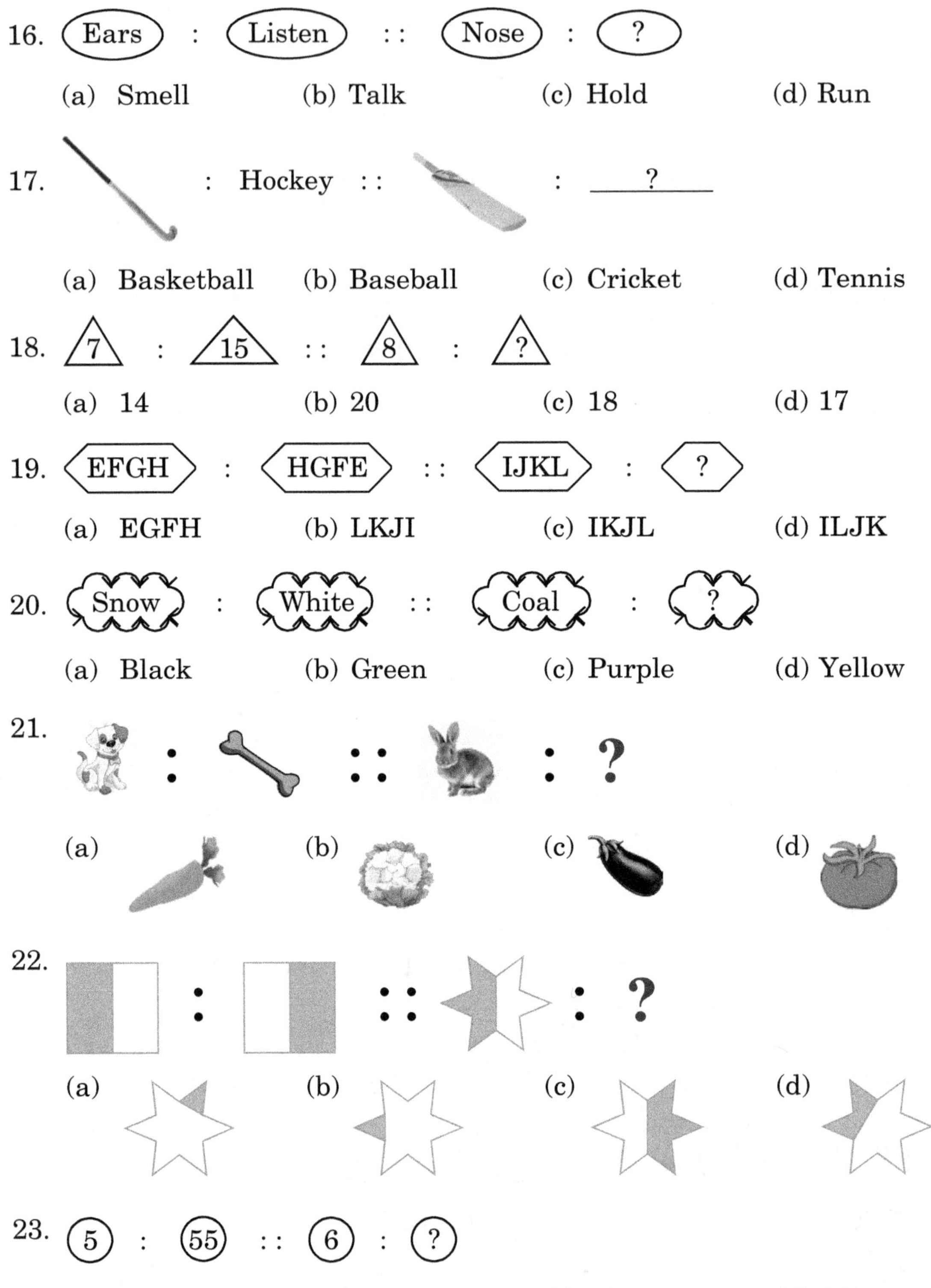

16. Ears : Listen :: Nose : ?

(a) Smell (b) Talk (c) Hold (d) Run

17. : Hockey :: : ?

(a) Basketball (b) Baseball (c) Cricket (d) Tennis

18. 7 : 15 :: 8 : ?

(a) 14 (b) 20 (c) 18 (d) 17

19. EFGH : HGFE :: IJKL : ?

(a) EGFH (b) LKJI (c) IKJL (d) ILJK

20. Snow : White :: Coal : ?

(a) Black (b) Green (c) Purple (d) Yellow

21. : :: : ?

(a) (b) (c) (d)

22. : :: : ?

(a) (b) (c) (d)

23. 5 : 55 :: 6 : ?

(a) 66 (b) 77 (c) 88 (d) 99

24. ABC : DEF :: PQR : ?

(a) XYZ (b) VWX (c) STU (d) DEF

25. Dolphin : Sea :: Tiger : ?

(a) Pond (b) Kennel (c) Home (d) Jungle

26. : :: : ?

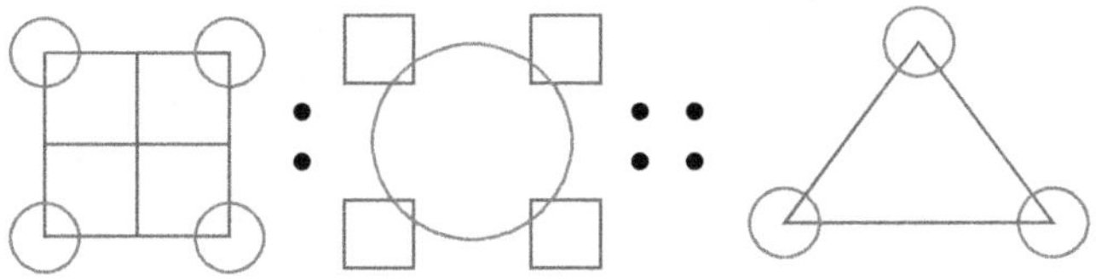

(a) 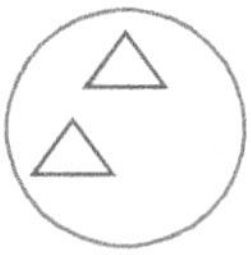 (b)  (c) 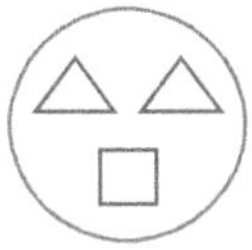 (d)

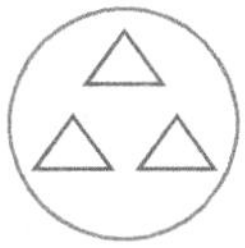

27. : :: ? :

(a) 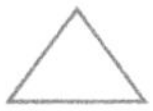 (b)  (c) 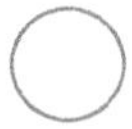 (d)

28. There is a certain relationship between the pair of figures on the either side of : :. Identify the relation and find the missing figure.

(Olympiad)

: :: : ?

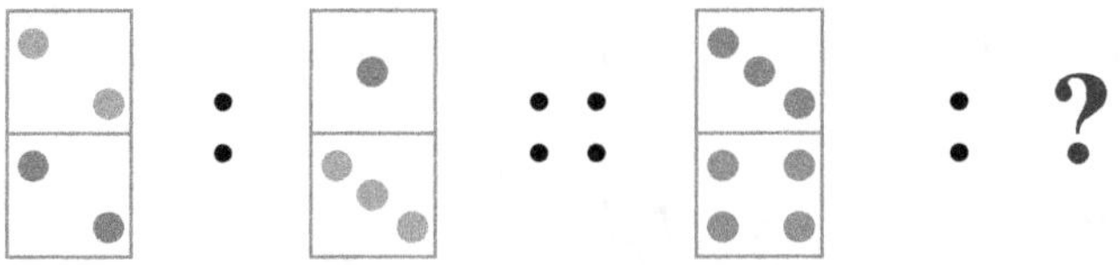

(a) 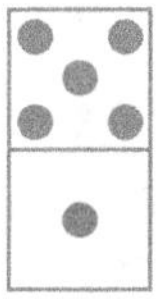 (b) 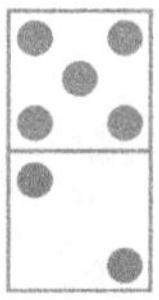 (c) 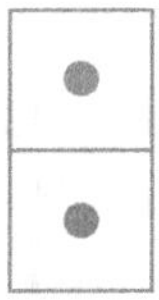 (d)

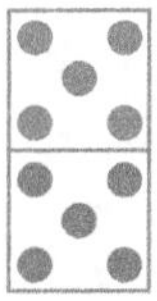

29. There is a certain relationship between the pair of figures on the either side of : :. Identify the relation between the pair and find the missing figure.

(Olympiad)

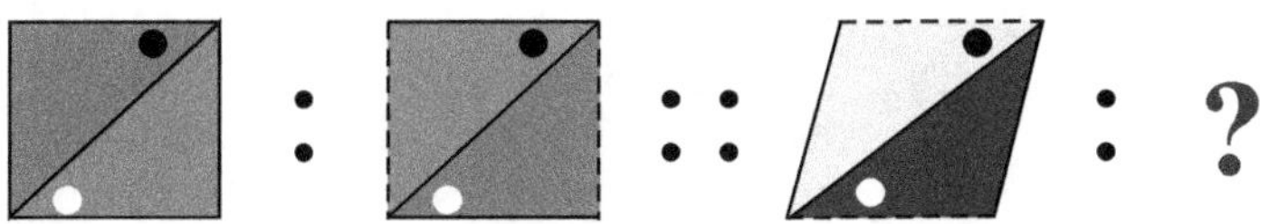

(a) 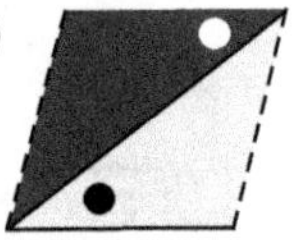 (b) 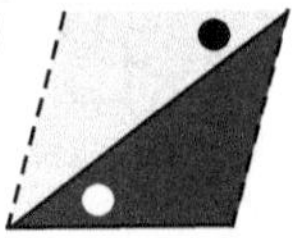 (c) 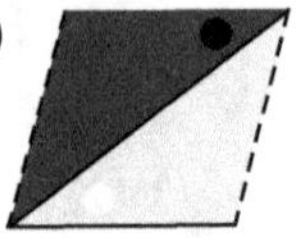 (d)

30. If [figure] is related to 12, then [figure] is related to

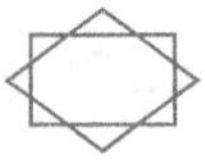

(Olympiad)

(a) 16 (b) 12 (c) 14 (d) 8

31. If [figure] is related to [figure], then [figure] is related to ____________.

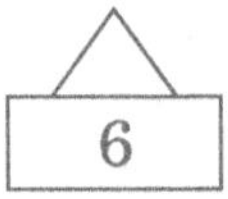

(Olympiad)

(a) 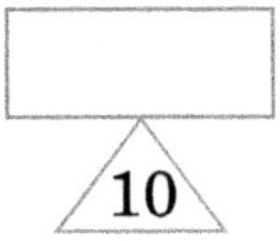 10 (b) 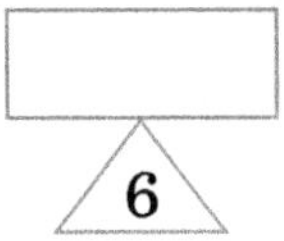 6 (c) 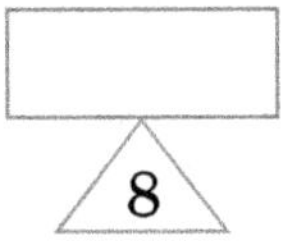 8 (d) 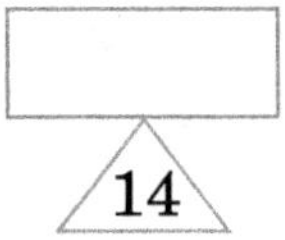 14

32. 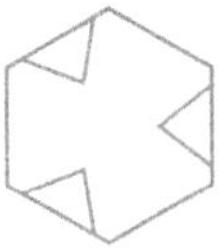 [figure] : [figure] :: [figure] : ?

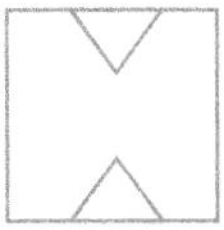

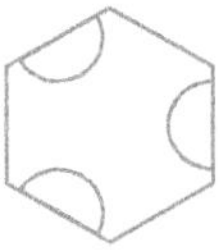

(a) 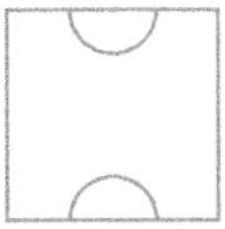 (b)  (c) 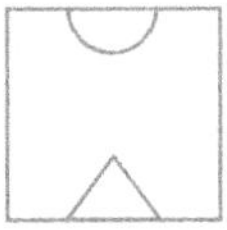 (d)

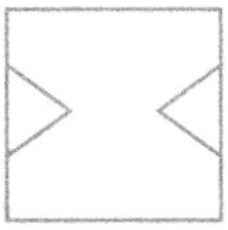

33. There is a certain relationship between the pair of figures on the either side of : :. Identify the relation and find the missing figure. (Olympiad)

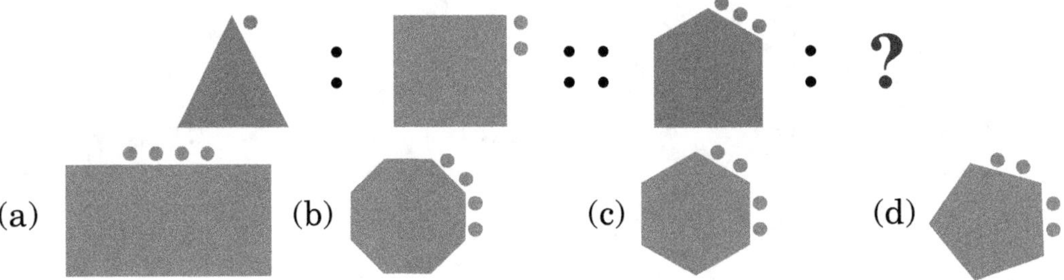

(a) (b) (c) (d)

Answers and Explanations

Level-1

1. **(a)** As, Doctor is related to hospital. Similarly, student is related to school.
2. **(c)** 2nd figure is the part of 1st figure.
3. **(a)** The dog lives inside the kennel as the fish lives inside the pond.
4. **(d)** The fish has fins as the bird has wings.
5. **(a)** The first cone is the opposite of second. Similarly, the fourth cone will be opposite of third.
6. **(c)** In the first pair of figures there are two circles and one triangle. Similarly, in the second pair of figures there are two triangles and one circle.
7. **(b)** As, in the second image of the first pair of figures, have one star more than the first one in opposite end. Similarly, in fourth image one star will be more than in the third figure in opposite end.
8. **(c)** Inner most figure in the repetition of outer most figure.
9. **(a)** The 2nd figure is the mirror image of the first one.
10. **(d)** The second one is the mirror image of the first one.
11. **(d)** As, $1 \times 9 = 9$

    Similarly, $2 \times 9 = 18$
12. **(c)** As, $3 \times 6 = 18$

    Similarly, $4 \times 6 = 24$
13. **(c)** As, $5 \times 5 = 25$

    Similarly, $6 \times 6 = 36$
14. **(a)** As, $3 \times 2 = 6$

    $\Rightarrow 6 + 1 = 7$

    Similarly,

    $4 \times 2 = 8$

    $\Rightarrow 8 + 1 = 9$
15. **(b)** $15 \div 5 = 3$

    $\Rightarrow 3 + 6 = 9$

    Similarly,

    $20 \div 5 = 4$

    $\Rightarrow 4 + 6 = 10$
16. **(c)** As, $10 \div 5 = 2$

    $\Rightarrow 2 - 1 = 1$

    Similarly, $15 \div 5 = 3$

    $\Rightarrow 3 - 1 = 2$
17. **(a)** As,

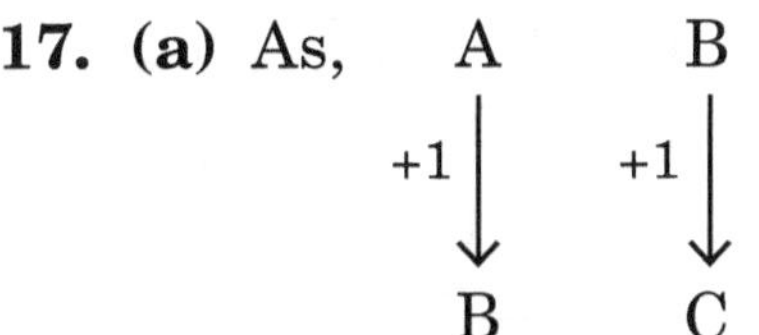

Similarly,

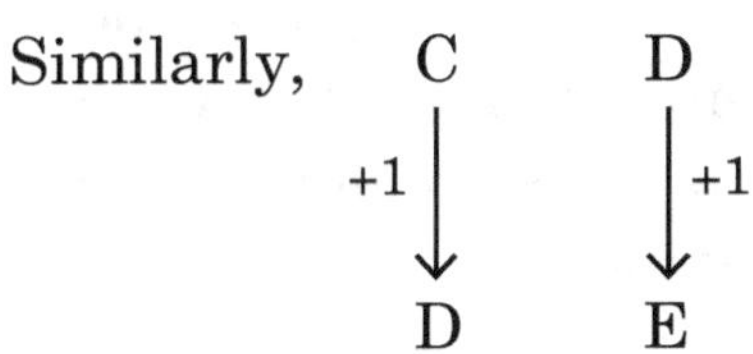

Here, each corresponding letter moves one step forward in English alphabet.

18. **(b)** As,

$P \xrightarrow{+1} Q \xrightarrow{+1} R \xrightarrow{+1} S$

Similarly,

$I \xrightarrow{+1} J \xrightarrow{+1} K \xrightarrow{+1} L$

19. **(c)** After MNO the next letter is P. Similarly, after QRS the next letter is T.

20. **(d)** DCBA is opposite sequence of ABCD. Similarly, SRQP is the opposite of PQRS.

21. **(b)** As, T for Tongue.

Similarly, L for Lungs.

22. **(a)** As, the young of a 'cat' is 'kitten'. In the same way, the young of a 'dog' is 'puppy'.

23. **(b)** As, the taste of honey is sweet. Similarly, the taste of Lemon is sour.

24. **(c)** As, the fish lives in pond. Similarly, the dog lives in kennel.

25. **(d)** As, big is similar to tall. Similarly, small is similar to short.

26. **(a)** As, car runs on road. Similarly, boat runs in water.

27. **(b)** As, mother and daughter both are female. Similarly, father and son both are male.

28. **(d)** As, the colour of water is blue. Similarly, the colour of grass is green.

29. **(a)** As, scissors helps in cutting clothes. Similarly, knife helps in cutting fruits.

30. **(d)** As, easy is opposite of difficult. Similarly, weak is opposite of strong.

Level-2

1. **(c)** The wheel shown in 2nd picture belongs to the bicycle.

2. **(d)** The inner image becomes outer image and outer image becomes inner image.

3. **(c)** In first pair of figures, the upper element gets larger and the lower element gets smaller to obtain the second figure.

4. **(b)** The inner element becomes outer and outer element becomes inner.

5. **(b)** The sequence is changing with one circle more than the first one in opposite side of the triangle.

6. **(c)** The first image is just the opposite image of the second one.

7. **(b)** As, 17 + 2 = 19

Similarly, 23 + 2 = 25

8. **(c)** As, 15 + 10 = 25

Similarly, 16 + 10 = 26

9. **(a)** As, 21 ÷ 3 = 7

Similarly, 33 ÷ 3 = 11

10. **(c)** As, ⓶ + 3 + 4 = 9

Similarly, ⓷ + 4 + 5 = 12

11. **(a)** As,

A	B	A	B
+2 ↓	+2 ↓	+2 ↓	+2 ↓
C	D	C	D

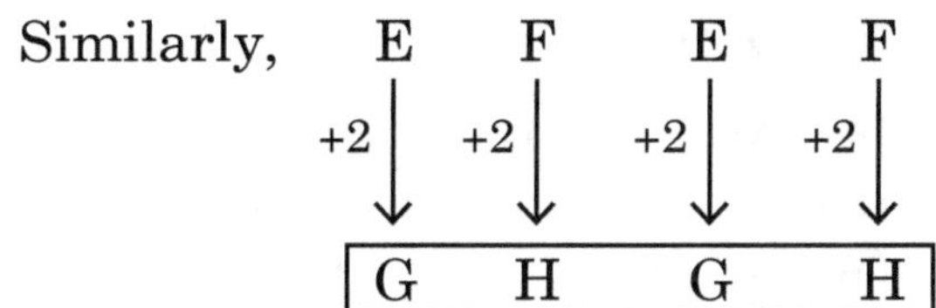

12. **(a)** As, A B A → B A B (+1, −1, +1)

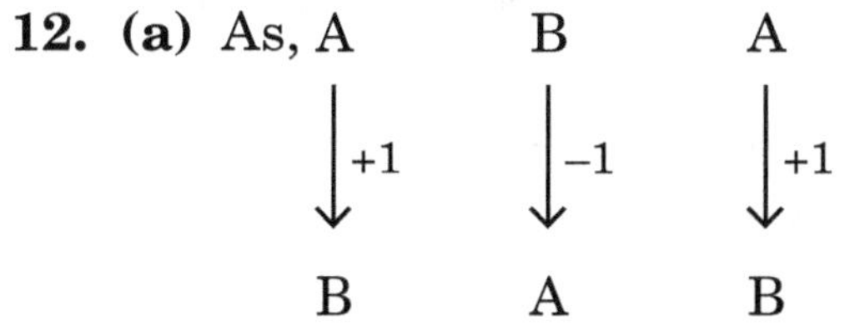

Similarly, M N M → N M N (+1, −1, +1)

13. **(c)** As, B B C → C C B (+1, +1, −1)

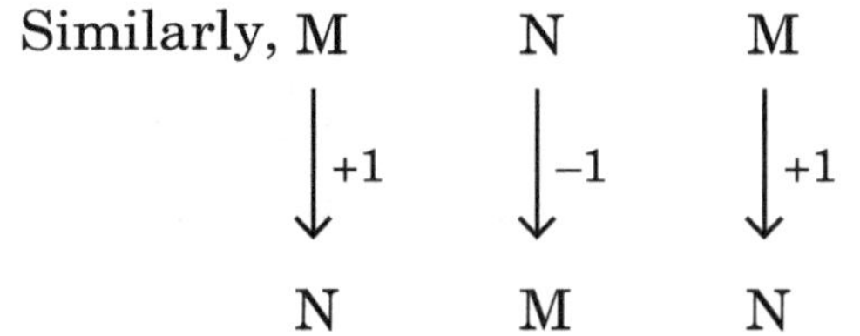

Similarly, A A B → B B A (+1, +1, −1)

14. **(c)** The letters have been reversed.

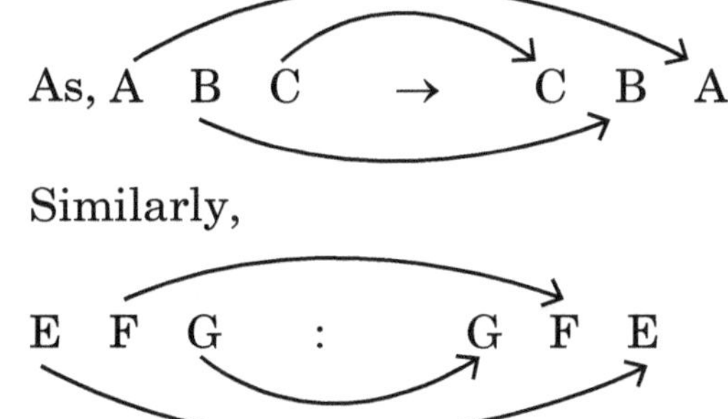

15. **(d)** The letter which gets repeated in the word.

As, Middle → d Similarly, Manner → n

16. **(a)** As, we listen with our ears. Similarly, we smell with our nose.

17. **(c)** As, hockey is played with hockey stick, Similarly, cricket is played with bat.

18. **(d)** As, $7 \times 2 = 14$

$14 + 1 = 15$

Similarly, $8 \times 2 = 16$

$16 + 1 = 17$

19. **(b)** As, H G F E is the reverse ordering of E F G H. Similarly, L K J I is the reverse ordering of I J K L.

20. **(a)** As, snow is white in colour. Similarly, coal is black in colour.

21. **(a)** As, the dog likes to eat bones. Similarly, the rabbit likes to eat carrot.

22. **(c)** Half of the pattern is shaded in reverse order in both the pair.

23. **(a)** As, $5 \times 11 = 55$

Similarly, $6 \times 11 = 66$

24. **(c)** As, DEF are the next continuing alphabets of ABC. Similarly, STU are the next continuing alphabets of PQR.

25. **(d)** As, dolphin lives inside the sea. Similarly, tiger lives in the jungle.

26. **(b)** In the first pair of figure, the square are having four circles and the circle having four squares. Similarly, in the second pair of figure, the triangle having three circles therefore, circle having three triangles.

27. **(a)** In the first pair of figure the second image is the 3 dimensional image of the first one. Similarly, in the second pair of figure, the prism is the 3 dimensional image of the triangle.

28. **(b)** In the first pair of image in two boxes there are total 4 dots. Similarly in the second pair of images there are total seven dots in the boxes.

29. **(c)** In the pair of figures, red becomes blue and blue becomes red. Similarly, in second pair of figures, yellow becomes blue and blue becomes yellow.

30. **(a)** As, ✡ this figure has two triangles with 6 sides so, $2 \times 6 = 12$

Similarly, 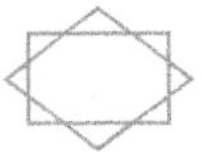 this figure has two squares with 8 sides, $2 \times 8 = 16$.

31. **(c)** Option (c) is correct.

32. **(a)** As, the first pair has three triangles in 1st figure and two triangles in second figure. Similarly, the second pair has three semi-circles in third figure and therefore, two semi-circles in fourth figure.

33. **(c)** As,

△ 3 sides ⟶ ▭ 4 sides

○ 1 circle ⟶ ○○ 2 circles

Similarly,

5 sides ⟶  6 sides

○○○ 3 circles ⟶ ○○○○ 4 circles.

CHAPTER 2

PATTERNS

OBJECTIVES

- Students will identify patterns in pictures/shapes, numbers and letters.
- They will develop to extend given patterns.
- They help students to be aware of patterns in their daily surroundings.
- They will help them to sort and group objects.
- Patterns serve as the foundation of algebraic thinking.

INTRODUCTION

A pattern is a repeated design or recurring sequence. It is a set of pictures/ shapes, letters or numbers arranged according to a certain rule.

Type I

Find the missing term or next term in (number or letter) series to continue the given series.

- Identify the order of series (descending or ascending order). Observe the pattern using operations: addition, subtraction, skip counting and reverse counting.
- Identify the order of alphabetical series either A to Z or Z to A.
- Numbering of alphabets series either A to Z or Z to A.
- Skipping letters/numbers.

Type II

Find the missing term in the pattern?

- Identify the missing term in the pattern by observing the rule followed in rest of the given terms.

Type III

Find the missing part in the figure pattern.

- Complete the figure pattern by drawing its incomplete part in the pattern.

(i) Picture / Shape-based Pattern

Example 1. What comes next in the pattern given?

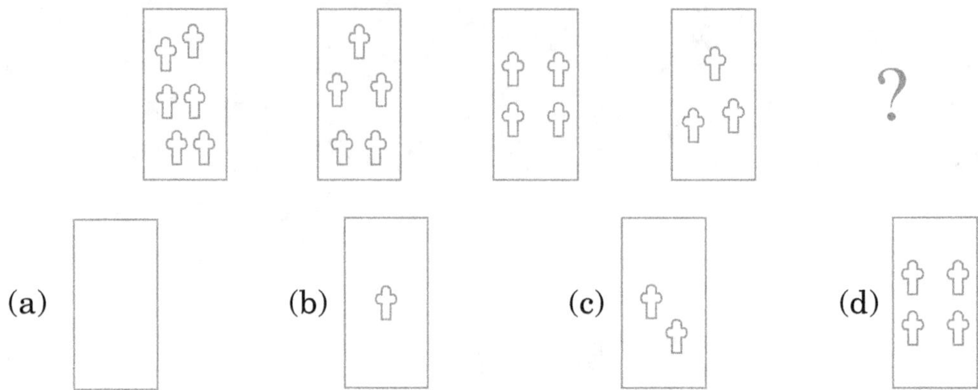

Ans. (c)

Explanation:

The elements are decreasing by one in each step. So, the correct answer is (c).

Example 2. Find the rule followed in the figure pattern and the missing figure.

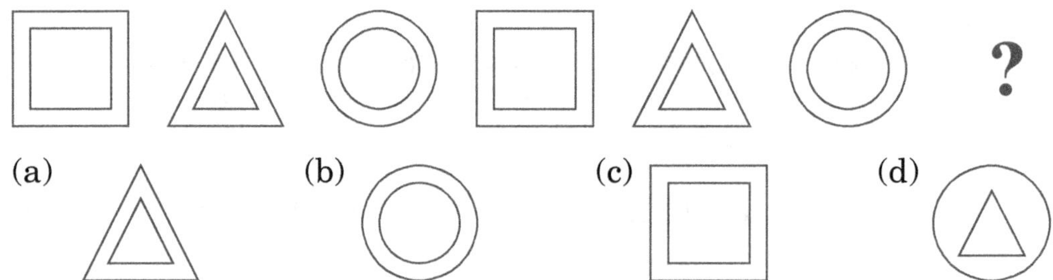

Ans. (c)

Each figure in the row repeats itself after two figures. So, the missing figure is (c).

(ii) Number-based Pattern

Example 3. What comes next in the given pattern?

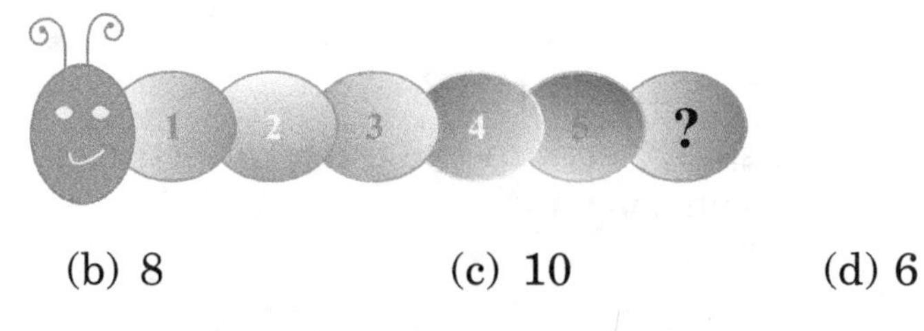

(a) 7 (b) 8 (c) 10 (d) 6

Ans. (d)

Numbers are given in ascending order. So, the correct answer is (d).

Example 4. Complete the number pattern.

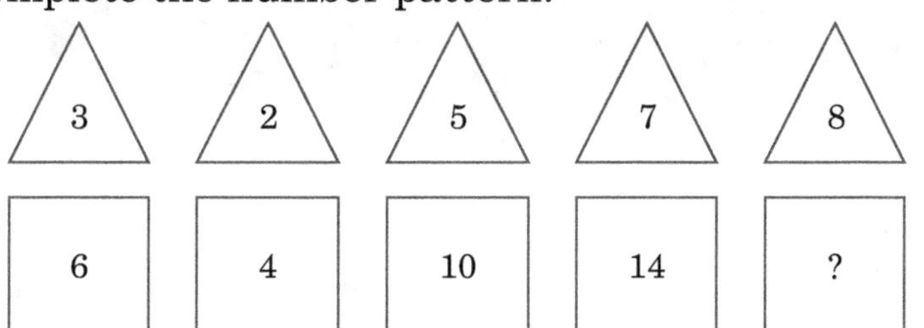

(a) 15 (b) 8 (c) 16 (d) 14

Ans. (c) The pattern is as follows:

3 + 3 = 6, 7 + 7 = 14

2 + 2 = 4, 8 + 8 = 16

5 + 5 = 10

(iii) Alphabet-based Pattern

Example 5. What comes next in the alphabet-pattern given.

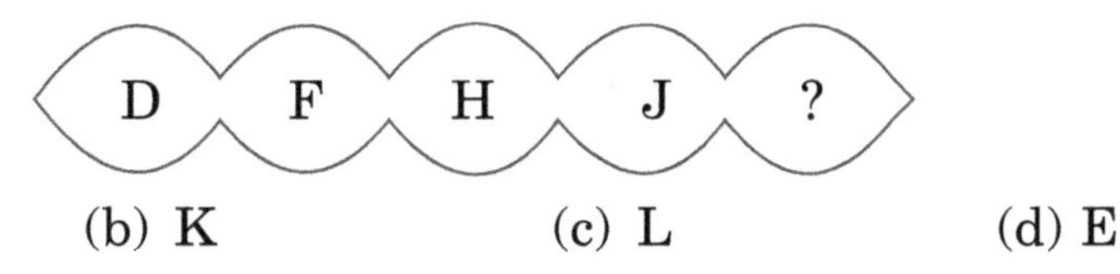

(a) M (b) K (c) L (d) E

Ans. (c)

Explanation:

Alphabets are moved on two steps forward.

$$D \xrightarrow{+2} F \xrightarrow{+2} H \xrightarrow{+2} J \xrightarrow{+2} (L)$$

So, the correct answer is (c).

Example 6. Which is the next letter?

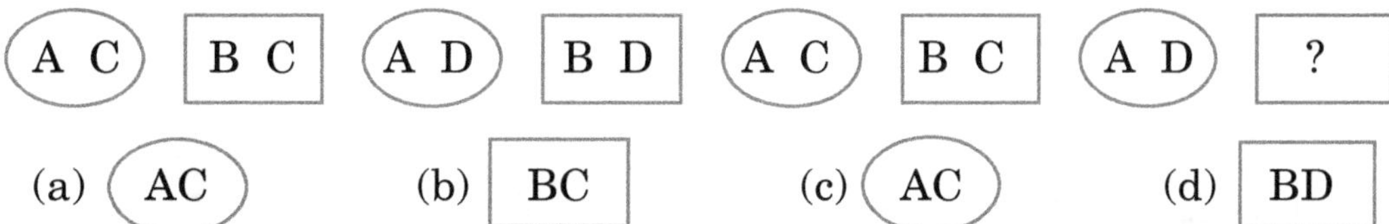

(a) AC (b) BC (c) AC (d) BD

Ans. (d) The pattern of letters is as follows:

A C B C A D B D A C B C A D B D

LEVEL-1

Direction (Qs. 1-3): Which is the next figure?

1.  ?

(a)  (b)  (c)  (d)

2.  ?

(a)  (b)  (c)  (d)

3.  ?

(a)  (b)  (c)  (d)

4. How many cars will be there in Pattern 5?

Pattern 1 Pattern 2 Pattern 3

(a) 11 (b) 12 (c) 14 (d) 9

5. How many bees will be there in Pattern 4?

Pattern 1 Pattern 2 Pattern 3

(a) 10 (b) 14 (c) 16 (d) 12

6. Which is the missing object?

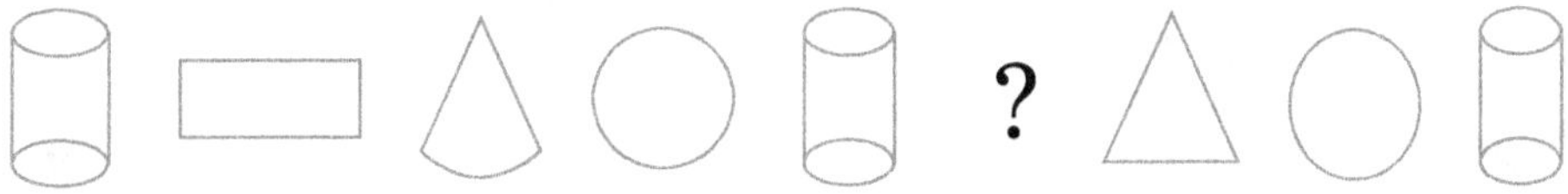

?

(a)  (b) 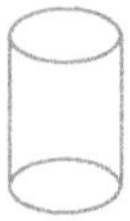 (c) (d)

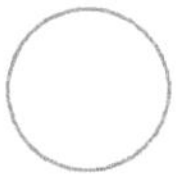

7. Find the next pattern ?

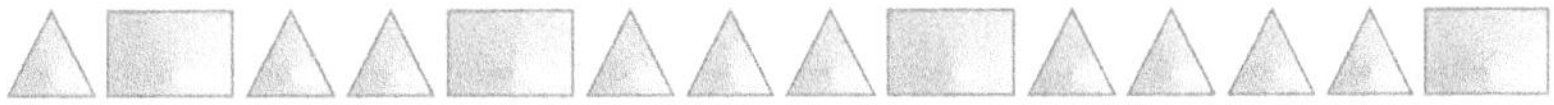

(a)  (b)

(c) 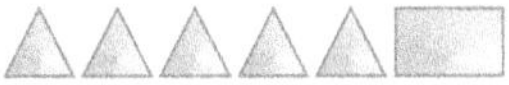 (d)

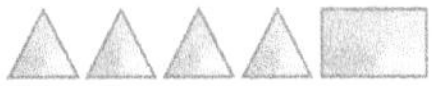

8. Find the missing pattern ?

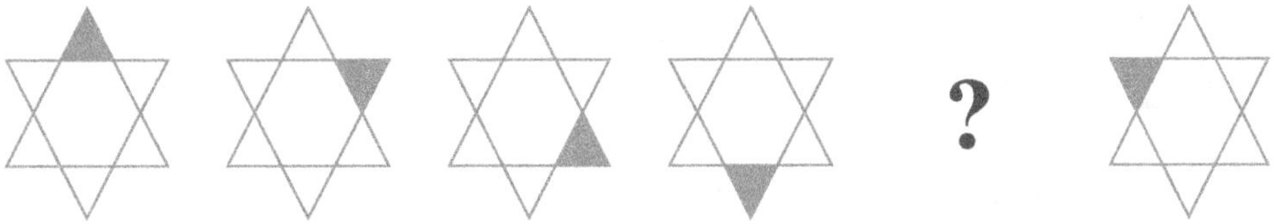

?

(a) 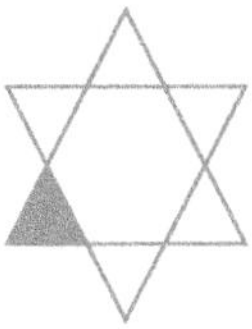 (b) 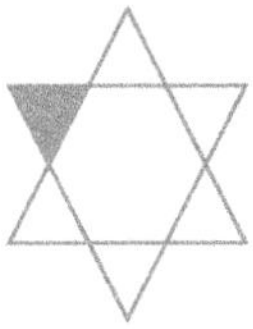 (c) 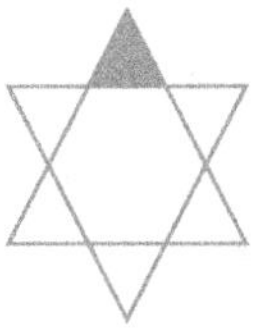 (d)

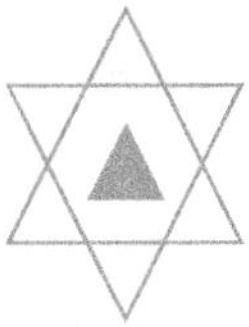

9. Which is the next pattern ?

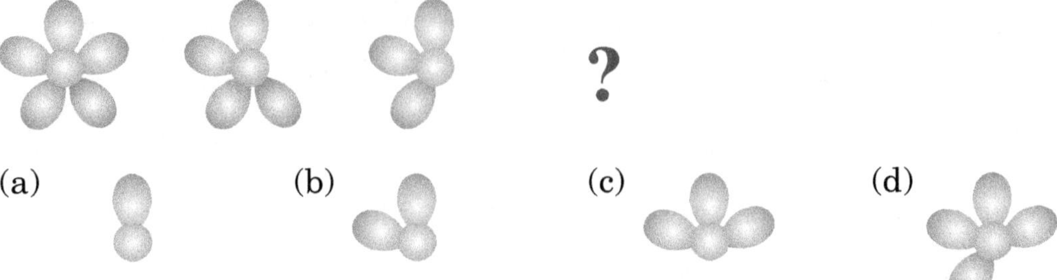

(a) (b) (c) (d)

10. Which is the next pattern ?

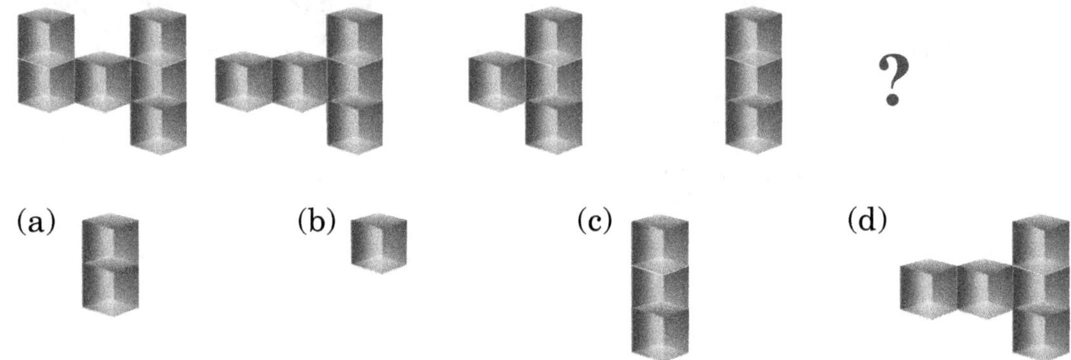

(a) (b) (c) (d)

11. Which is the next pattern ?

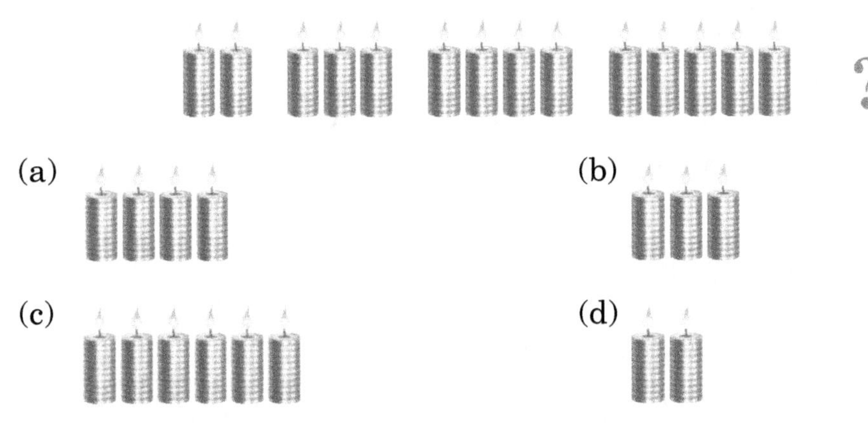

(a) (b) (c) (d)

12. Find the next pattern ?

13. Which is the next pattern ?

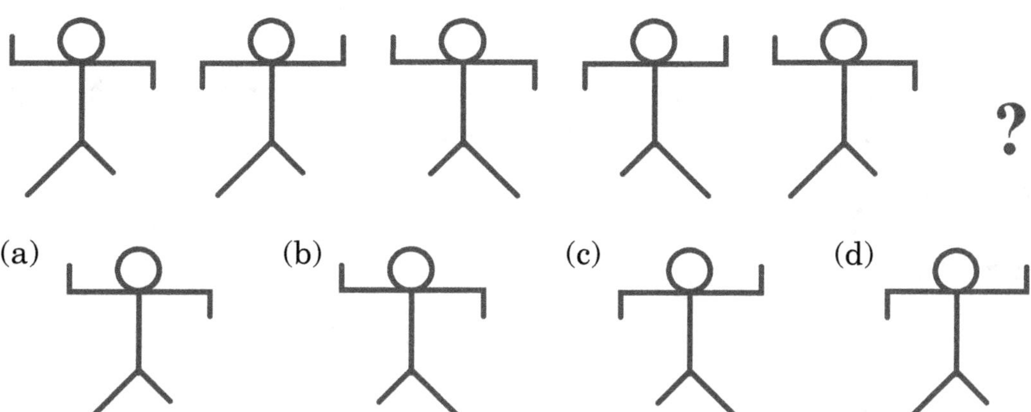

Direction (Qs. 14-17): Find the missing number in the given pattern.

14.

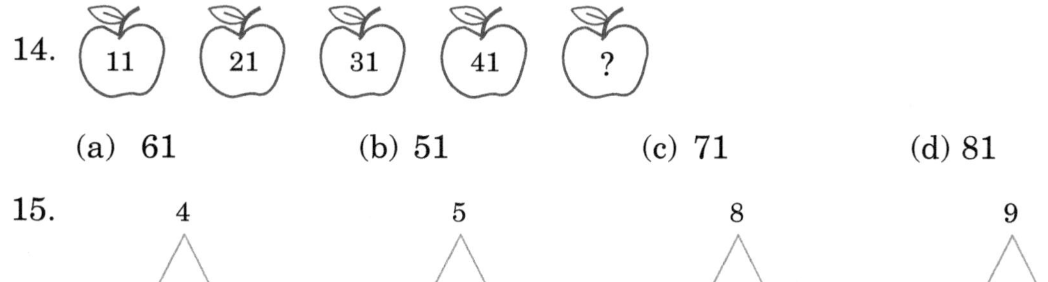

(a) 61 (b) 51 (c) 71 (d) 81

15.

4	5	8	9
4 2	5 2	5 2	4 4
10	12	15	?

(a) 12 (b) 15 (c) 17 (d) 13

16.

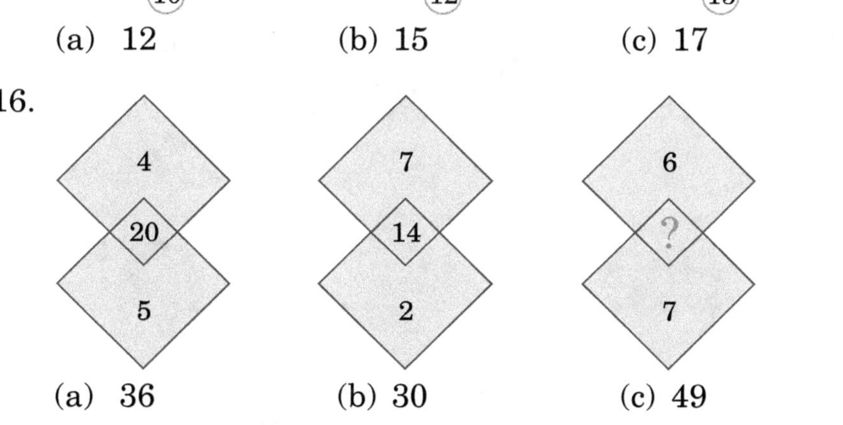

(a) 36 (b) 30 (c) 49 (d) 42

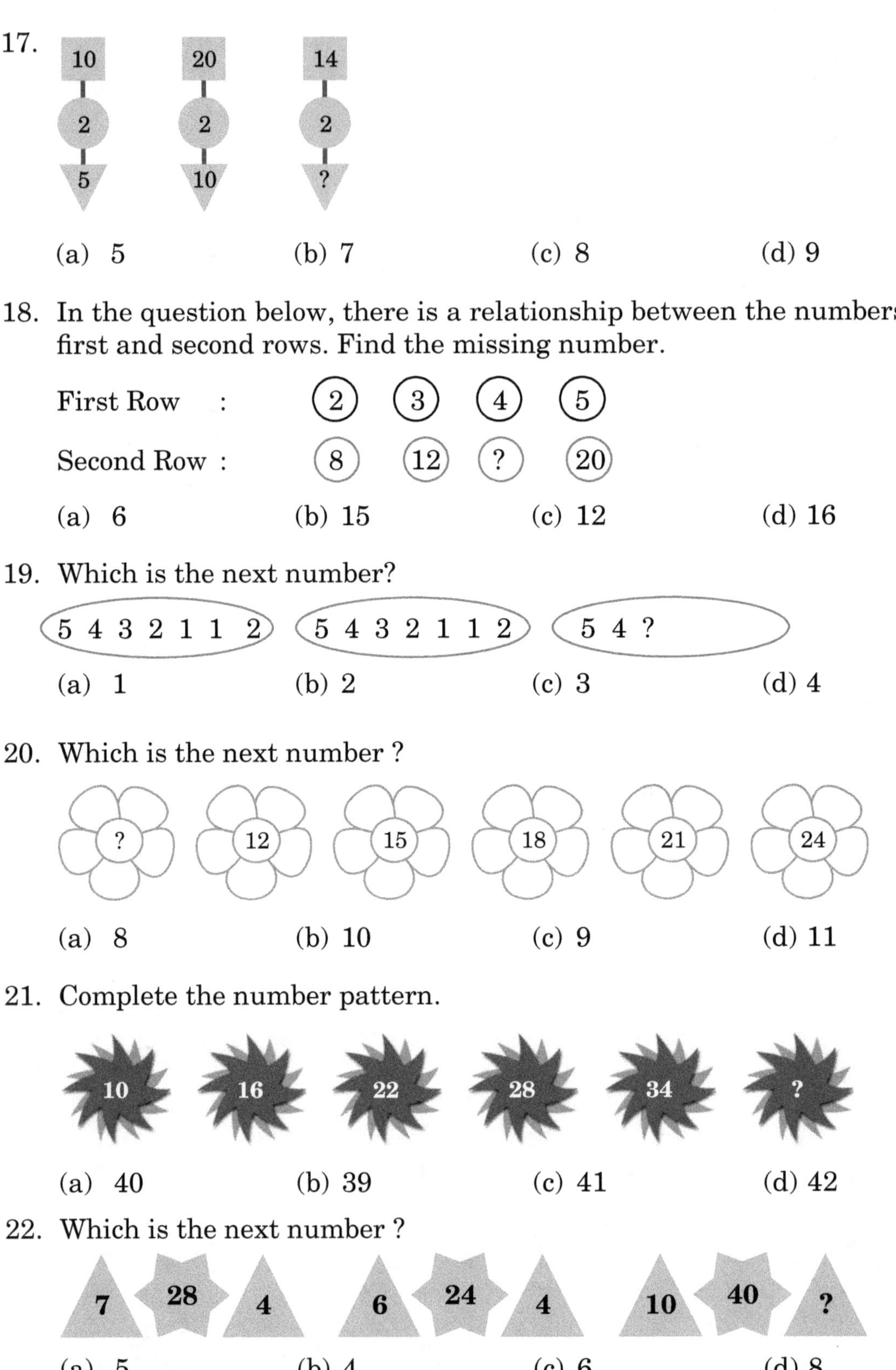

17.

(a) 5 (b) 7 (c) 8 (d) 9

18. In the question below, there is a relationship between the numbers in the first and second rows. Find the missing number.

First Row : 2 3 4 5

Second Row : 8 12 ? 20

(a) 6 (b) 15 (c) 12 (d) 16

19. Which is the next number?

5 4 3 2 1 1 2 5 4 3 2 1 1 2 5 4 ?

(a) 1 (b) 2 (c) 3 (d) 4

20. Which is the next number ?

(a) 8 (b) 10 (c) 9 (d) 11

21. Complete the number pattern.

(a) 40 (b) 39 (c) 41 (d) 42

22. Which is the next number ?

(a) 5 (b) 4 (c) 6 (d) 8

23. What is the next term ?

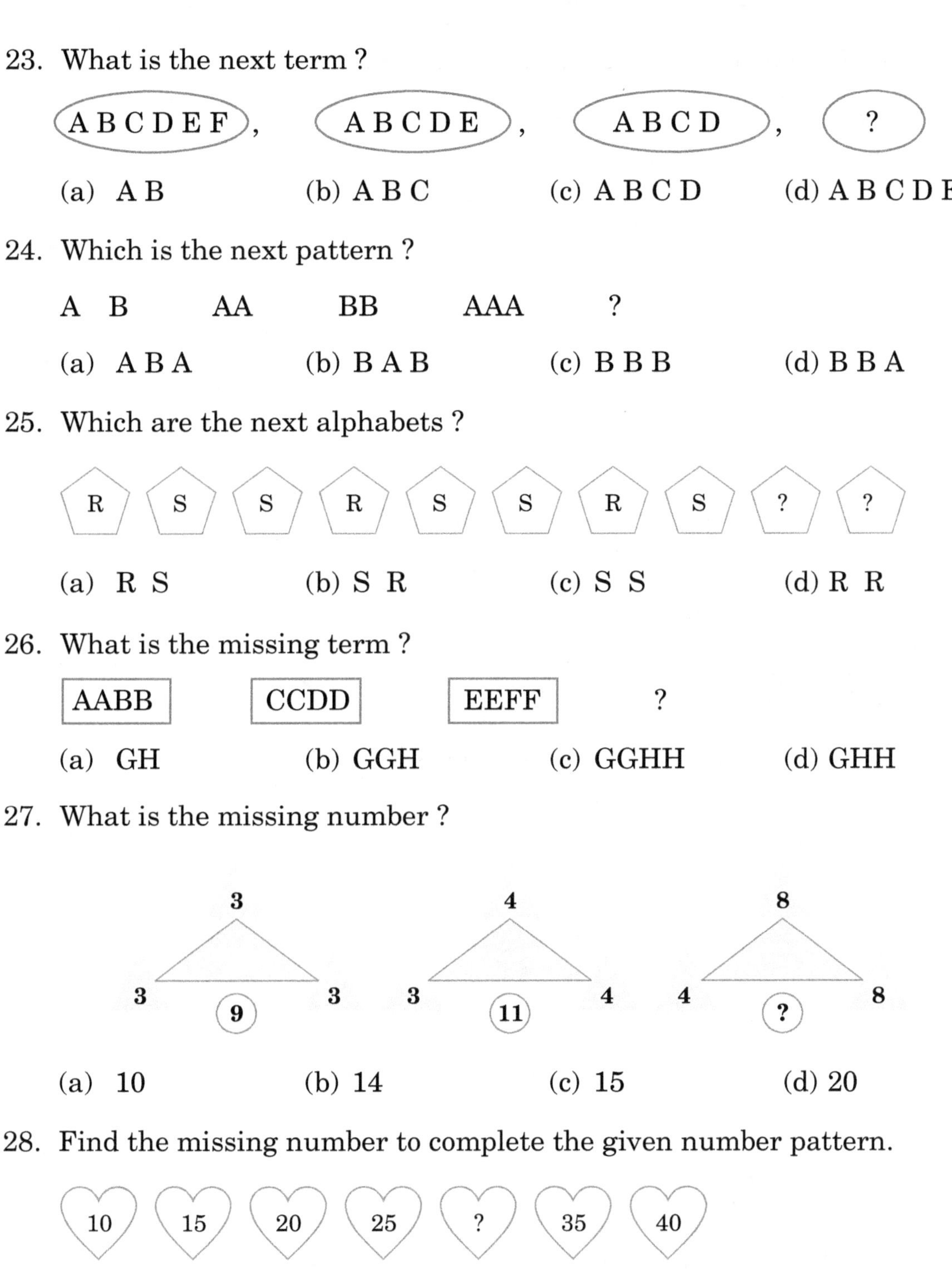

(a) A B (b) A B C (c) A B C D (d) A B C D E

24. Which is the next pattern ?

A B AA BB AAA ?

(a) A B A (b) B A B (c) B B B (d) B B A

25. Which are the next alphabets ?

(a) R S (b) S R (c) S S (d) R R

26. What is the missing term ?

(a) GH (b) GGH (c) GGHH (d) GHH

27. What is the missing number ?

(a) 10 (b) 14 (c) 15 (d) 20

28. Find the missing number to complete the given number pattern.

(a) 35 (b) 15 (c) 30 (d) 45

29. Find the missing number in the given pattern.

125

25 5

200

20 10

93

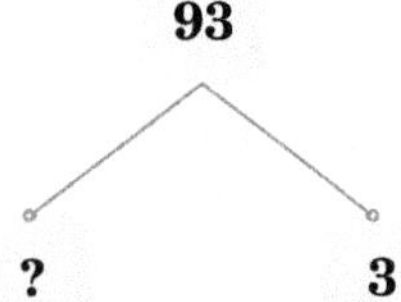

(a) 43 (b) 55 (c) 85 (d) 31

30. What will be the next number in the given pattern?

(a) 42 (b) 52 (c) 82 (d) 45

LEVEL-2

1. Find the next pattern.

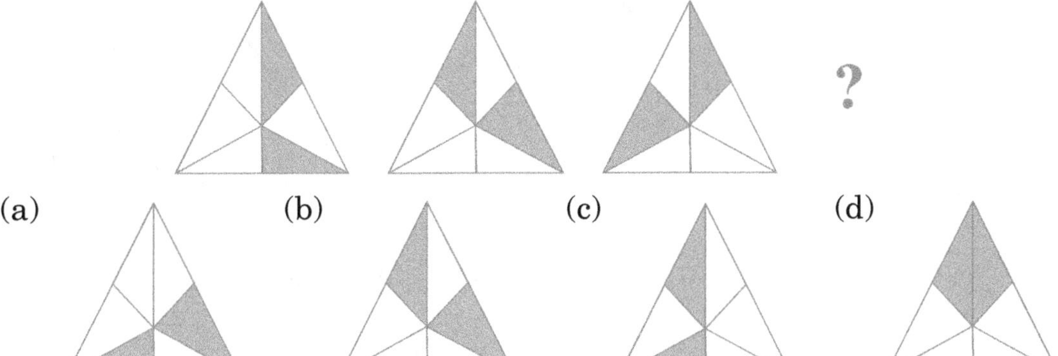

2. Find the next figure in the series given below.

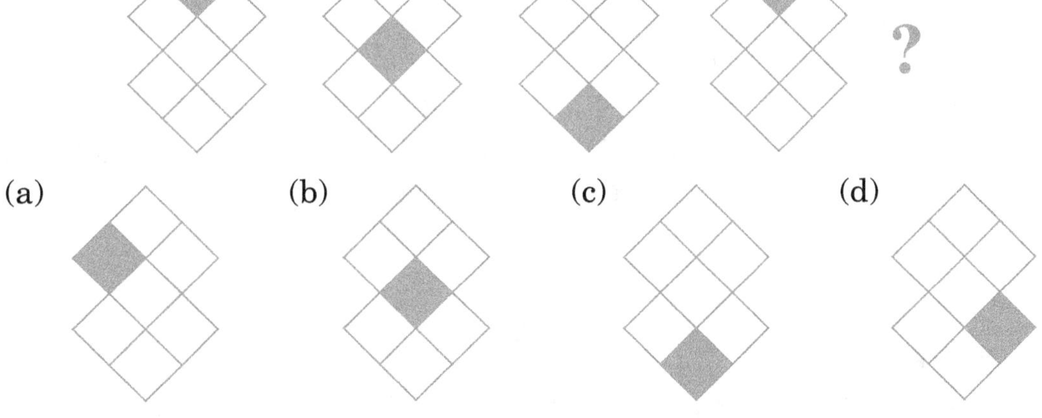

3. Find the next pattern.

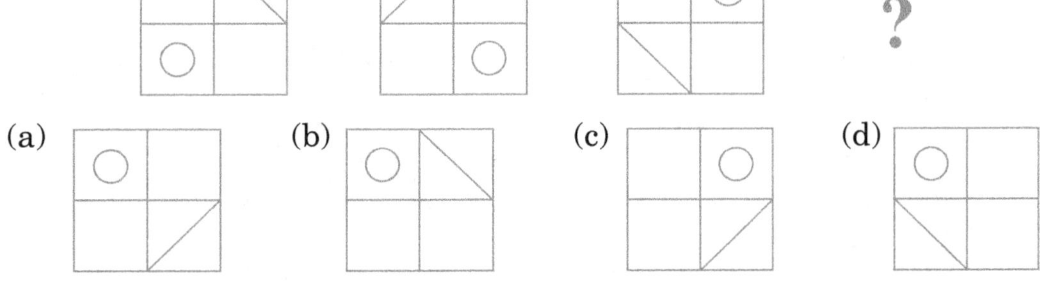

4. Find the next figure.

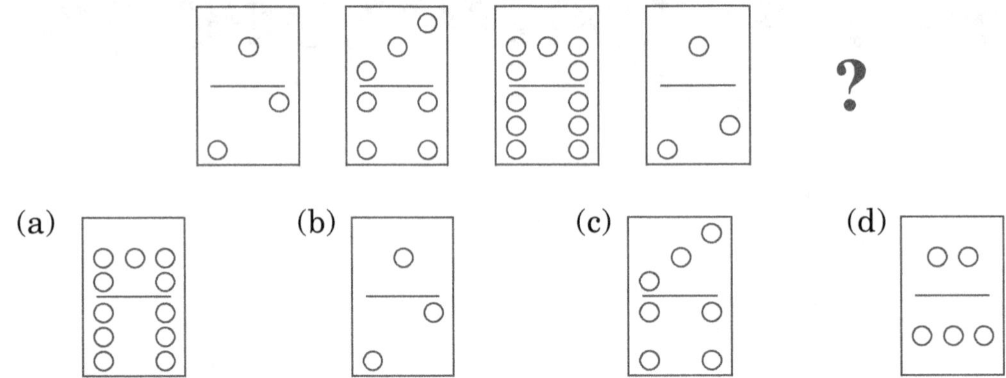

5. Which pattern is following in the given number series?

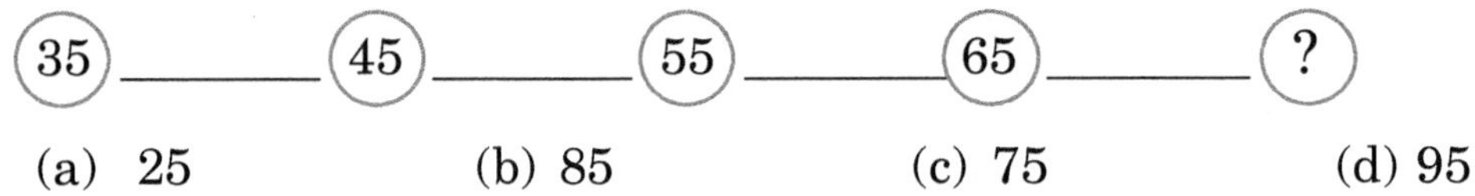

(a) 25 (b) 85 (c) 75 (d) 95

6. Fill the correct number in empty box.

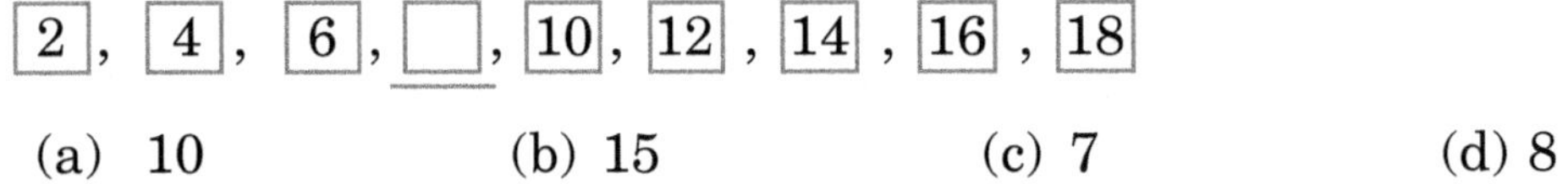

(a) 10 (b) 15 (c) 7 (d) 8

7. The factory smoke stacks puff each time the horn is blown. What pattern do you see in the picture? What do think will happen at the 4th horn blows?

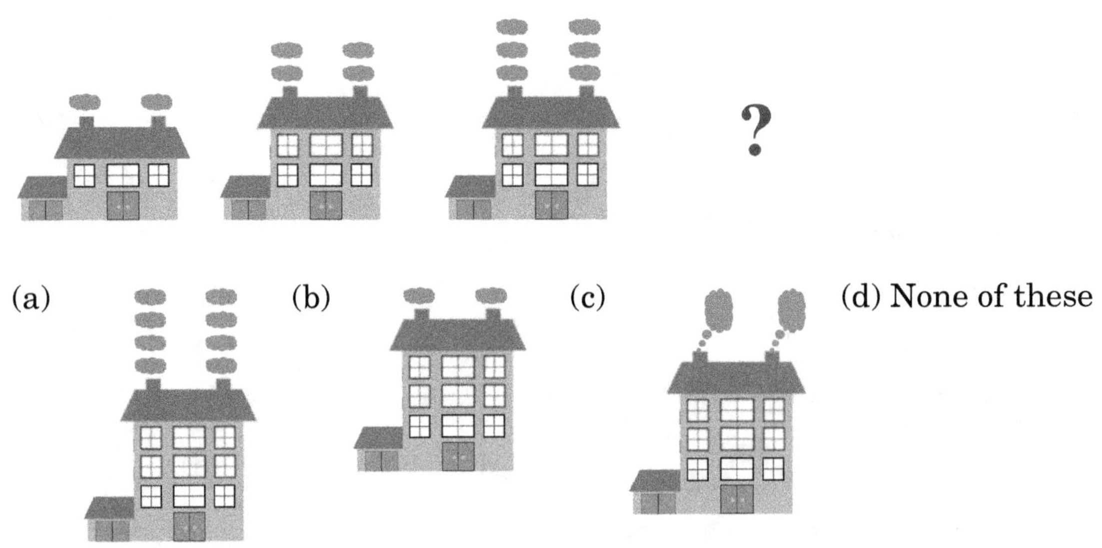

(d) None of these

8. Find the missing number in number pattern-II, if the series in both patterns follows the same rule.

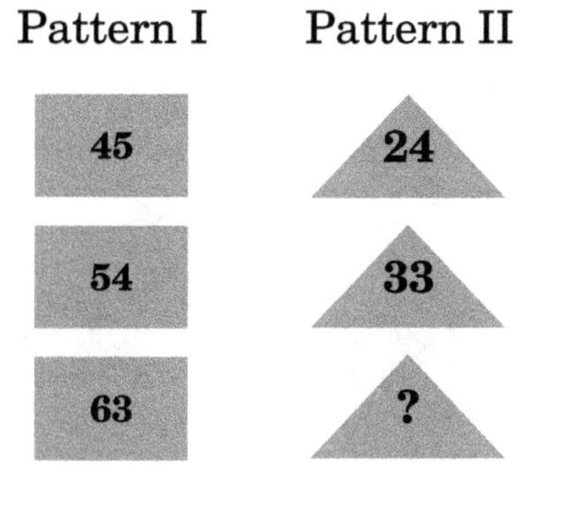

(a) 32 (b) 42 (c) 41 (d) 40

9. Find the missing number in the given figure.

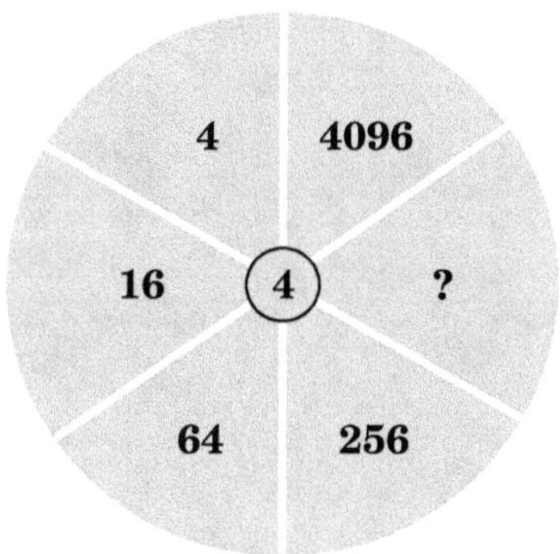

(a) 1024 (b) 1246 (c) 1296 (d) 0

10. Find the missing figure in the given series.

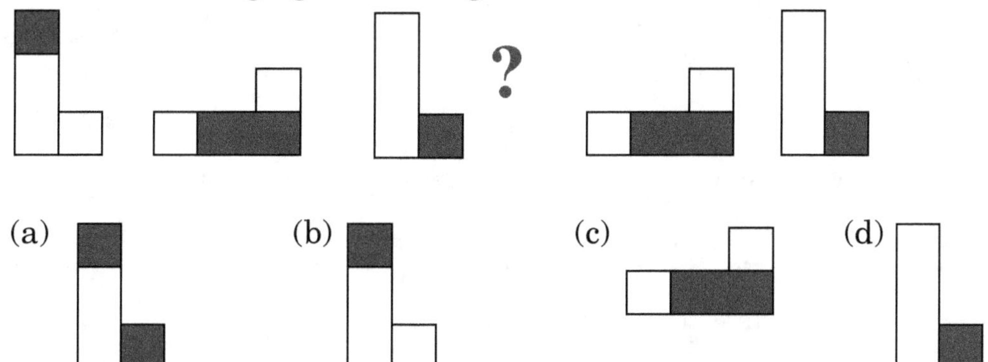

11. Complete the pattern that comes next in series.

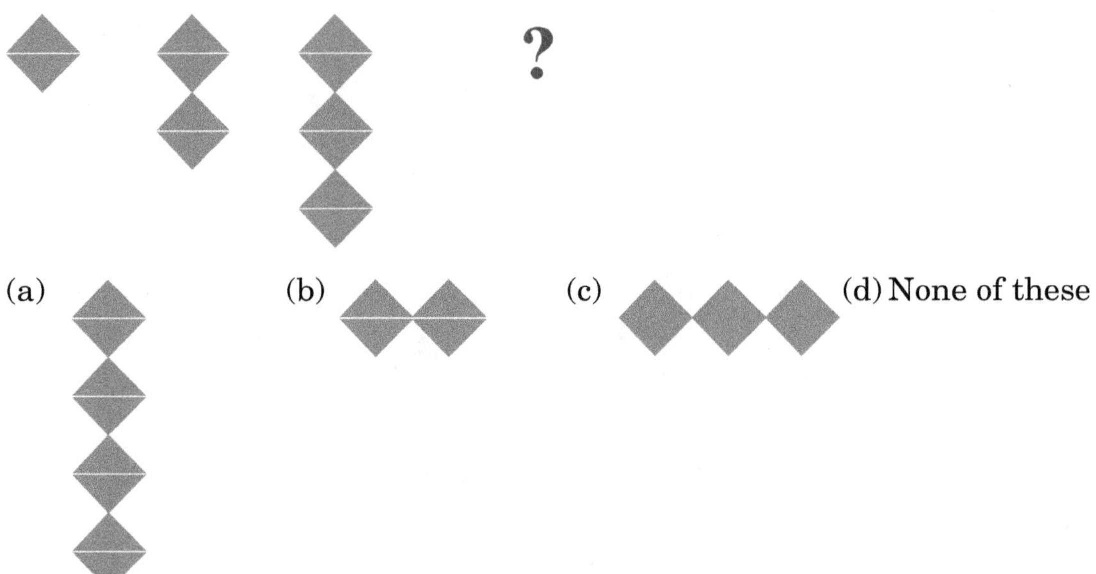

(a) (b) (c) (d) None of these

12. Complete the pattern by using the technique of repeating pattern.

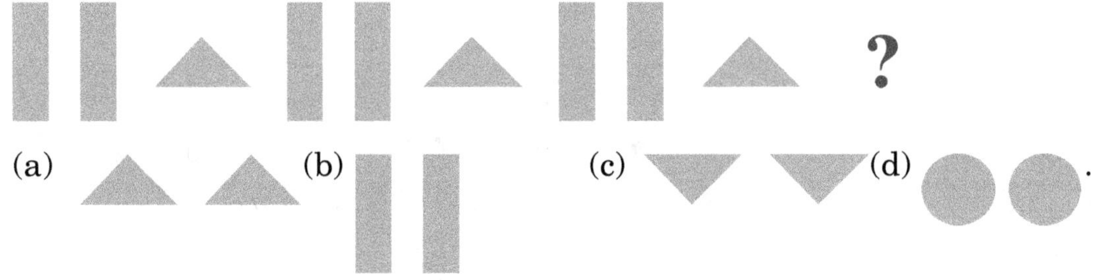

(a) (b) (c) (d)

13. Which is the next figure ?

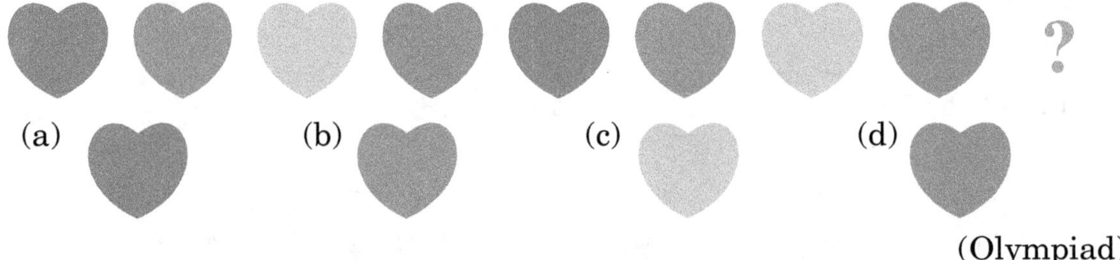

(a) (b) (c) (d)

(Olympiad)

14. The next figure in the given figure pattern is _________.

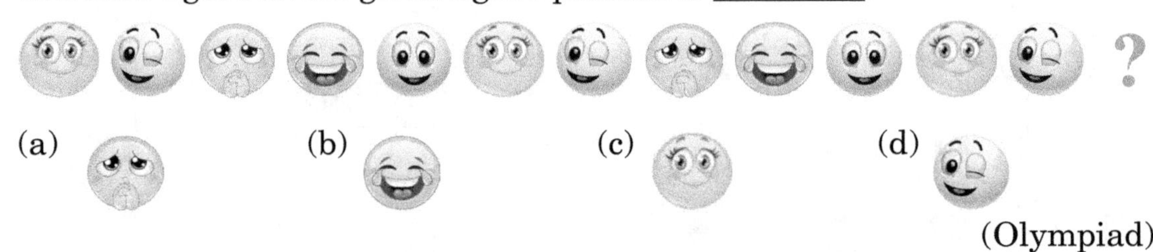

(a) (b) (c) (d)

(Olympiad)

15. Which of the following parts will complete the pattern in Figure (X)?

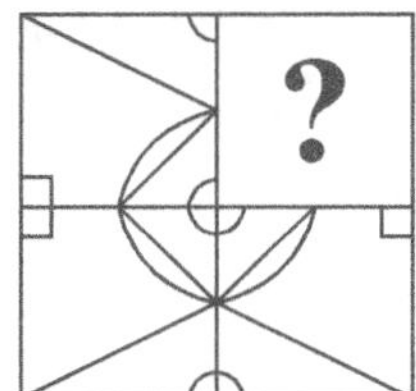

Figure (X)

(a) (b) (c) (d)

(Olympiad)

16. Identify the missing figure in the given figure pattern.

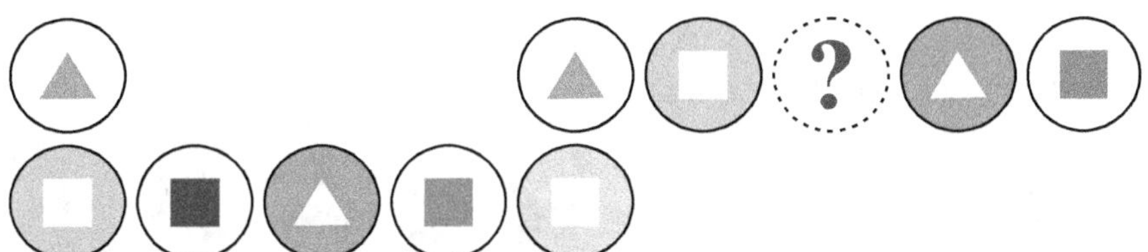

(a) (b) (c) (d)

(Olympiad)

17. Identify the missing shape which will complete the figure pattern.

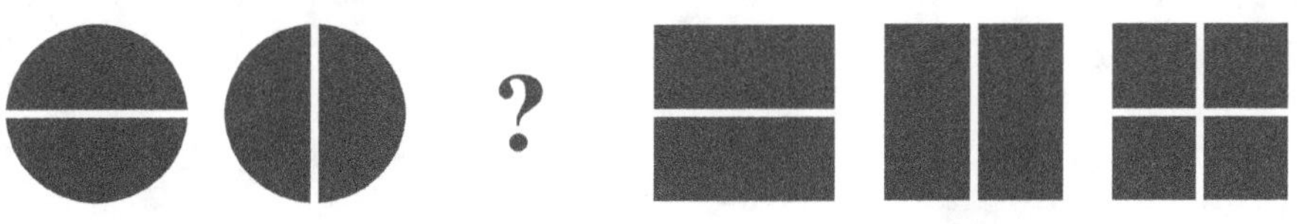

(a) 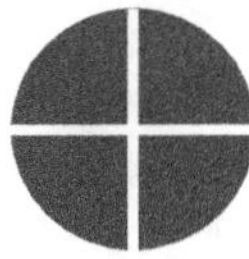 (b)  (c) 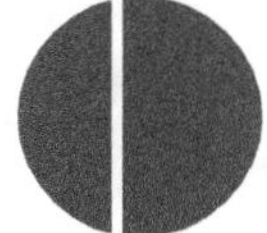 (d) 

(Olympiad)

18. Identify the figure which will complete the given figure series?

(a) (b) (c) (d)

(Olympiad)

19. What is the missing number?

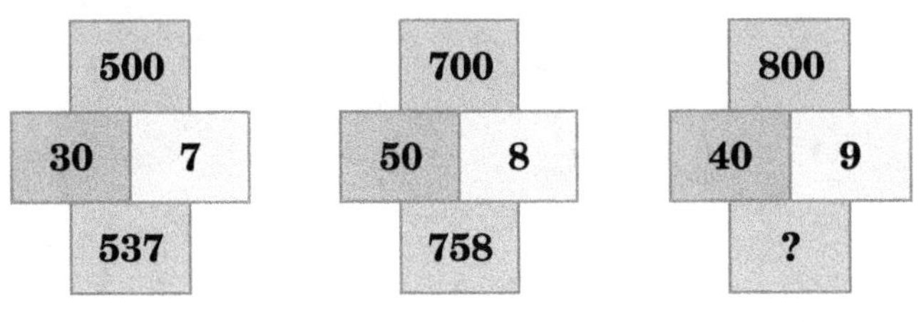

(a) 498 (b) 849 (c) 984 (d) 489

(Olympiad)

20. Find the missing term in the pattern below.

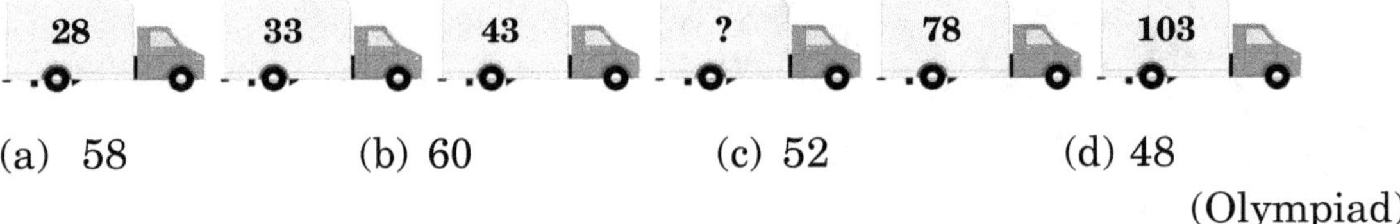

(a) 58 (b) 60 (c) 52 (d) 48

(Olympiad)

21. How many times does number 7 occur in counting from 7 to 80?

(a) 20 (b) 15 (c) 17 (d) 18

(Olympiad)

22. The missing number in the given number pattern is ________.

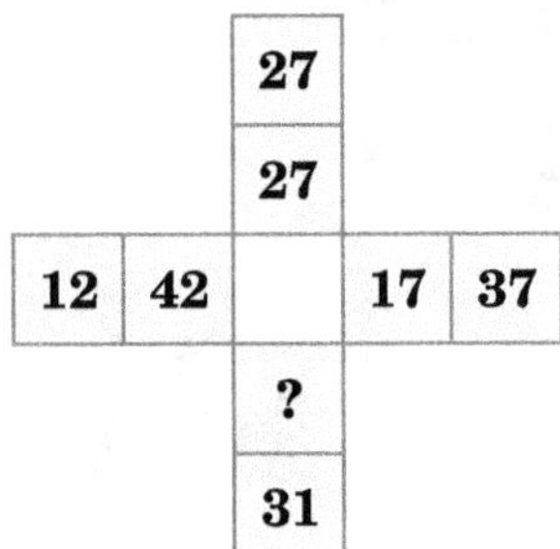

(a) 32 (b) 23 (c) 85 (d) 15

(Olympiad)

23. If the time in given below clocks follows a certain pattern, then what will be the time on the last clock?

(a) 7 : 10 (b) 6 : 40 (c) 7 : 00 (d) 5 : 20

(Olympiad)

24. ________ will replace the (?) in the given number pattern.

(a) 95 (b) 90 (c) 85 (d) 105

(Olympiad)

25. Complete the number pattern given below.

(a) 18 (b) 16 (c) 17 (d) 19

(Olympiad)

26. Which is the missing block?

4 4	1 7	
? 1 2 5		2 6

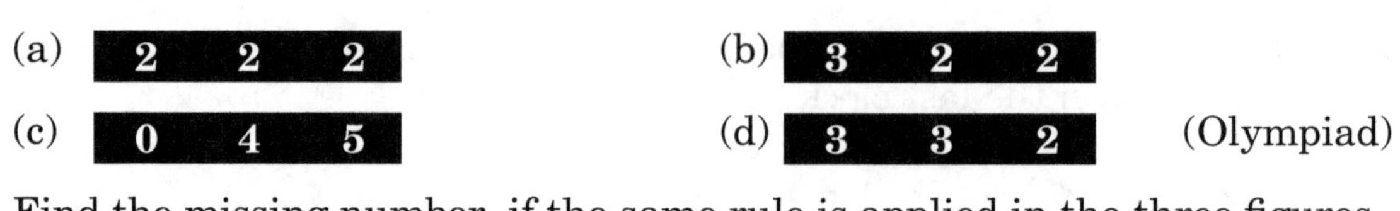

(Olympiad)

27. Find the missing number, if the same rule is applied in the three figures.

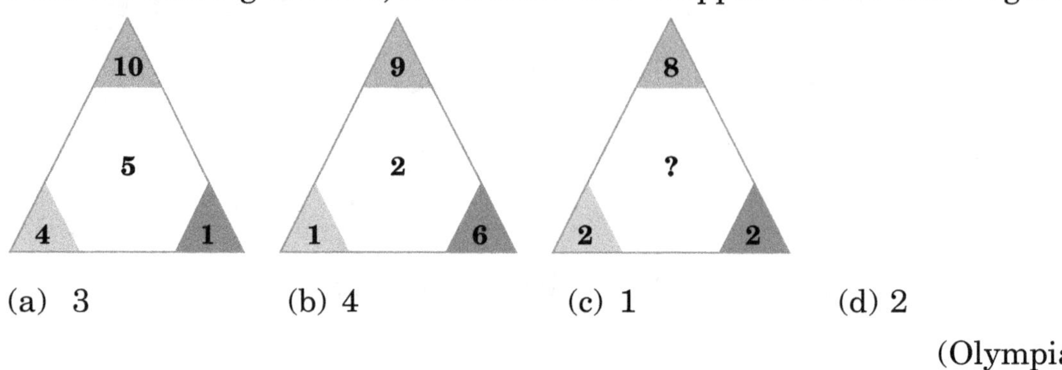

(a) 3 (b) 4 (c) 1 (d) 2

(Olympiad)

28. 8 / 3 11 8 / 2 10 11 / 4 15 ? / 4 9

(a) 8 (b) 6 (c) 5 (d) 13

29. What is the missing number ?

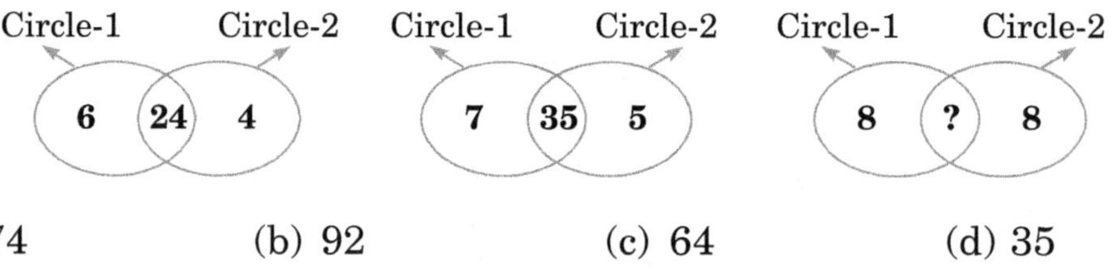

(a) 74 (b) 92 (c) 64 (d) 35

30. Find the rule followed in the figure pattern and the missing figure.

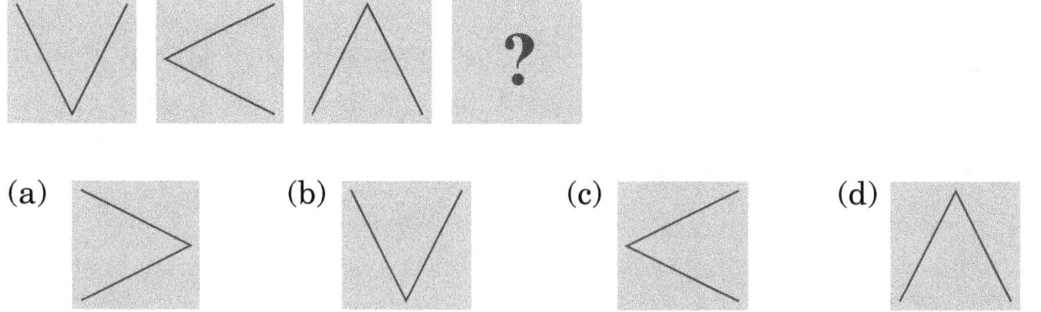

Answers and Explanations

Level-1

1. **(c)** Each figure repeats itself after a figure.

2. **(b)** The pattern is as follows:

   Teddy Bear ⟶ Doll ⟶ Joker ⟶ Doll ⟶ Teddy Bear ⟶ Joker ⟶ Teddy Bear ⟶ Doll ⟶ Joker ⟶ Doll ⟶ Teddy Bear

3. **(c)** The Pattern is as follows:

   Dog ⟶ Cat ⟶ Mouse ⟶ Mouse ⟶ Cat ⟶ Dog ⟶ Dog ⟶ Cat ⟶ Mouse ⟶ Mouse

4. **(d)** Here,

   Number of cars in Pattern 1 = 1

   Number of cars in Pattern 2 = 3

   Number of cars in Pattern 3 = 5

   So, the pattern is as follows

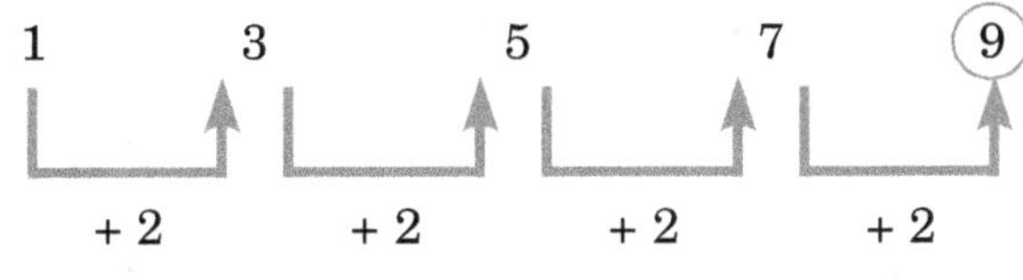

   ∴ Number of cars in pattern 5 = 9

5. **(a)** Here,

   Number of bees in Pattern 1 = 4

   Number of bees in Pattern 2 = 6

   Number of bees in Pattern 3 = 8

   So, the pattern is as follows:

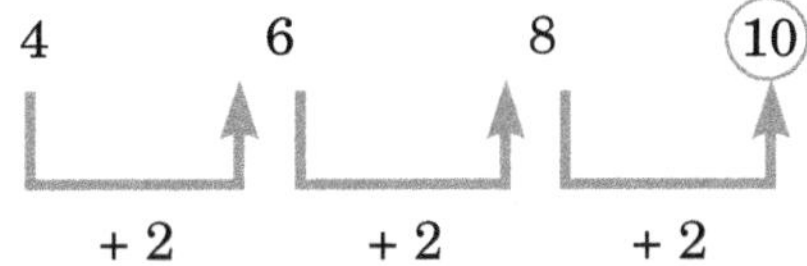

   ∴ Number of bees in Pattern 4 = 10

6. **(c)** The pattern repeates itself after 4 shapes.

7. **(c)** The pattern is :

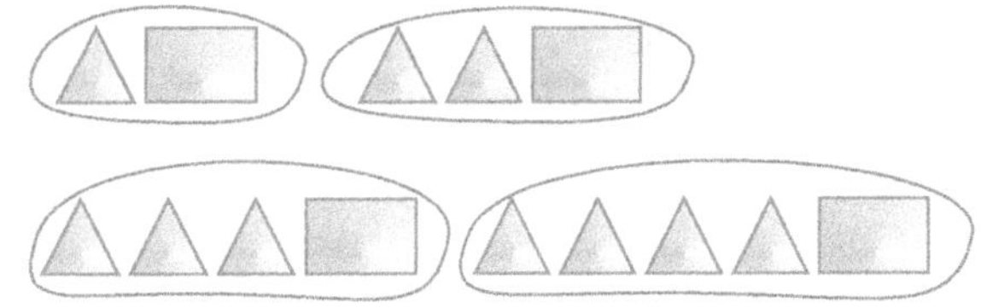

   So, Next pattern is:

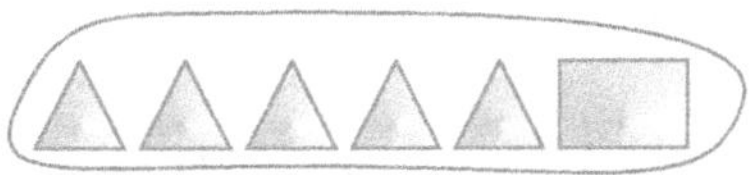

8. **(a)** Shaded triangle is moving clockwise.

9. **(b)** Petals are decreasing by one in each step.

10. **(a)** One square box is reducing at every step.

11. **(c)** One candle is increasing at every step.

12. **(b)** One leaf is reducing of one side alternately.

13. **(d)** Each figure repeats itself after every three figures.

14. **(b)** We get each next number by adding 10 in its previous number.

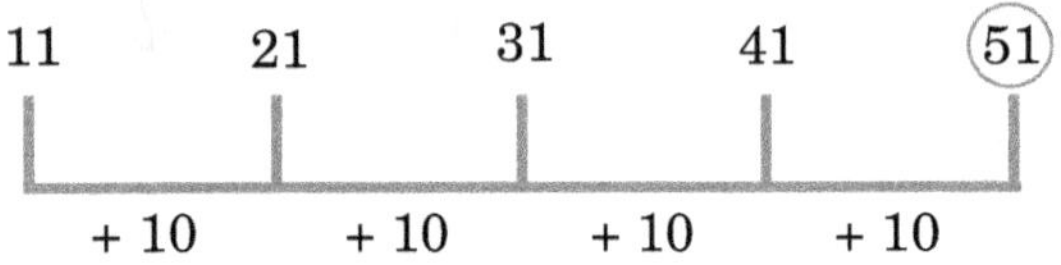

15. **(c)** Bottom number is obtained by adding the corner numbers.

4 + 4 + 2 = 10

5 + 5 + 2 = 12

8 + 5 + 2 = 15

9 + 4 + 4 = 17

16. **(d)** Middle number is obtained by adding 4 five times.

4 + 4 + 4 + 4 + 4 = 20

Middle number is obtained by adding 7 two times.

7 + 7 = 14

Similarly, Middle number is obtained by adding 6 seven times.

6 + 6 + 6 + 6 + 6 + 6 + 6 = 42

17. **(b)** Number in ☐ is obtained by adding

Number in ▽ two times.

5 + 5 = 10, 10 + 10 = 20, 7 + 7 = 14

18. **(d)** Number in second row is obtained by adding number of first row 4 times.

2 + 2 + 2 + 2 = 8, 3 + 3 + 3 + 3 = 12

4 + 4 + 4 + 4 = **16**, 5 + 5 + 5 + 5 = 20

19. **(c)**

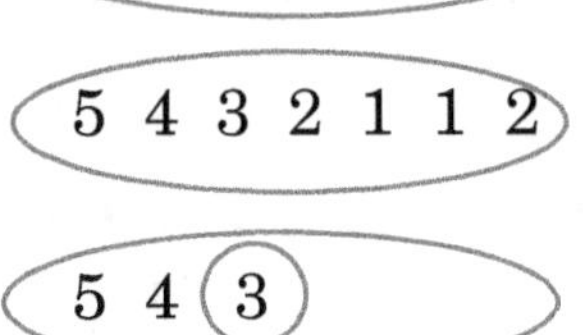

20. **(c)**

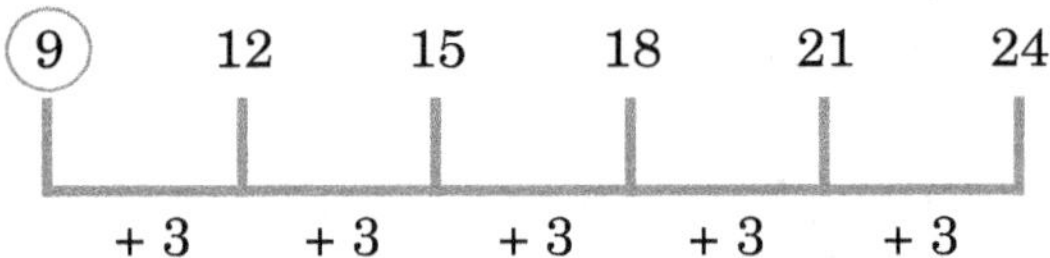

21. **(a)** Each number is obtained by adding six in previous number.

10 + 6 = 16; 16 + 6 = 22;

22 + 6 = 28; 28 + 6 = 34,

34 + 6 = 40

22. **(b)** As, 7 + 7 + 7 + 7 = 28 (Add 7 four times)

and, 6 + 6 + 6 + 6 = 24

(Add 6 four times)

Similarly,

10 + 10 + 10 + 10 = 40

(Add 10 four times)

23. **(b)** One letter is removing at every step.

24. (c)

repeated one time repeated two times

A B AA BB AAA BBB

repeated one time repeated two times

25. (b) Each letter repeats itself after two letters.

26. (c) Letters are arranged in consecutive order and repeated.

27. (d) Bottom number is obtained by adding the corner numbers.

$3 + 3 + 3 = 9$

$4 + 4 + 3 = 11$

$8 + 8 + 4 = \boxed{20}$

28. (c) The pattern is as follows:

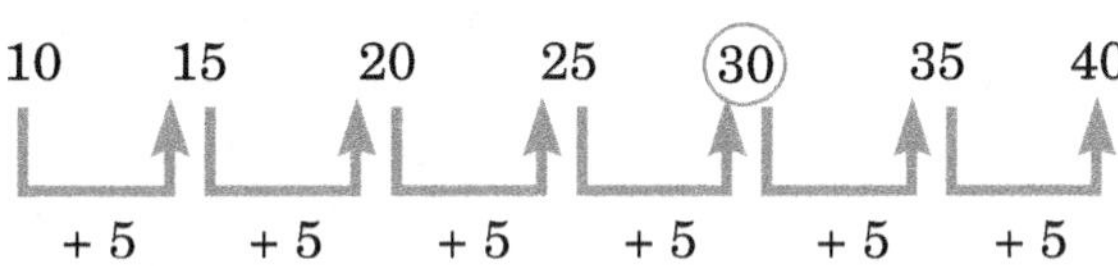

29. (d) As, $125 \div 25 = 5$

and, $200 \div 20 = 10$

Similarly, $93 \div ? = 3$

$? = 93 \div 3, ? = \boxed{31}$

30. (a) The pattern is as follows:

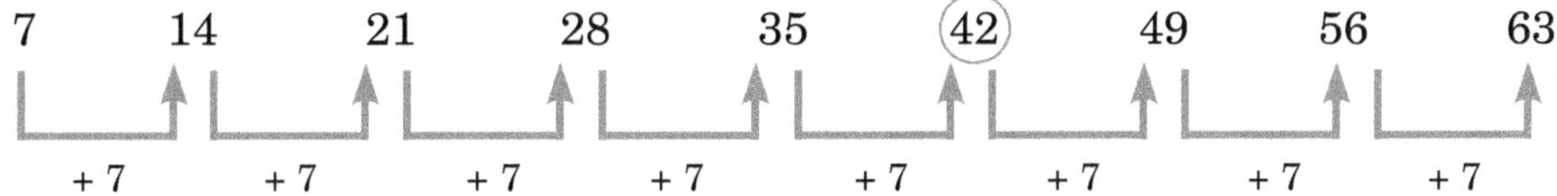

Level-2

1. **(c)** Shaded triangles are moving anticlockwise.
2. **(b)** Shaded square is moving from top to bottom.
3. **(a)** Slant line and circle are moving anticlockwise.
4. **(c)** Each figure repeats itself after two figures.
5. **(c)** The pattern is as follows:

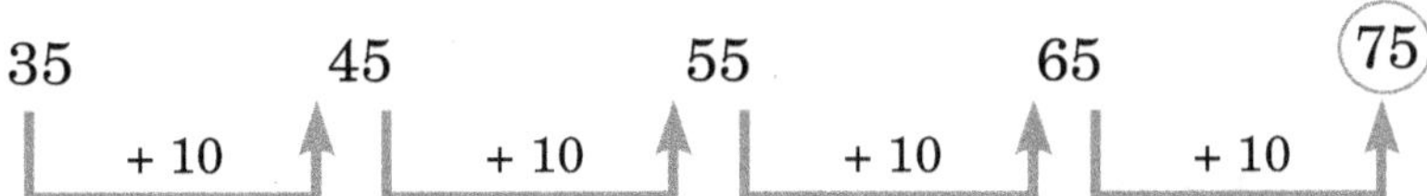

6. **(d)** In the given sequence, the rule of adding 2 in each number is followed.

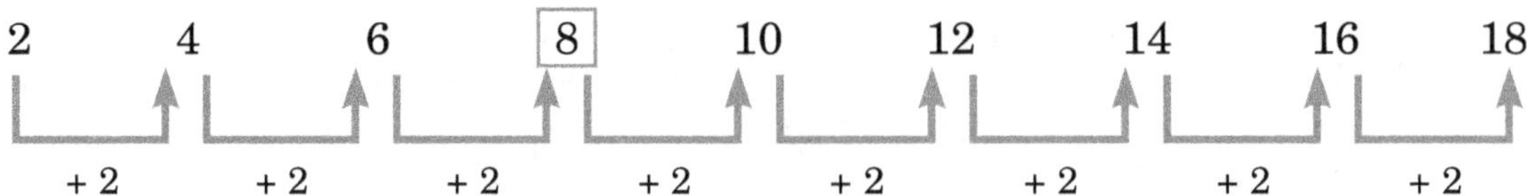

7. **(a)** In this series adding of 2 smoke clouds in each figure is followed.

8. **(b)** As,

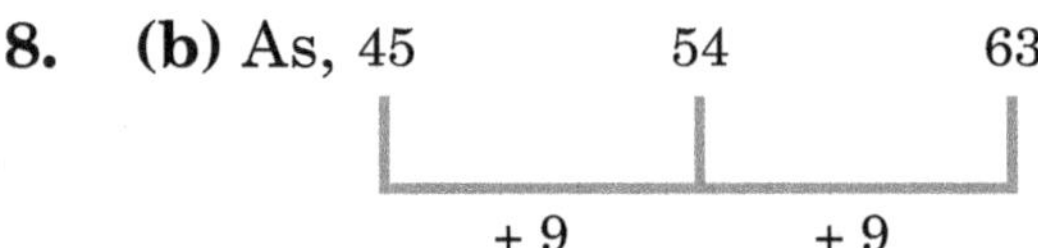

Similarly,

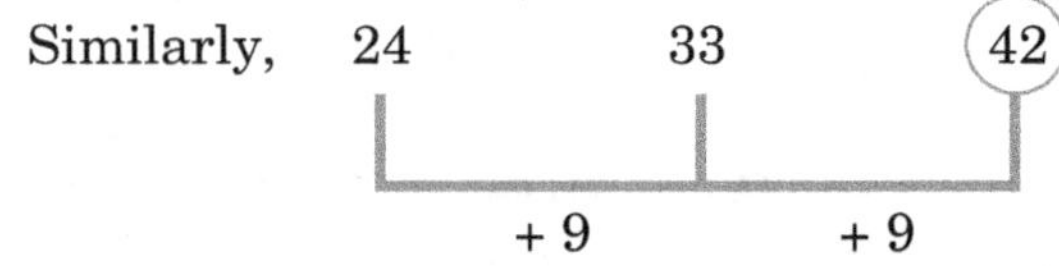

9. **(a)** As,

$4 \times 1 = 4$

$4 \times 4 = 16$

$16 \times 4 = 64$

$64 \times 4 = 256$

$256 \times 4 = 1024$ (circled)

$1024 \times 4 = 4096$.

10. **(b)** The pattern repeats itself after 2 steps.

11. **(a)** Pattern is increasing by adding 1 in each step.

12. **(b)** Each figure repeats itself after a figure.

13. **(a)** Each figure repeats after three figures.

14. **(a)** Each figure repeats after four figures.

15. **(b)** Option figure (b) will complete the pattern in figure (X).

16. **(a)** Option figure (a) is the missing figure in the given figure pattern.

17. **(a)** Option figure (a) is the missing shape.

18. **(a)** Each figure repeats after every three figures.

19. **(b)** As,

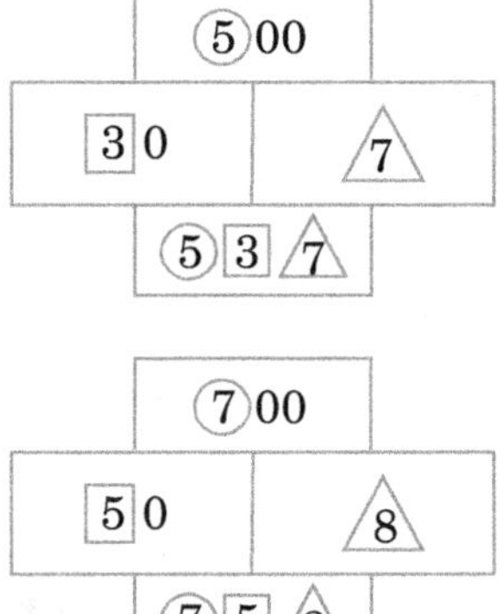

Similarly,

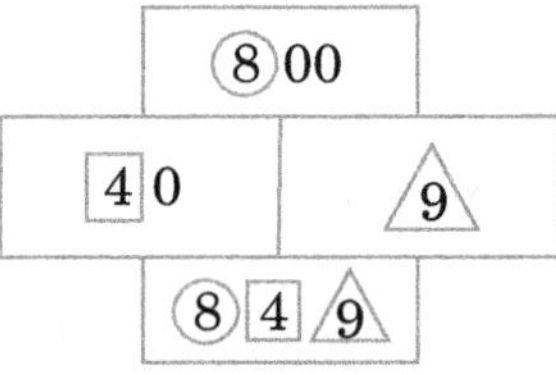

20. **(a)** The pattern of the series is as follows:

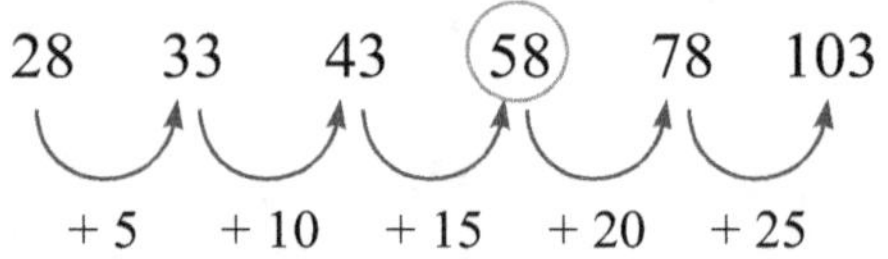

21. (d) Integers: 7, 17, 27, 37, 47, 57, 67, 70, 71, 72, 73, 74, 75, 76, **77**, 78, 79 = 18 times

└→ Count as two

22. (b) As,

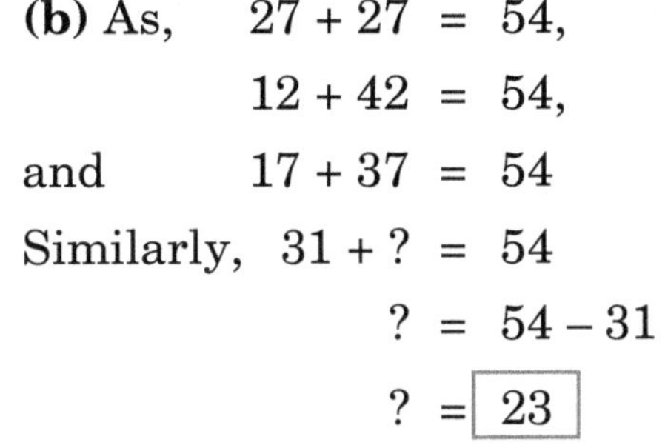

23. (a) 7 : 10 will be the time on the last clock.

24. (a) The pattern of the series is as follows:

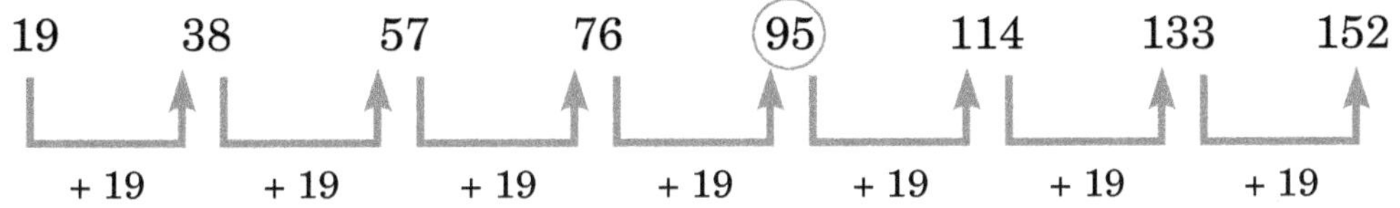

25. (b) The pattern of the series is as follows:

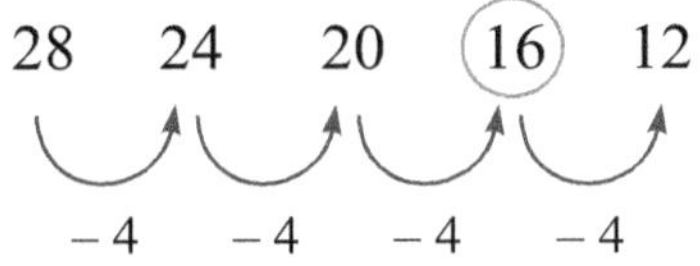

26. (d) As,

4 + 4 = (8)	1 + 7 = (8)
3 + 3 + 2 = (8)	2 + 6 = (8)
1 + 2 + 5 = (8)	

27. (b) As in 1st figure,

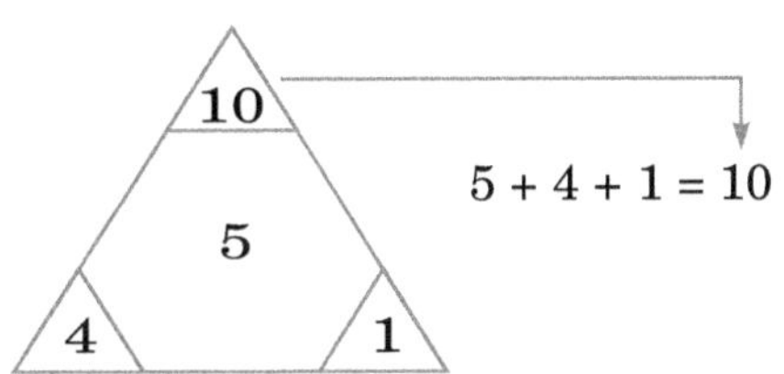

In 2nd figure,

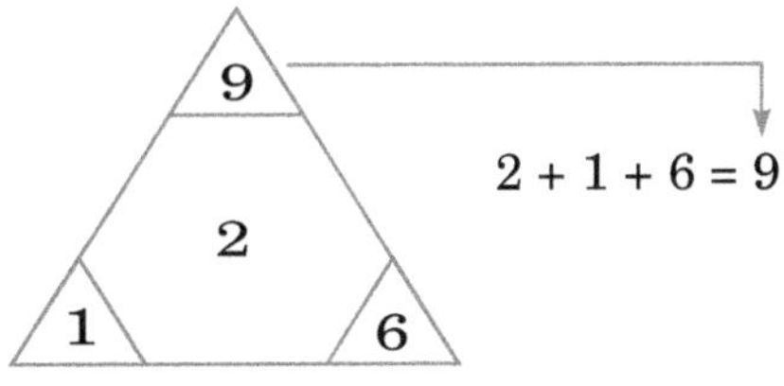

Similarly,
In 3rd figure,

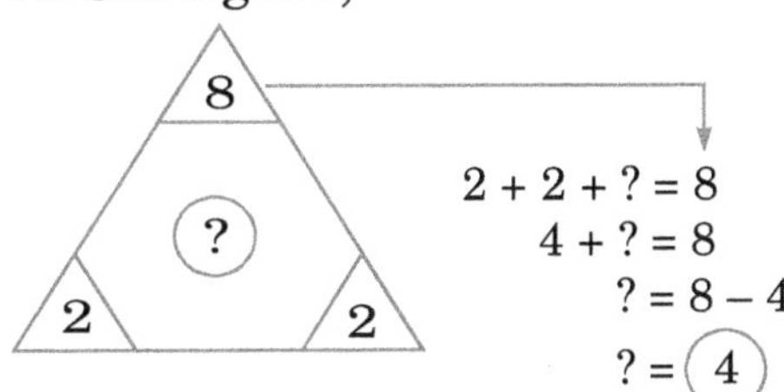

28. (c) The pattern is as follows:

$11 - 3 = 8$

$10 - 2 = 8$

$15 - 4 = 11$

$9 - 4 = 5$

29. (c) Middle number is obtained by multiplying number in Circle 1 and Circle 2.

$6 \times 4 = 24$

$7 \times 5 = 35$

$8 \times 8 = \textcircled{64}$

30. (a) Inner figure is rotating clockwise. So the missing figure is (a).

CHAPTER 3

SEQUENCE

OBJECTIVES

- Students will learn to arrange words/events in a meaningful order
- They will develop the ability to know association and order.
- Students will learn how arithmetic, geometric and other sequences relate to the real world.

INTRODUCTION

A sequence is a set of related events, movements, or items that follow each other in a particular order.

TYPES OF SEQUENCE

TYPE-I

Sequence of Words

In this particular type of problem, certain interrelated words are given and numbered, followed by various sequences of the numbers denoting them, as alternatives.

Students are required to arrange these words in a logical sequence based on a common property and then choose the correctly graded sequence from the given data.

Examples:

1. Arrange the words given below in a meaningful sequence.

   1. Key 2. Door 3. Lock 4. Room 5. Switch on

   (a) 5, 1, 2, 4, 3 (b) 4, 2, 1, 5, 3 (c) 1, 3, 2, 4, 5 (d) 1, 2, 3, 5, 4

Ans. (c)

Explanation:

The correct order is:

1 3 2 4 5

Key ⟶ Lock ⟶ Door ⟶ Room ⟶ Switch on

2. Arrange the given words in a meaningful sequence.

1. Skull 2. Shoulder 3. Neck 4. Face 5. Legs

(a) 1, 2, 3, 4, 5 (b) 1, 4, 3, 2, 5 (c) 1, 3, 4, 2, 5 (d) 1, 4, 2, 3, 5

Ans. (b) The meaningful sequence is

1 4 3 2 5

Skull ⟶ Face ⟶ Neck ⟶ Shoulder ⟶ Legs

3. Arrange the given words in a meaningful sequence.

1. Animal 2. Cow 3. Grass 4. Mammal 5. Milk

(a) 4, 1, 2, 5, 3 (b) 1, 4, 2, 5, 3 (c) 1, 4, 2, 3, 5 (d) 4, 1, 2, 3, 5

Ans. (c) The meaningful sequence is:

1 4 2 3 5

Animal ⟶ Mammal ⟶ Cow ⟶ Grass ⟶ Milk

4. Arrange the given pictures in the proper sequence by using their alphabets.

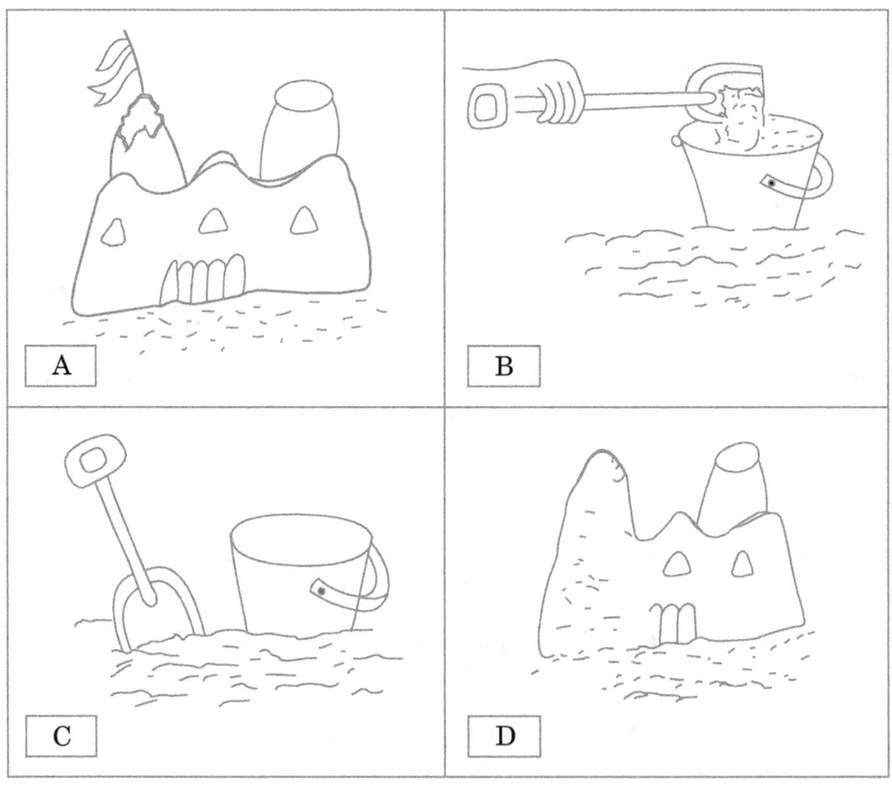

(a) ABCD (b) DCBA (c) BCAD (d) CBDA

Ans. (d) CBDA is the proper sequence

TYPE-II

FORMATION OF WORDS

In these type of questions, certain words are given and students are required to observe them in order as they are asked to do.

Examples:

1. V A R S T E ⇒ Choose the correct order of letters which are required to
   1 2 3 4 5 6
   form the correct word.

   (a) 2, 3, 1, 6, 4, 5 (b) 3, 2, 4, 5, 6, 1

   (c) 4, 5, 2, 3, 1, 6 (d) 6, 3, 4, 5, 2, 1

Ans. (c)

Explanation: Here, we've to create the correct word and 'V' has been labelled as 1, 'A' as 2, 'R' as 3, 'S' as 4, 'T' as 5 and 'E' as 6.

On observing, we can see the correct word is STARVE. So, option (c) is correct.

2. In the following question, a group of letters is given which are numbered 1, 2, 3, 4 and 5. Below are given four alternatives containing combinations of these numbers. Select that combination of numbers so that letters arranged accordingly, form a meaningful word.

R	U	S	G	A
1	2	3	4	5

   (a) 1, 5, 4, 2, 3 (b) 5, 3, 4, 1, 2 (c) 3, 2, 4, 5, 1 (d) 4, 5, 3, 2, 1

Ans. (c)

Explanation: On observing, we can see the correct word is SUGAR.

So, option (c) is correct.

LEVEL-1

1. Arrange the letters to a proper sequence to form a meaningful word.

A C H L K
1 2 3 4 5

(a) 2 3 1 4 5 (b) 1 3 2 4 5 (c) 3 2 4 1 5 (d) 2 3 1 5 4.

2. Arrange the given pictures in the proper sequence by using their alphabets?

A. She listens to a story after dinner

B. Helly is having her dinner

C. She is sleeping

(a) A, B, C (b) B, A, C (c) B, C, A (d) A, C, B

3. If the day before yesterday was Saturday, then what is the day today?

(a) Friday (b) Thursday (c) Wednesday (d) Monday

4. How many combinations of two-digit numbers having 8 can be made from the following numbers?

8, 5, 2, 1, 7, 6

(a) 11 (b) 10 (c) 7 (d) 15

5. In the given following series how many 1 3 7 have appeared together?

3 1 7 3 7 7 1 3 7 1 7 3 5 1 3 7 7 1 9 0 6 2 9 3 7

(a) 5 (b) 7 (c) 2 (d) 0.

6. If it is Tuesday today, it was ______________ yesterday and it will be ______________ tomorrow.

(a) Friday, Saturday (b) Monday, Wednesday

(c) Thursday, Friday (d) Monday, Friday

7. How many 3's are there in the following sequence?

9 3 6 2 3 9 5 9 3 7 8 9 1 6 3 9 6 3 9

(a) 5 (b) 7 (c) 8 (d) 6

8. Today Palak is trying to make a pizza. Arrange the following pictures in the proper sequence to know how Palak makes her pizza?

1

2

3

4

(a) 4, 3, 2, 1 (b) 1, 2, 3, 4 (c) 3, 4, 1, 2 (d) 1, 3, 4, 2

9. Arrange the following words in a proper and logical order sequence.

1. Trillion 2. Thousand 3. Billion 4. Hundred 5. Million

(a) 4, 2, 5, 3, 1 (b) 1, 2, 3, 4, 5 (c) 5, 4, 3, 2, 1 (d) 3, 4, 1, 2, 5

10. Arrange the letters in a proper sequence to form a meaningful word.

L	W	O	R	E	F
2	4	3	6	5	1

(a) 1, 2, 3, 4, 5, 6 (b) 2, 4, 3, 6, 5, 1 (c) 5, 6, 4, 3, 2, 1 (d) 6, 4, 3, 5, 2, 1

11. Arrange the letters in a proper sequence to form a meaningful word.

G	M	O	A	N
1	2	3	4	5

(a) 2, 3, 4, 5, 1 (b) 2, 4, 5, 1, 3

(c) 5, 4, 3, 2, 1 (d) 5, 4, 2, 1, 3

12. Arrange the letters in a proper sequence to form a meaningful word.

M	S	I	E	L
1	2	3	4	5

(a) 2, 1, 3, 5, 4 (b) 1, 2, 3, 4, 5

(c) 4, 5, 3, 1, 2 (d) 2, 5, 1, 3, 4

13. In the following series how many times 3, 2, 7 have appeared together.

3 1 3 2 7 7 1 3 7 1 7 3 5 1 3 2 7 1 9 0 6 2 9 3 7

(a) 5 (b) 7 (c) 2 (d) 0

14. If it is Thursday today, it was ________________ yesterday when I was dancing with my brother at home and it will be ________________ tomorrow when I will join my swimming classes again.

(a) Wednesday, Friday (b) Monday, Saturday

(c) Thursday, Friday (d) Monday, Friday

15. How many combinations of two-digit numbers having 9 can be made from the following numbers?

    9, 5, 2, 1, 7, 6

    (a) 11 (b) 12 (c) 10 (d) 20

16. Arrange the correct sequence of months.

$\mathrm{S_EP}$	$\mathrm{M^AY}$	$\mathrm{D_EC}$	$\mathrm{A^UG}$	$\mathrm{F_EB}$
1	2	3	4	5

    (a) 31452 (b) 12345 (c) 52413 (d) 54321

17. Arrange the letters in a proper sequence to form a meaningful word.

    R E W A T

    1 2 3 4 5

    (a) 12345 (b) 34521 (c) 32145 (d) 54321

LEVEL-2

1. Arrange the given pictures of seasons in a proper sequence by using their alphabets.

(a) DCBA (b) ABCD (c) BACD (d) ACBD

2. Today Tani is trying to make tea. Given are some pictures, arrange them in the proper sequence to know how she makes her tea?

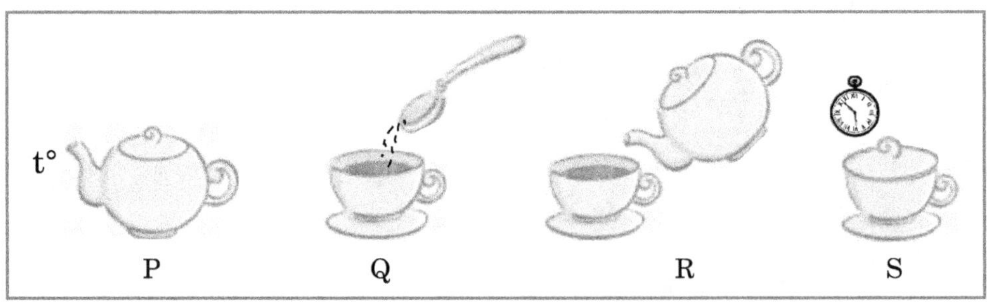

(a) PSQR (b) SRQP (c) PQRS (d) QRSP

3. Arrange the given pictures of a school in a proper sequence by using their numbers.

(a) 3142 (b) 2413 (c) 1234 (d) 4312

4. Arrange the given pictures in a proper sequence using their alphabets.

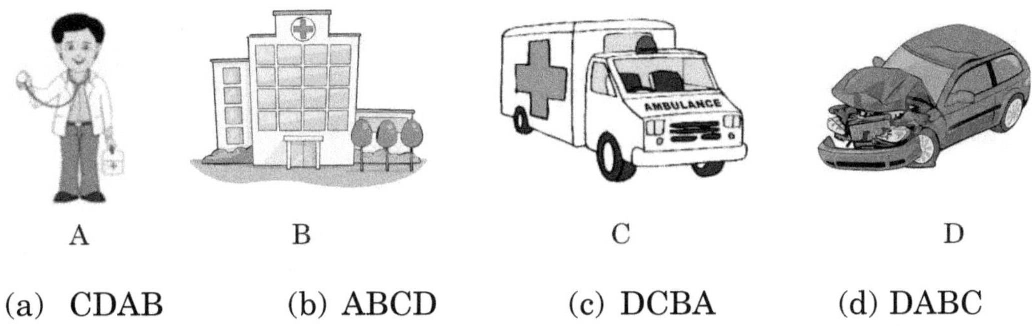

(a) CDAB (b) ABCD (c) DCBA (d) DABC

5. Arrange the given pictures in a proper sequence by using their alphabets.

(a) RSPQ (b) SRPQ (c) QPSR (d) SRQP

6. Arrange the given pictures in a proper sequence (small to big) by using their numbers.

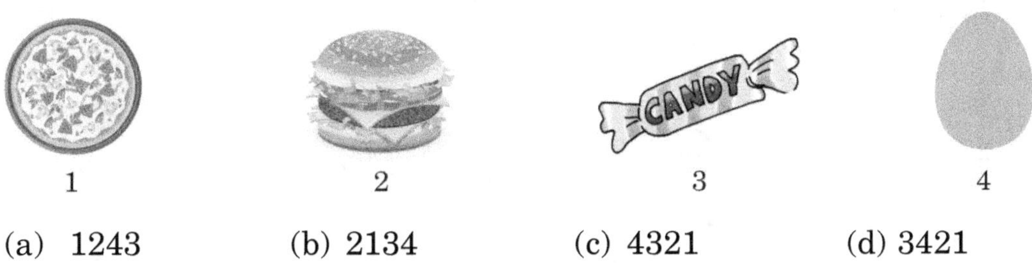

(a) 1243 (b) 2134 (c) 4321 (d) 3421

7. Arrange the given pictures of clocks (in descending order) in a proper sequence by using their alphabets?

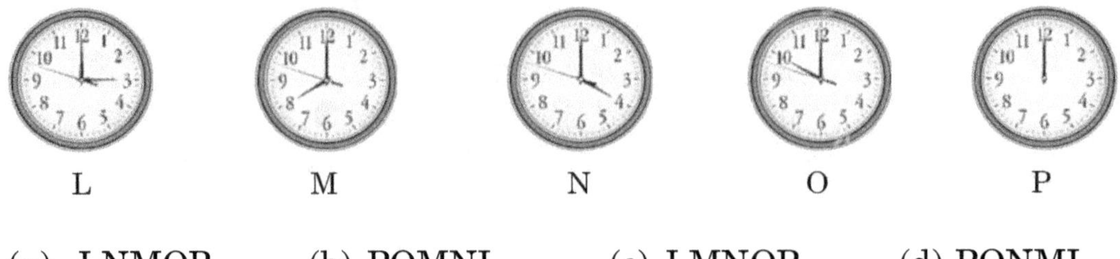

(a) LNMOP (b) POMNL (c) LMNOP (d) PONML

8. Arrange the given pictures of fruits (in ascending order) in a proper sequence by using their alphabets?

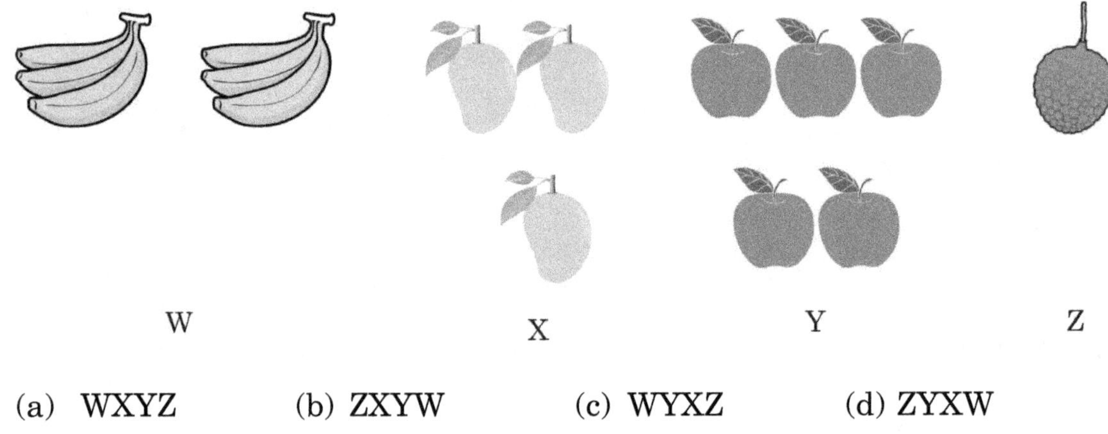

(a) WXYZ (b) ZXYW (c) WYXZ (d) ZYXW

9. Arrange the given pictures of age (small to big) in the proper sequence by using their numbers?

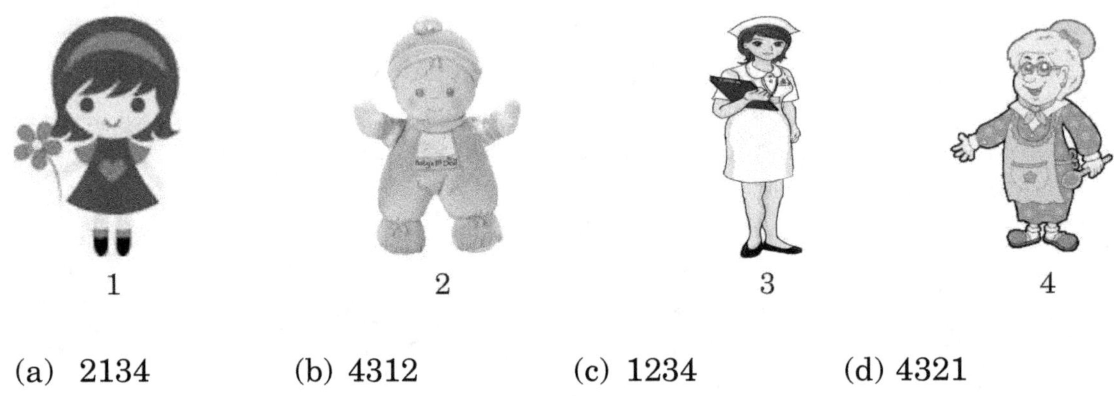

(a) 2134 (b) 4312 (c) 1234 (d) 4321

10. Arrange the given pictures of bodyparts (top to bottom) in the proper sequence by using their numbers?

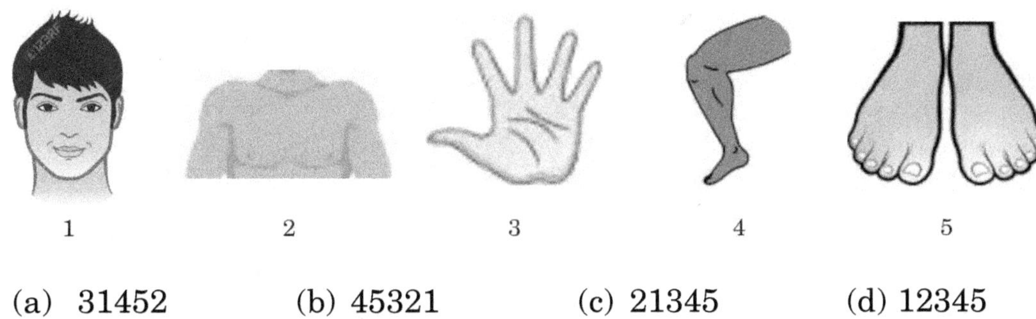

(a) 31452 (b) 45321 (c) 21345 (d) 12345

11. Arrange the given pictures of animals size (big to small) in the proper sequence by using their numbers?

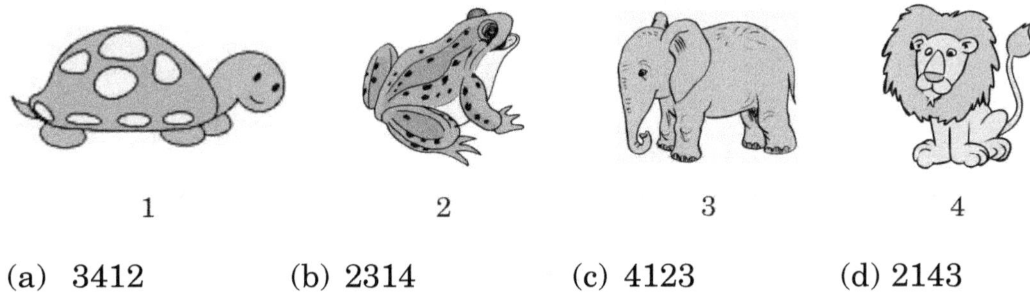

(a) 3412 (b) 2314 (c) 4123 (d) 2143

12. Arrange the given pictures of a rose in a proper sequence by using their alphabets?

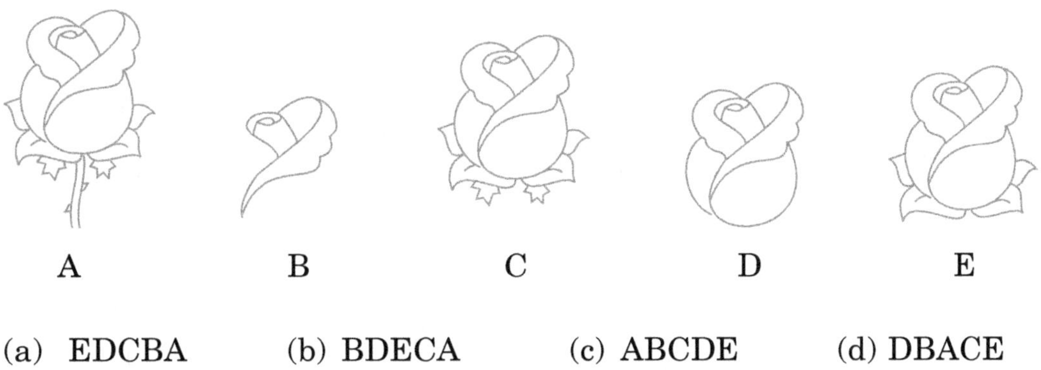

(a) EDCBA (b) BDECA (c) ABCDE (d) DBACE

13. Arrange the given pictures of a cat in a proper sequence by using their alphabets?

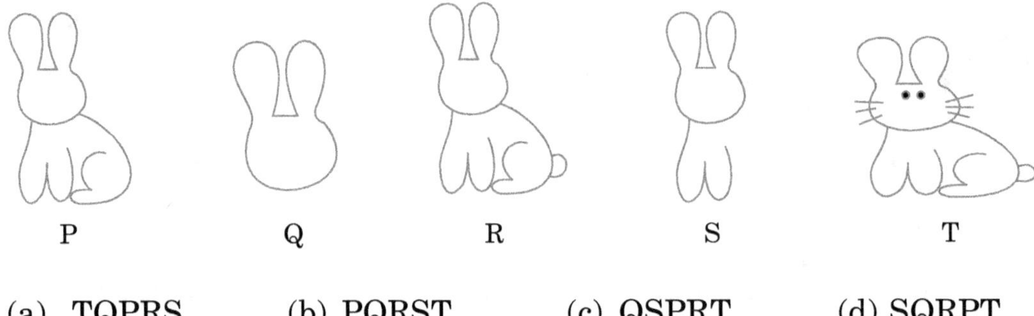

(a) TQPRS (b) PQRST (c) QSPRT (d) SQRPT

14. Arrange the given pictures in the proper sequence by using their alphabets?

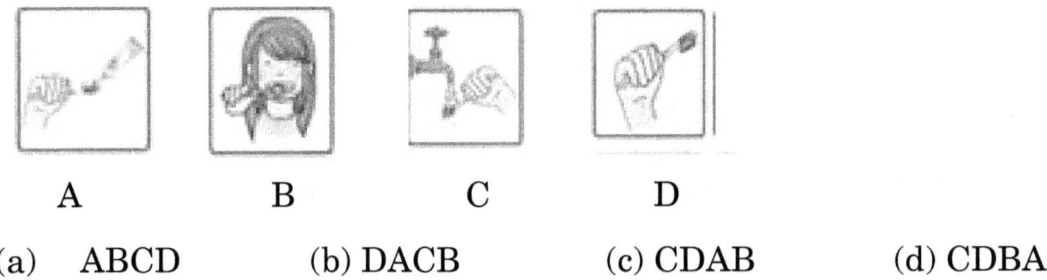

(a) ABCD (b) DACB (c) CDAB (d) CDBA

15. Arrange the given pictures in the proper sequence by using their alphabets?

(a) QRSTP (b) PQRST (c) SPQTR (d) SPTQR

16. Arrange the given pictures in the proper sequence by using their alphabets?

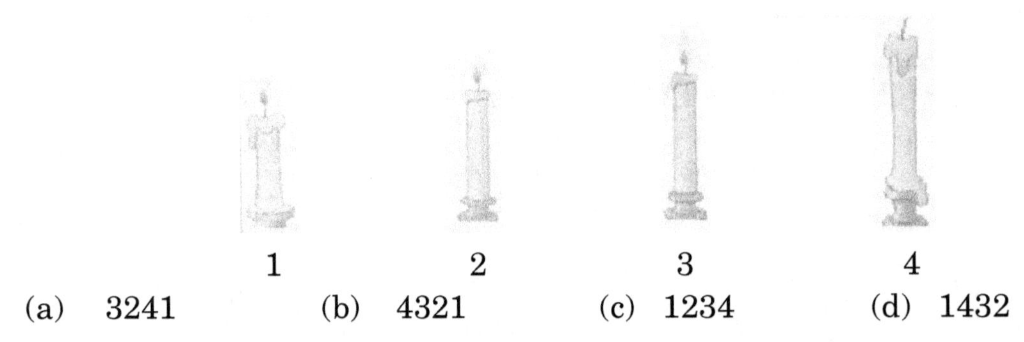

(a) 3241 (b) 4321 (c) 1234 (d) 1432

Answers and Explanations

Level-1

1. **(a)** The meaningful word is CHALK
2. **(b)** B, A, C is the correct sequence.
3. **(d)** Monday, if the day before yesterday was Saturday, So, today is Monday.
4. **(a)** The possible two-digit numbers are: 68, 78, 18, 28, 58, 88, 85, 82, 81, 87, 86. These are 11 in numbers.
5. **(c)** 3 1 7 3 7 7 **1 3 7** 1 7 3 5 **1 3 7** 7 1 9 0 6 2 9 3 7 at these places 1 3 7 appeared together
6. **(b)** If today is Tuesday then yesterday was Monday. So, tomorrow will be Wednesday.
7. **(a)** 9 **3** 6 2 **3** 9 5 9 **3** 7 8 9 1 6 **3** 9 6 **3** 9 in total there are five 3's in given equation.
8. **(c)** 3, 4, 1, 2 is the proper sequence.
9. **(a)** 4, 2, 5, 3, 1 is the logical order sequence.

   4. Hundred 2. Thousand
   5. Million 3. Billion
   1. Trillion

10. **(a)** 1 2 3 4 5 6

    F L O W E R

11. **(b)** The meaningful word is 'MANGO'
12. **(a)** The meaningful word is 'SMILE'.
13. **(c)** 3 1 3 2 7 1 3 7 1 7 3 5 1 3 2 7 7 1 9 0 6 2 9 3 7 at these places 3 2 7 appeared together.
14. **(a)** If today is Thursday then yesterday was Wednesday. So, tomorrow will be Friday.
15. **(a)** The possible two-digit numbers are: 69, 79, 19 29, 59, 99, 95, 92, 91, 97 and 96.

    These are 11 in numbers.

16. **(c)** 52413 is the correct sequence of months.
17. **(b)** The meaningful word is 'WATER'.

Level-2

1. **(c)** BACD is the proper sequence of seasons.
2. **(c)** PQRS is the proper sequence of making tea.
3. **(b)** 2413 is the proper sequence of a school.
4. **(c)** DCBA is the proper sequence.
5. **(a)** RSPQ is the correct sequence.
6. **(d)** 3421 is the proper sequence from small to big.

7. **(b)** POMNL is the correct sequence of clocks in descending to ascending order.
8. **(b)** ZXYW is the proper sequence of fruits in ascending to descending order.
9. **(a)** 2134 is the proper sequence.
10. **(d)** 12345 is the correct sequence of body parts.
11. **(a)** 3412 is the proper sequence of animals.
12. **(b)** BDECA is the correct sequence of a rose.
13. **(c)** QSPRT is the proper sequence of a cat.
14. **(b)** DACB is the proper sequence.
15. **(c)** SPQTR is the proper sequence.
16. **(b)** 4321 is the proper sequence.

ODD ONE OUT

OBJECTIVES

- To train the students to find things that are similar or different.
- To distinctly identify things on the basis of their shape, size, colour etc.
- To help students make connections between the words and to know the process involved in it etc.

INTRODUCTION

Odd one out is the only one different from all in some manner. The student is required to choose this one item which does not fit into the given group.

Steps to Solve

Step 1: Look carefully each of pictures, numbers, words and figures.

Step 2: Find the common feature among them.

Step 3: Choose the item which does not has common feature.

Types of Odd One Out

(i) Picture or figure-based odd one out

Directions: Examples (1 to 5): Select the odd one out.

1. (a) (b) (c) (d)

Ans. (d)

Explanation:

All others have four objects while option (d) has five objects. So, the correct answer is d.

2. (a) (b)  (c) 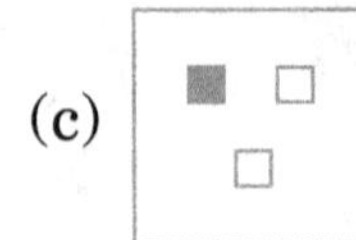 (d) 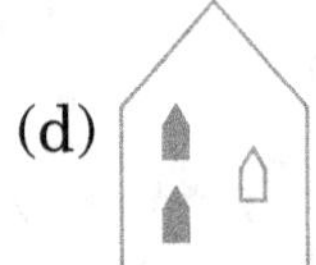

Ans. (d) Except (d), in all other figures there are one small shaded figure.

(ii) Number-based odd one out

3. (a) 5 (b) 10 (c) 12 (d) 20

Ans. (c)

Explanation:

All others except (c) are multiples of 5. So, the correct answer is (c).

(iii) Alphabet-based odd one out

4. (a) A (b) R (c) P (d) Q

Ans. (a)

Explanation:

All others except (a) are consonant, while A is a vowel. So, the correct answer is (a).

(iv) Word-based odd one out

5. (a) Mug (b) Bucket (c) Soap (d) Bed

Ans. (d)

Explanation:

All the objects except (d) belong to bathroom. So, the correct answer is (d).

LEVEL-1

Direction (Qs. 1-30): Choose the option, which does not match the other three.

1. (a)  (b)  (c)  (d) 

2. (a)  (b)  (c) 

(d) 

3. (a)  (b) 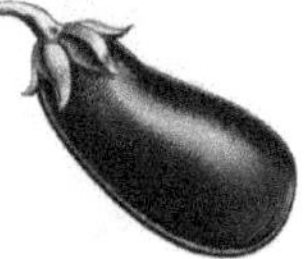 (c)  (d) 

4. (a)  (b)  (c)  (d) 

5. (a)  (b)  (c)  (d) 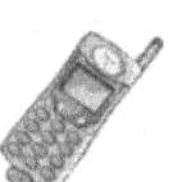

6. (a)  (b)  (c)  (d) 

7. (a)  (b)  (c)  (d) 

8. (a)  (b)  (c)  (d) 

9. (a) 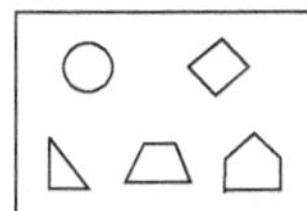 (b) 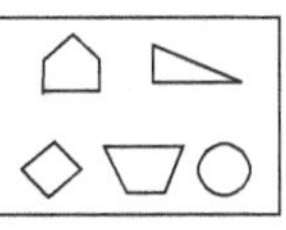 (c) 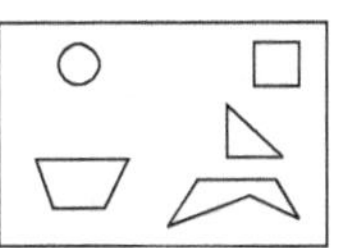 (d) 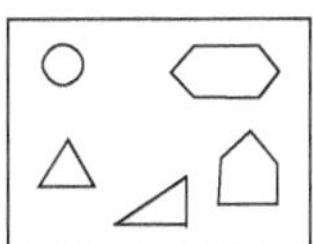

10. (a)  (b)  (c)  (d) 

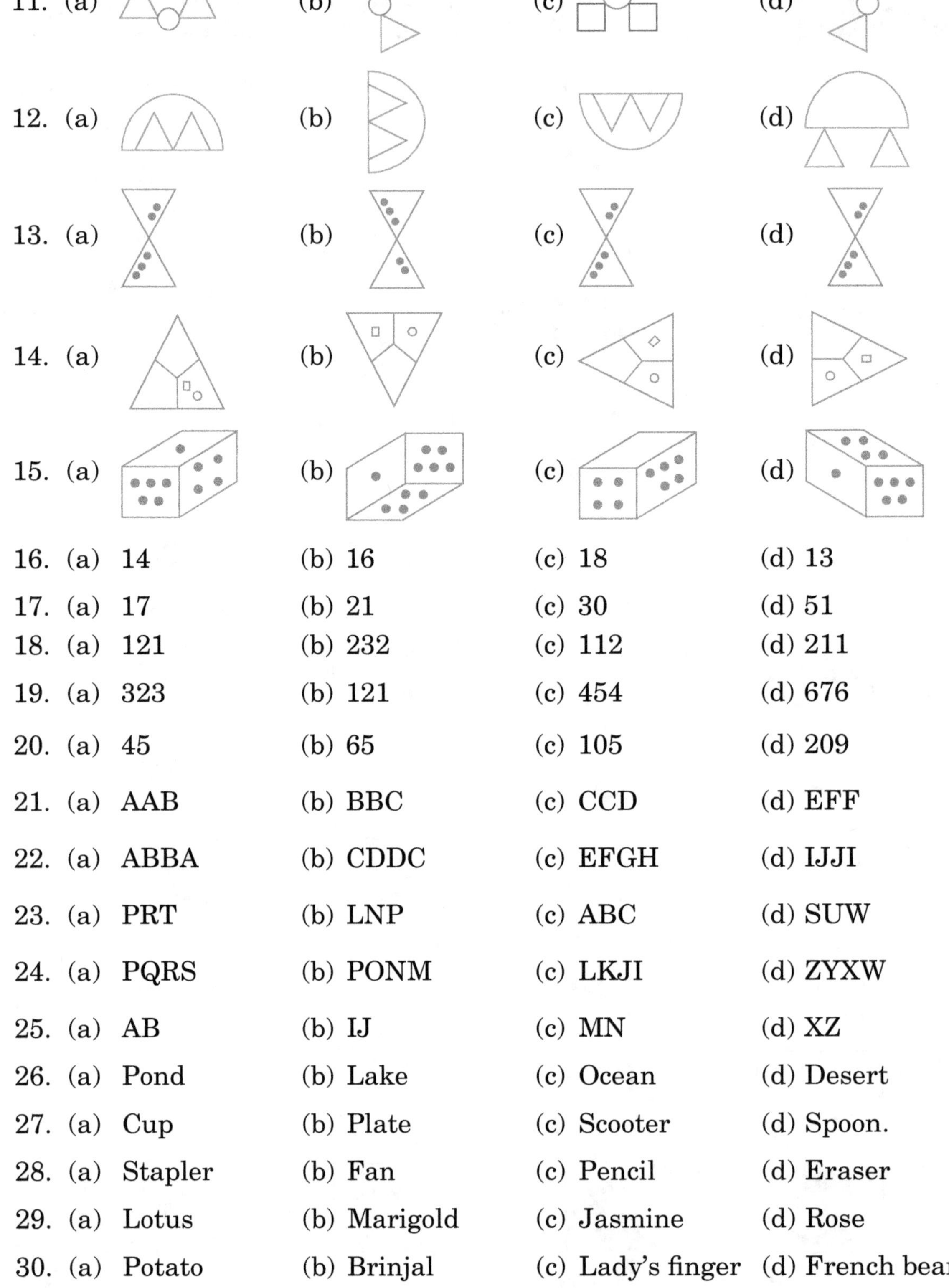

11. (a) (b) (c) (d)

12. (a) (b) (c) (d)

13. (a) (b) (c) (d)

14. (a) (b) (c) (d)

15. (a) (b) (c) (d)

16. (a) 14 (b) 16 (c) 18 (d) 13

17. (a) 17 (b) 21 (c) 30 (d) 51

18. (a) 121 (b) 232 (c) 112 (d) 211

19. (a) 323 (b) 121 (c) 454 (d) 676

20. (a) 45 (b) 65 (c) 105 (d) 209

21. (a) AAB (b) BBC (c) CCD (d) EFF

22. (a) ABBA (b) CDDC (c) EFGH (d) IJJI

23. (a) PRT (b) LNP (c) ABC (d) SUW

24. (a) PQRS (b) PONM (c) LKJI (d) ZYXW

25. (a) AB (b) IJ (c) MN (d) XZ

26. (a) Pond (b) Lake (c) Ocean (d) Desert

27. (a) Cup (b) Plate (c) Scooter (d) Spoon.

28. (a) Stapler (b) Fan (c) Pencil (d) Eraser

29. (a) Lotus (b) Marigold (c) Jasmine (d) Rose

30. (a) Potato (b) Brinjal (c) Lady's finger (d) French bean

LEVEL-2

Direction (Qs. 1-25): Choose the option, which does not match the other three.

1. (a) 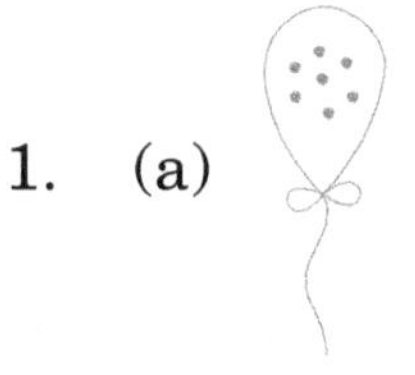 (b) 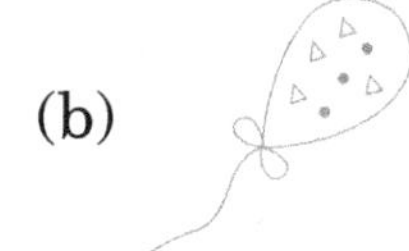 (c) 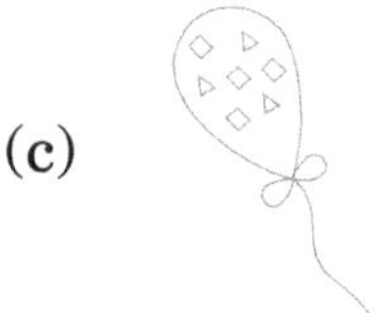 (d) 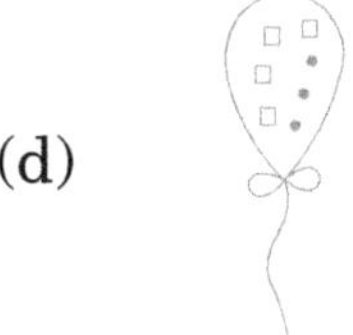

2. (a) 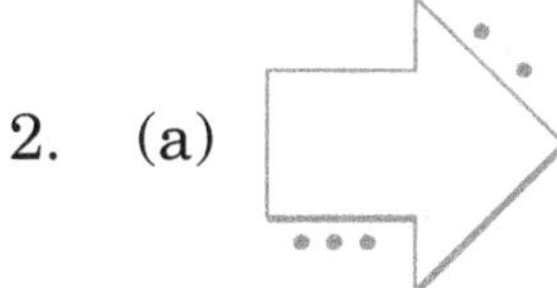 (b) 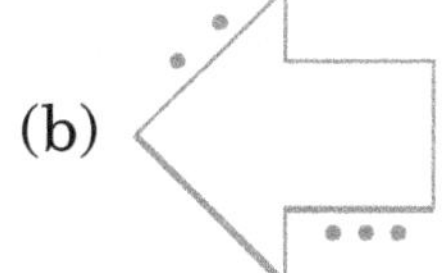 (c) 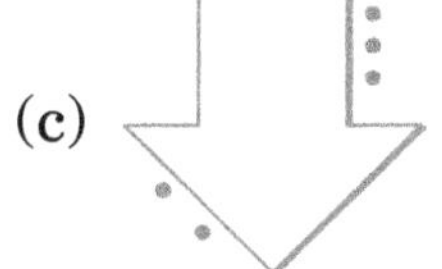 (d) 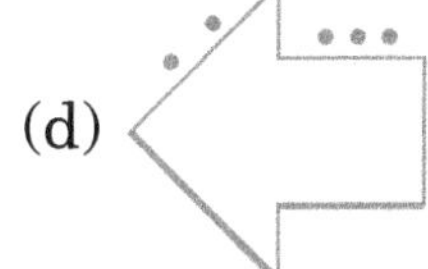

3. (a) 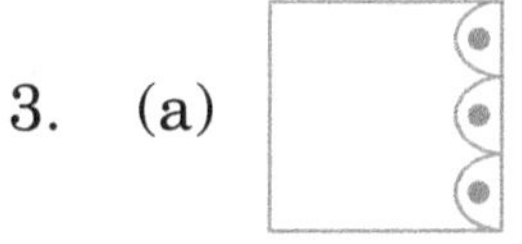 (b) 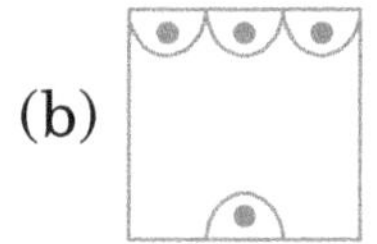 (c) 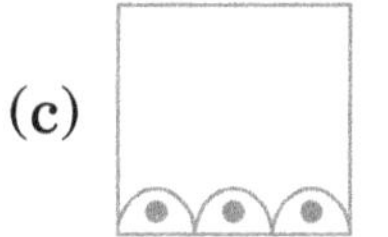 (d) 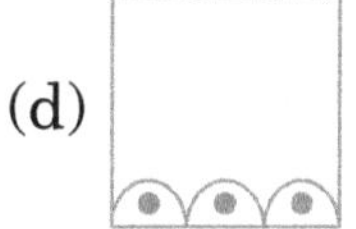

4. (a) 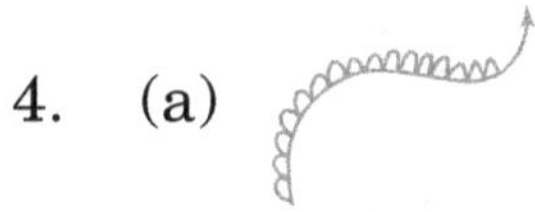 (b) 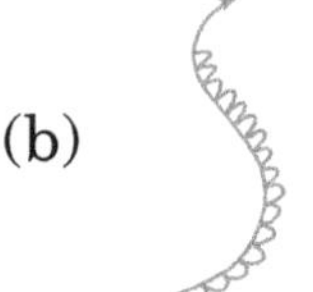 (c) 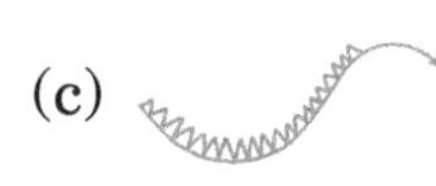 (d) 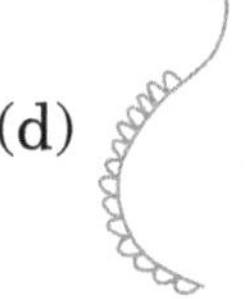

5. (a) 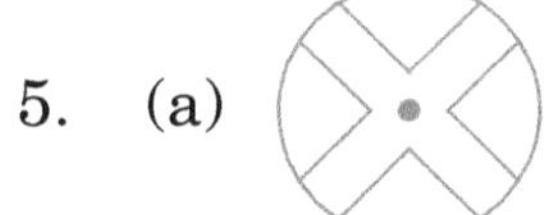 (b) 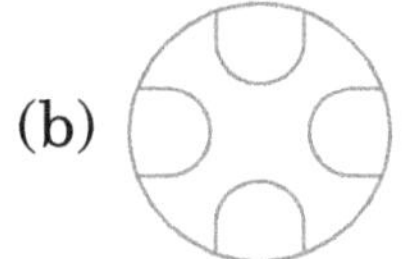 (c) 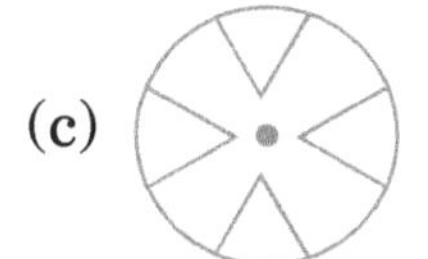 (d) 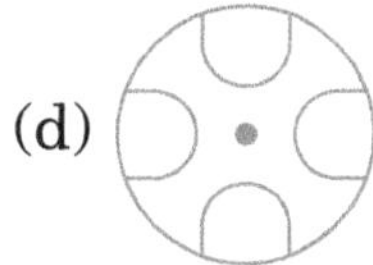

6. (a)  (b) 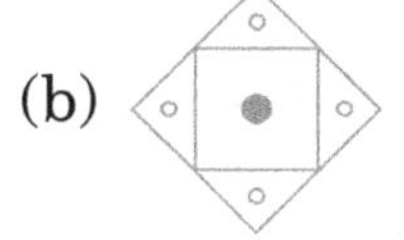 (c) 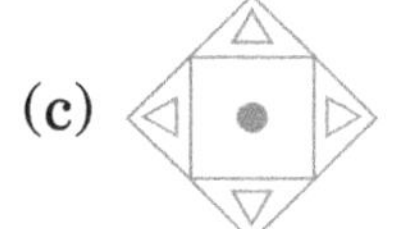 (d) 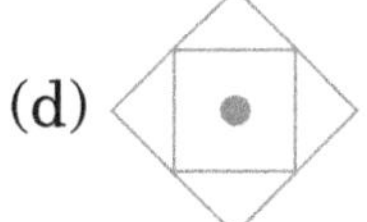

7. (a) (b)  (c) 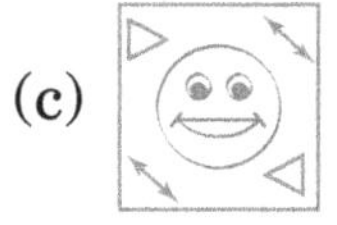 (d) 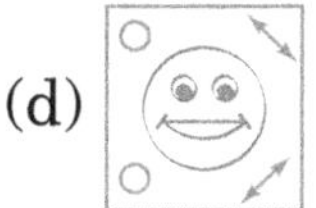

8. (a) (b) 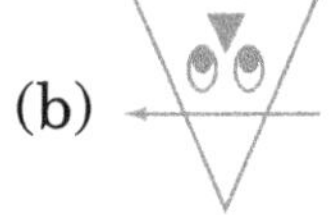 (c) 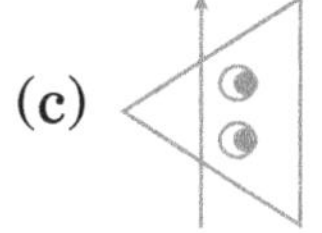 (d) 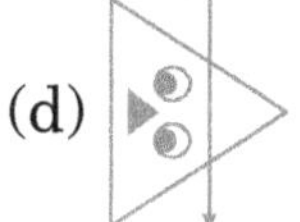

9. (a) 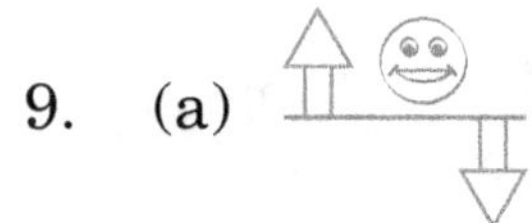 (b) 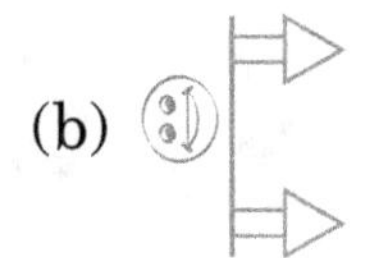 (c) 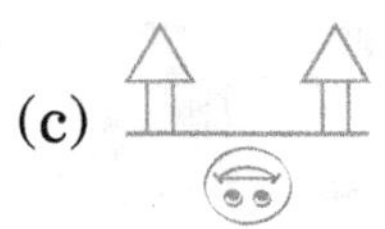 (d) 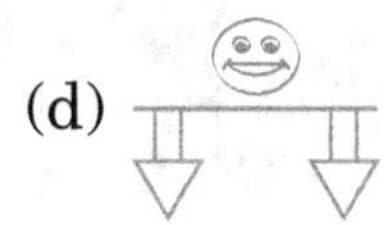

10. (a) (b) (c) 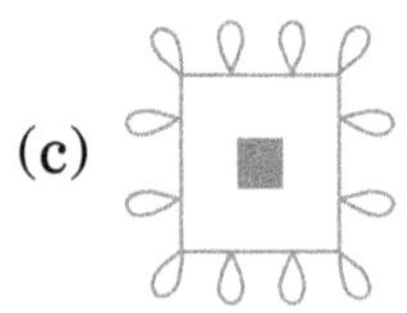 (d) 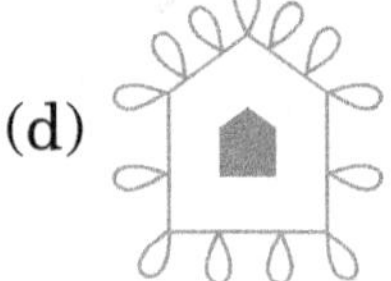

11. (a) 115 (b) 226 (c) 633 (d) 449

12. (a) 321 - 123 (b) 456 - 654 (c) 789 - 987 (d) 678 - 867

13. (a) 772 (b) 997 (c) 882 (d) 662

14. (a) 111 (b) 444 (c) 775 (d) 777

15. (a) 654 (b) 123 (c) 456 (d) 789

16. (a) Aba (b) Efg (c) Hih (d) Jkj.

17. (a) tUt (b) mNm (c) QrQ (d) pQp

18. (a) bcD (b) efG (c) klm (d) pqR

19. (a) ICICI (b) MNOMN (c) PQPQP (d) YZYZY

20. (a) bbc (b) kfc (c) den (d) ofc

21. (a) August (b) July (c) June (d) October

22. (a) Cow (b) Snake (c) Elephant (d) Tiger

23. (a) Cat (b) Dog (c) Cow (d) Tiger

24. (a) Sofa (b) Table (c) Chair (d) Seat

25. (a) Boot (b) Shoe (c) Sandal (d) Glove

26. Raj planted a tree in his garden. Some apples fell down from the tree. Which of the following apples would have fallen from the tree?

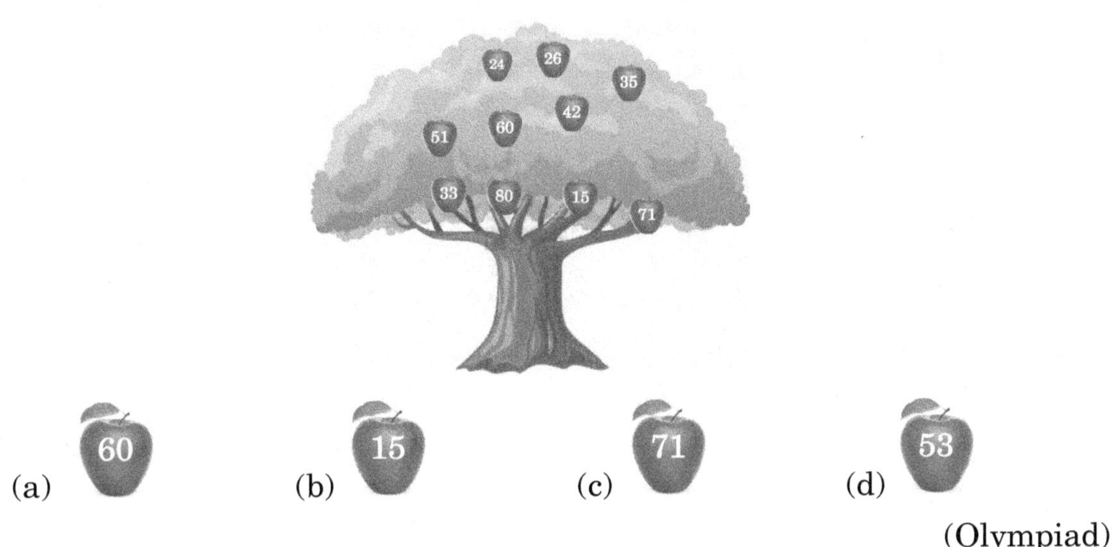

(Olympiad)

27. Find the figure which is the same as that of Fig.(X)?

Fig. (X)

(a) (b) (c) (d)

(Olympiad)

28. Select the odd one out.

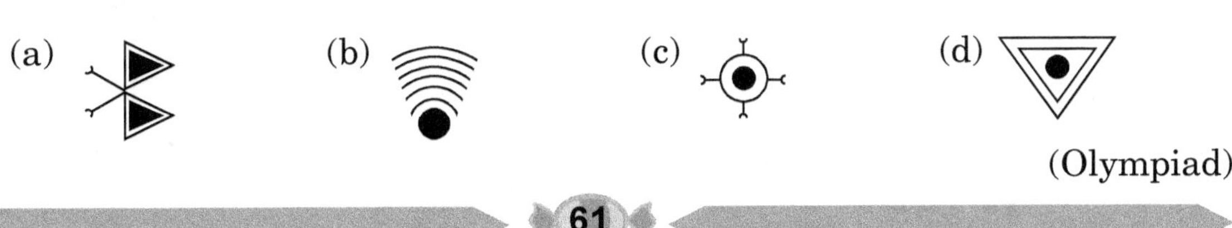

(Olympiad)

29. Select the odd one out.

(a) (b) (c) (d)

(Olympiad)

30. Three out of four figures form a group. Identify the figure that does not fit into the group.

(a) (b) (c) (d)

(Olympiad)

31. Find the odd one out.

(a) (b) (c) (d)

(Olympiad)

32. Find the odd one out.

(a) (b) (c) (d)

(Olympiad)

33. Find the odd one out

(a) 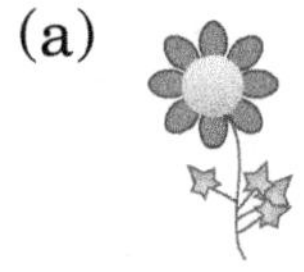 (b) (c) 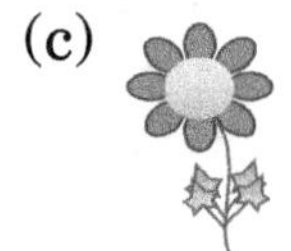 (d) 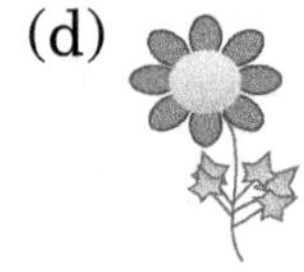

(Olympiad)

Answers and Explanations

Level-1

1. **(b)** Only fish lives in the water.
2. **(c)** All others are eatable things except juice.
3. **(b)** All the three are fruits but in option (b) brinjal is a vegetable.
4. **(a)** Except snake all other use their legs for moving.
5. **(d)** Mobile is a gadget and all others are wooden items.
6. **(c)** All others are kitchenware except lamp.
7. **(d)** Fan is a home appliance, rest are musical instruments.
8. **(a)** All others are parts of has but toe is part of foot.
9. **(d)** In option (d), ⬭ this figure has one extra side.
10. **(d)** All others except (d) are squares.
11. **(c)** All others consist of circle and two triangles but in option (c) triangle is replaced by square.
12. **(d)** In all other figures the triangles are inside the semi circle but in the last image the triangles are outside the semi circle.
13. **(b)** All others have same pattern except option (b).
14. **(a)** In all other pictures, the circle and the square are placed in different segments of the triangle.
15. **(c)** In option (c), dice does not have any dots on one side of it.
16. **(d)** Except the number 13, rest are even numbers.
17. **(c)** Except the number 30, rest are odd numbers.
18. **(b)**

    As, $1 + 2 + 1 = 4$

    $1 + 1 + 2 = 4$

    and $2 + 1 + 1 = 4$

    but, $2 + 3 + 2 = 7$

    So, 232 is odd one out.
19. **(a)** Except 323, in all others, the middle number is greater than the first and third number.
20. **(d)** Except 209, in all other options the one's place digit is 5.

    4$\underline{5}$, 6$\underline{5}$, 10$\underline{5}$
21. **(d)** Except (d), in all other options first two letters are repeated.
22. **(c)** Except (c), in all other the options first and last letters are same and middle two letters are repeated.
23. **(c)**

    As, P $\xrightarrow{+2}$ R $\xrightarrow{+2}$ T

    L $\xrightarrow{+2}$ N $\xrightarrow{+2}$ P

    and S $\xrightarrow{+2}$ U $\xrightarrow{+2}$ W

    But, A $\xrightarrow{+1}$ B $\xrightarrow{+1}$ C
24. **(a)** Only option (a) has a correct sequencing of alphabets. Rest are in reverse order.
25. **(d)** As, A $\xrightarrow{+1}$ B, I $\xrightarrow{+1}$ J and M $\xrightarrow{+1}$ N

    But X $\xrightarrow{+2}$ Z
26. **(d)** Except option (d), all others are sources of water.
27. **(c)** Except option (c), all other options are kitchenware.

28. **(b)** Except option (b), all others are office stationery.

29. **(a)** Only lotus blossoms in the pond.

30. **(a)** Only potato grows in the soil.

Level-2

1. **(a)** The first balloon has only one pattern of drawing on it while the others have two patterns on them.

2. **(d)** In this figure, the dots appear on the same side of the triangle whereas in others the position of the dots is opposite.

3. **(b)** In this diagram there is an extra half circle and dot present on the other side of the square.

4. **(c)** The pattern of leaf is in the opposite side of the curved line.

5. **(b)** The middle dot is absent in this figure.

6. **(d)** The corners of the square are not filled by any pattern.

7. **(d)** The arrows of this image placed on the same side but arrows of the other picture are placed diagonally.

8. **(c)** The image does not have the triangle inside it unlike other three images.

9. **(a)** The direction of the arrows is in opposite direction.

10. **(b)** Except (b) others have inner figure.

11. **(c)** Except (c), in all other options the hundredth's and tenth's place are occupied by similar numbers.

12. **(d)** Except (d), in all other options first and third term of each pair has been reversed.

13. **(b)**Except (b), in all other numbers have 2 in their one's place.

14. **(c)** Except (c), in all other options have similar number in all the three places, i.e. one's, tenth's and hundredth's.

15. **(a)** All the numbers are placed in ascending order while in option (a), numbers are placed in descending order.

16. **(b)** In option (b), the alphabets are in sequence.

17. **(c)** Except option (c), in all others, middle letter is in capital letter and first and third letter are in small letter.

18. **(c)** Except option (c), in all other options, the last letter is in capital letter.

19. **(b)** Except option (b), each letter repeats itself after a letter.

20. **(a)** Only in option (a) the first two letters are repeated.

21. **(c)** Except option (c), all others have 31 days.

22. **(b)** Only snake does not have legs.

23. **(d)** Tiger is a wild animal while others are pet animals.

24. **(b)**Only table is not for sitting.

25. **(d)** Only glove is worn on hand.

26. **(d)** It is clearly shown from the tree that "53" numbered apple would have fallen from the tree.

27. **(b)** In option (b), figure is the same as that of Fig.(X).

28. **(b)** Option (b) is different from others.

29. **(a)** All others are winter clothes except raincoat.

30. **(c)** Option (c) is different from others.

31. **(c)** Option (d) is different from the others.

32. **(c)** Except option (c) all others have four sides.

33. **(d)** All others are having four leaves while in option (d) flower is having five leaves.

CHAPTER 5

POSITION/RANKING TEST

OBJECTIVES

- To enhance structural and locational abilities.
- To trace out specific mentioned positions according to a certain given pattern.

INTRODUCTION

Position or Ranking is a place of something in a certain given conditions.

Type I:

- Identify the position of an object/a person from the left end or right end and rank them from the top or from the bottom.

Type II:

- In this type, identify positions of two persons/objects by interchanging.

Type III:

- Identify the position of an object/a person with respect to the position or rank of other person.

Type IV:

- Identify the position of an object/a person after removing some object/ person from the series.

Steps to Solve

★ **Step 1:** See carefully all items given in the figure.

★ **Step 2:** Identify the position of an object/ a person from left end or right end.

★ **Step 3:** Think and choose the right option.

Examples:

1. 

The position of the ice-cream in the circle is ___________ ?

(a) 3rd from the left end (b) 6th from the left end

(c) 4th from the right end (d) In the centre

Ans. (b)

Explanation:

Circled ice-cream is 6th from the left end.

2. 

The 4th flower from the right end is flower ___________.

(a) E (b) D (c) F (d) C

Ans. (a)

Explanation:

It is clearly shown from the given flowers that E is fourth from the right end.

3. Which flower is fourth to the right of flower R?

(a) S (b) G (c) F (d) E

(Olympiad)

Ans. (b) Flower G is fourth to the right of flower R.

4. If the table is removed from the arrangement shown below, then which item is third to the left of the fourth item from the right end?

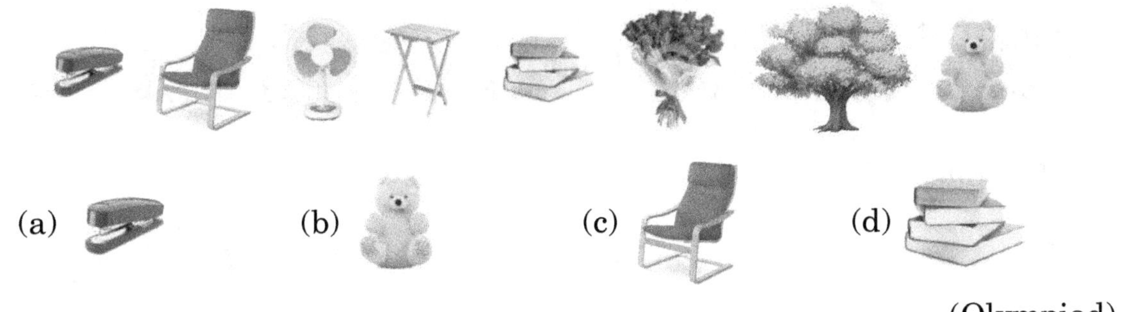

(Olympiad)

Ans. (a) Stapler is third to the left of the fourth item from the right end.

5. Study the given pictures carefully.

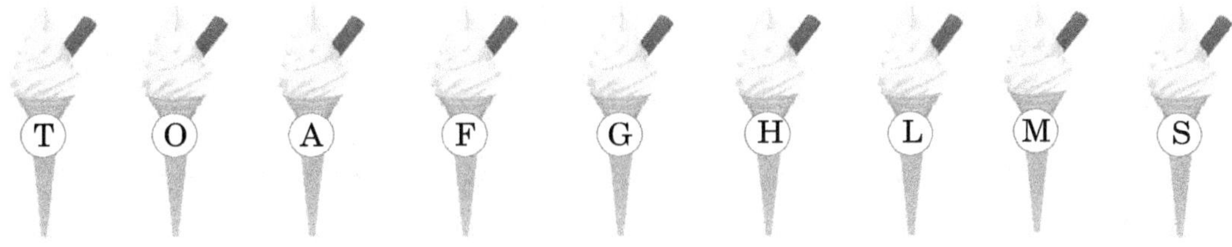

Which letter is fourth to the left of the third letter from the right end?

(a) O (b) T (c) A (d) L

(Olympiad)

Ans. (c) Letter A is fourth to the left of the third letter from the right end.

LEVEL-1

1. Which letter comes in the ninth position from left.

Left → M N O P M N O P M N O P ← Right

(a) M (b) N (c) O (d) P

2. Which alphabet is fifth to the left of alphabet C?

J K L A B C X Y P

(a) B (b) P (c) J (d) K

Direction (Qs 3 to 6): Look at the images given below carefully and answer the following questions.

M O B L K J G H I

3. Which letter is present in the middle position in the above series of mango?

(a) M (b) K (c) L (d) I

4. What is the rank of mango with the letter B from right end?

(a) 4 (b) 5 (c) 7 (d) 6

5. Which letter is present on the right of the letter that ranks 3rd position from right?

(a) M (b) O (c) H (d) I

6. Write the opposite arrangement of letters present in the 4th and 8th rank from right?

(a) OJ (b) KI (c) LP (d) ML

Direction (Qs. 7 to 10): Look at the images given below carefully and answer the following questions.

Ishan Riya Ritiwik Pinki Shreya Nitin Sammy

7. Who is standing between Pinki and Nitin?

   (a) Ishan (b) Sammy (c) Shreya (d) Ritwik

8. Who is standing in the sixth position from the bus?

   (a) Ishan (b) Sammy (c) Shreya (d) Nitin

9. Who is standing on the left of Ritwik and his/her position from the bus?

   (a) Sammy, 2nd (b) Nitin, 6th (c) Pinki, 4th (d) Shreya, 5th

10. How many children are there in between 2nd and 7th position starting from the Bus?

    (a) 2 (b) 4 (c) 5 (d) 8

Direction (Qs 11 to 15): After finishing a running race, 5 friends are talking among themselves about the results of the race. The statement of each of them is given below. Look at the picture and read the statements carefully and answer the following questions.

Rehan Mayank Danish

Saishah Riya

Statement-1: Danish said, "I was first".

Statement-2: According to Riya she was in between Danish and Mayank.

Statement-3: Riya said, Saishah was in front of her.

Statement-4: Rehan was the last person to reach the destination and followed Saishah.

Statement-5: Mayank exactly occupied the central position of the race.

11. Who was lying among the friends?

(a) Danish (b) Saishah (c) Mayank (d) Riya

12. What was Mayank's rank in the race?

(a) 4th (b) 3rd (c) 5th (d) 2nd

13. What was Saishah's rank in the race?

(a) 3rd (b) 5th (c) 2nd (d) 4th

14. How many children are running after Danish?

(a) 3 (b) 2 (c) 4 (d) 5

15. How many children are there in between Riya and Rehan?

(a) 2 (b) 3 (c) 4 (d) 5

Direction (Qs. 16 to 20): In the picture given below some money and their values are shown. Carefully look at each picture and give answer to the question.

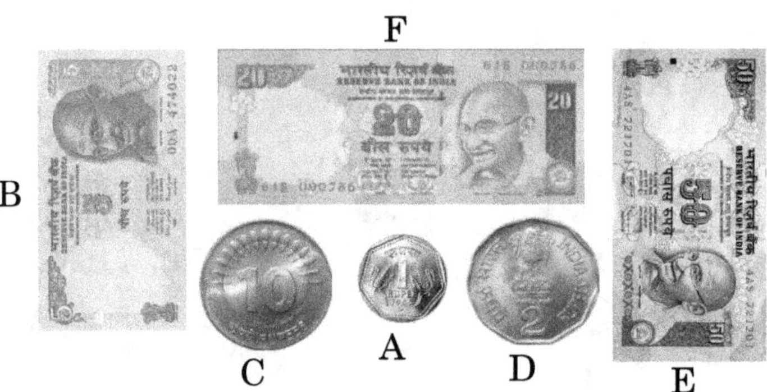

16. What is the value of the coins and notes in descending order?

(a) E, B, D, C, F, A (b) B, F, E, C, D, A

(c) E, F, C, B, D, A (d) D, F, B, E, C, A

17. After ranking in descending order, calculate the sum of money ranked in 2nd and 5th position.

(a) 25/- (b) 22/- (c) 15/- (d) 10/-

18. Which value ranks the third position from the lowest value?

(a) 5/- (b) 2/- (c) 50/- (d) 10/-

19. Calculate the amount you will get by adding the money value ranking in the 1st position and the 5th position from left after arranging them in descending order.

(a) 50/- (b) 22/- (c) 52/- (d) 10/-

20. What is the position of 20 rupee note from the right end in descending order?

(a) Second from the left end.

(b) Fifth from the right end.

(c) Fifth from the left end.

(d) Second from the right end.

LEVEL-2

Direction (Qs. 1 & 2): Given below are some alphabets in a particular order. Observe them carefully and answer the following questions.

Left	T	B	A	Q	R	P	M	S	N	Right

1. Identify the letters which are ranked at 4th, 6th and 9th position from the left. What will be the letters?

   (a) QPN (b) NPQ (c) PNQ (d) QNP

2. Arrange the letters which are ranked at 2nd, 3rd, 7th and 9th position in ascending order of English alphabets?

   (a) NMBA (b) BAMN (c) MNAB (d) ABMN

Direction (Qs. 3-6): In a class room there are few girls sitting in a row on the basis of their ranks position in the class room, answer the following questions. In each row there is only one student.

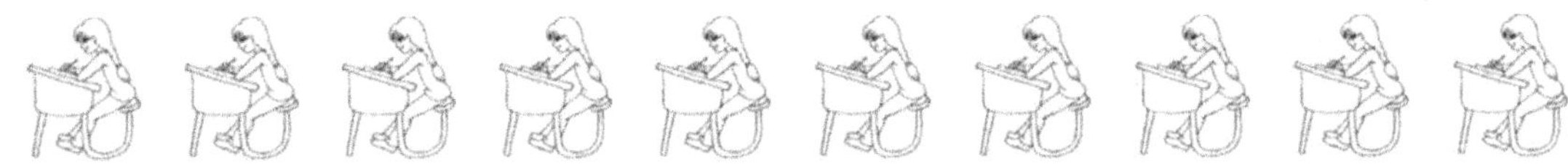

Ananya Pressha Avni Neha Riya Anita Pinki Ritu Shreya Disha

3. Riya is sitting in the row between Neha and Anita. Anita ranks 6th from the left. So, what is Neha's rank in the class?

   (a) 4th (b) 6th (c) 5th (d) 8th

4. Pinki is sitting immediately left to Anita and Disha is sitting fourth from the left of Anita. Find Disha's rank in the class room?

   (a) 1st (b) 10th (c) 6th (d) 4th

5. What is the position of Avni from the right end of the row?

   (a) 9th (b) 3rd (c) 8th (d) 4th

6. How many girls are sitting between Ananya and Shreya?

   (a) 8 (b) 9 (c) 7 (d) 10

Direction (Qs. 7-10): In a football match two teams (A and B) were playing in which the players were asked to kick some free goals. Five members from each team have been selected and arranged in chronological order with their team name. Every players must get a chance to kick the ball and after each player of team A, the players of team B could make a kick. Now, watch the picture given below carefully and answer some of the questions given below.

The order of kicks are

Start	Team A	Team B	Team A	Team B	Team A	Team B	Team A	Team B	Team A	Team B	End
	A 1	B 1	A 2	B 2	A 3	B 3	A 4	B 4	A 5	B 5	

7. How many free kicks were shot altogether?

   (a) 4 (b) 10 (c) 5 (d) 9

8. Who has kicked the second last kick?

   (a) A 2 (b) B 4 (c) A 5 (d) B 4

9. Who will kick at the 8th rank from the end?

   (a) A 3 (b) A 2 (c) B 3 (d) B 2

10. Whose rank is sixth from the start?

    (a) B 3 (b) A 3 (c) A 2 (d) B 2

11 Medha ranks sixteenth from the top and third from the bottom in a class. How many students are there in the class?

(a) 16 (b) 17 (c) 21 (d) 18

Direction (Qs. 12 & 13): There is a series of numbers given below. Observe them carefully and answer the following statement-based questions.

Left	2	4	8	12	16	6	18	12	10	14	Right

12. If the number at the second rank from left will be multiplied by 3 we will get

    (a) The number at the 8th rank from left.

    (b) The number at the 8th rank from right.

    (c) The number at the 9th rank from right.

    (d) The first number from left.

13. What is the number fourth from the left and 7th from the right?

    (a) 4 (b) 8 (c) 12 (d) 16

Direction (Qs. 14 & 15): Below given two different words. Look at them carefully and answer the following questions.

S E R E N D I P I T Y

O B S E Q U I T O U S

14. If we arrange the third letter of the first word, fourth letter of the second word and again sixth letter of the first word what do we get?

    (a) A pen (b) A colour (c) A plant (d) An animal

15. If we arrange the sixth letter of the first word, fourth letter of the second word and again fifth letter of the first word whose living place do we get?

    (a) An Owl (b) A Monkey (c) A Fish (d) A Lion

16. How many stairs are there between 6th stair and 15th stair?

(a) 5 (b) 7 (c) 8 (d) 10

(Olympiad)

17. The number of blue flowers to the right of middle flower is ________ ?

(a) 1 (b) 4 (c) 3 (d) 2

(Olympiad)

18. Which child is nearest to the house?

Amit Raj Karan Tanuj

(a) Amit (b) Raj (c) Karan (d) Tanuj

(Olympiad)

19. If the chair and the book are interchanged in their positions, then element ________ will be fourth to the left of the chair?

P Q R T S U V W X

(a) T (b) R (c) W (d) V

(Olympiad)

20. Which person is the 6th position from the ice-cream shop?

(a) Amit (b) Mohit (c) Raj (d) Beena

(Olympiad)

21. Some boys are standing in a line.

If Mohit and Gautam interchange their positions, then which boy will be third from the right end?

(a) Mohit (b) Gautam (c) Raj (d) Varun

(Olympiad)

Answers and Explanations

Level-1

1. **(a)** M letter comes in the ninth position from left.
2. **(c)** J alphabet is fifth to the left of alphabet C.
3. **(b)** The mango with letter K is exactly in the middle of the series as it ranks in the fifth position from both the ends.
4. **(c)** Mango with letter B is the 7th from the right end.
5. **(c)** The letter is H which appears on the right of the letter that ranks 3rd from right.
6. **(a)** The letter ranks 4th position from right is J and the letter ranks 8th position is O. Hence, the arrangement of letters will be OJ.
7. **(c)** Shreya is standing between Pinki and Nitin.
8. **(d)** Nitin is standing in the sixth position from the bus.
9. **(c)** Pinki is standing on the right of Ritwik and her position is 4th from the bus.
10. **(b)** There are 4 children in between 2nd and 7th position starting from the bus.
11. **(d)** Riya was lying as she was in second position and was followed by Mayank.
12. **(b)** Mayank's rank is 3rd in the race.
13. **(d)** As, Saishah was in front of Rehan who came last in the race of five children and her rank was 4th in the race.
14. **(c)** As, the number of children participated were five and Danish ranked first. So, there are four children after Danish in the race.
15. **(a)** Riya ranked 2nd and Rehan ranked 5th in the race. So, there are two more children who were ranked 3rd and 4th.
16. **(c)** E, F, C, B, D, A is the correct sequence i.e.

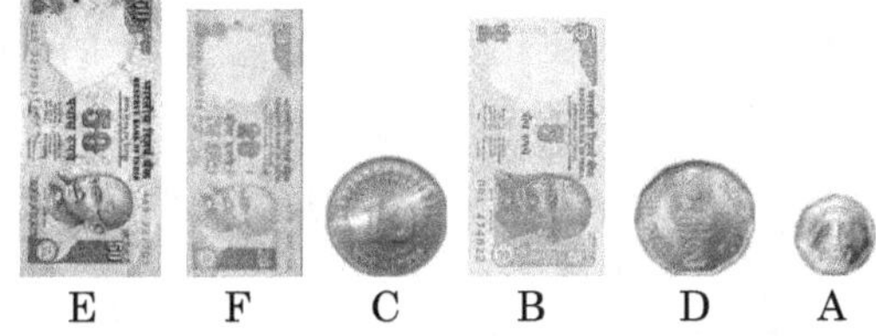

17. **(b)** The value of money in the 2nd position is 20 and in the 5th position is 2, So, the sum is 20 + 2 = 22/-.
18. **(a)** 5/- ranks the third position from the lowest value.
19. **(c)** 52/- is the amount.
20. **(b)** 20 rupee note is fifth from the right end in descending order.

Level-2

1. **(a)** The letter in the 4th, 6th and 9th ranks from left are Q, P and N respectively.
2. **(d)** The letters which are ranked at 2nd, 3rd, 7th and 9th position is B, A, M and N respectively. Now, arrange them in ascending order i.e., ABMN.
3. **(a)** Riya is sitting between Neha and Anita. If Anita's rank is 6th from the left of the row then Neha's rank is 4th in the class.
4. **(b)** Disha is sitting fourth to the left of Anita. So, Disha is sitting 10th position in the row.
5. **(c)** Avni is 8th position from the right end of the row.
6. **(c)** 7 girls are sitting between Ananya and Shreya.
7. **(b)** There are altogether 10 kicks in the match.
8. **(c)** The second last kick was made by the player A 5.
9. **(b)** The player at the 8th rank from the end was A 2.
10. **(a)** The player at the sixth rank from the start was B 3.
11. **(d)** (Rank of Medha from the top + rank of Medha from the bottom) –1

    $\Rightarrow (16 + 3) - 1$

    $\Rightarrow 19 - 1 = 18.$

    So, there are 18 students in the class.
12. **(a)** The number in the second rank is 4 and the result of its multiplication is 12 which is in the 8th position from the left.
13. **(c)** 12 is the number fourth from the left and 7th from the right.
14. **(b)** If we arrange the letters in the given sequence as:

    third letter of the first word – R

    fourth letter of the second word – E

    sixth letter of the first word – D

    So, together they form 'RED' which is a colour.
15. **(d)** If we arrange the letters in the given sequence, we get

    sixth letter of the first word – D

    fourth letter of the second word – E

    fifth letter of the first word – N

    So, together they form 'DEN' which is the living place of a lion.
16. **(c)** 8

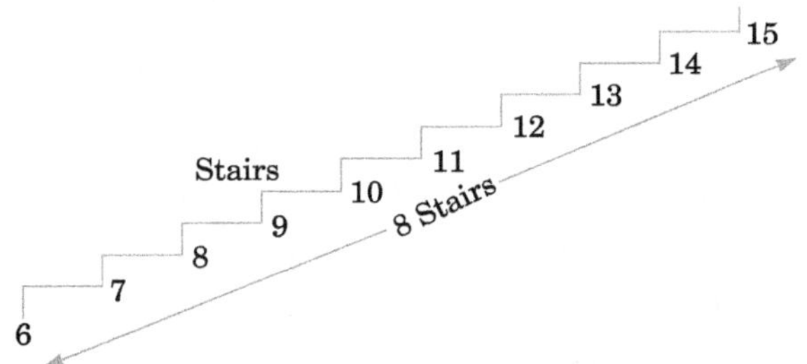

17. **(d)** The number of blue flowers to the right of middle flower is 2.
18. **(a)** Amit is nearest to the house.
19. **(b)** Element R will be fourth to the left of the chair.
20. **(c)** Raj is the 6th position from the ice-cream shop.
21. **(a)** If Mohit and Gautam inter-change their positions, then Mohit will be third from the right end.

CODING DECODING

OBJECTIVES

- To transmit an information from one place to other using some codes so as to reach to other person safely.
- To judge a child's ability to decipher the rule that codes a particular word and number.

INTRODUCTION

A Code is a 'system of signals'. Coding is a method of transmitting a message between the sender and the receiver without a third person knowing it.

Before transmitting, the data is encoded and at receiver side encoded data is decoded in order to obtain original data by determining common key in encoded data.

TYPES OF CODING-DECODING

1. Letter Coding
2. Number Coding
3. Substitution Coding

Type I: Letter Coding

In this type, the real alphabets are replaced by certain other alphabets according to a specific rule to form its code. Students are required to detect the common rule and answer the questions accordingly.

Case 1: Direct letter coding:

Example 1:

In a certain code, RAN is written as SBO and BAT is CBU, then how will be RAT be written in that code?

(a) SAU (b) RBT (c) SBU (d) UBS

Ans. (c)

Explanation:

Letter	R	A	N	B	T
Code	S	B	O	C	U

By direct code method, we get

$R \longrightarrow S$, $A \longrightarrow B$, $T \longrightarrow U$

So, RAT will be written as SBU.

Case 2: To form the code for another word (CODING)

Example 2:

In a certain language, SUN is coded as TVO, then how is FUN coded in that code?

(a) FVO (b) GVO (c) NUF (d) OVG

Ans. (b)

As, S U N (+1, +1, +1) → T V O   Similarly, F U N (+1, +1, +1) → G V O

So, FUN would be coded as GVO

Type II: Number Coding

In these questions, either numerical code values are assigned to a word or alphabetical code letters are assigned to the numbers. Students are required to analyse the code as per the question.

Example 1:

If in a certain code, FOUR is written as 3256 and MARE is written as 4167, how is MORE written in that code?

(a) 3416 (b) 4267 (c) 4326 (d) 7624

Ans. (b)

Explanation:

The alphabets are coded as shown:

F	O	U	R	M	A	E
3	2	5	6	4	1	7

So, In MORE,

M ⟶ 4, O ⟶ 2, R ⟶ 6, E ⟶ 7

Thus, the code for MORE is 4267.

Type III: Substitution Coding

In this type of questions, letter of words are substituted for either a new letter or a numeric.

Example 2:

If 'pen' is 'table', 'table' is 'fan', 'fan' is 'chair' and 'chair' is 'roof', then which of the following will a person sit?

(a) Fan (b) Chair (c) Roof (d) Table

Ans. (c)

Explanation:

A person will sit on the 'chair' and 'chair' is called 'roof'.

So, the person will sit on the 'roof'.

LEVEL-1

1. If East is called South, South is called North and North is called East, then where does the sun rises?

   (a) North (b) West (c) East (d) South

2. If cup is called spoon, spoon is called knife and knife is called plate, then we drink tea or coffee in _______ ?

   (a) plate (b) knife (c) cup (d) spoon

3. If "Pen" is called Pencil, "Pencil" is called Eraser and Eraser is called "Sharpener", then what do we use for erasing a drawing done by Pencil?

   (a) Eraser (b) Pen (c) Sharpener (d) Pencil

4. If Parrot is called Frog, Frog is called Lion and Lion is called Eagle, then who lives in DEN?

   (a) Lion (b) Eagle (c) Frog (d) Parrot

5. If △ can be written as 3 and □ can be written as 4 then ⌂ can be written as ______ ?

   (a) 3 (b) 6 (c) 5 (d) 4

6. If Monkey is called Mosquito, Mosquito is called Fish and Fish is called Frog, then who lives only in water?

   (a) Monkey (b) Mosquito (c) Fish (d) Frog

7. If Holi is colour, colour is diwali and diwali is dance. Then, we play the game of colours in which festival?

   (a) Diwali (b) Colour (c) Dance (d) Holi

8. If Rabbit is Mouse, Mouse is called Tortoise, and Tortoise is called Lion, then who won the race between rabbit and tortoise?

   (a) Tortoise (b) Lion (c) Rabbit (d) Mouse

9. The codes are given for the following colours, then which is the last colour of Indian Flag?

Green - 5

Blue - 4

Red - 3

Saffron - 2

(a) 2 (b) 3 (c) 4 (d) 5

10. If Dog is called Cat, Cat is called Cow and Cow is called Kitten, then we get milk from _______ ?

(a) Kitten (b) Cow (c) Dog (d) Cat

11. If Apple is called Mango, Mango is called Orange, Orange is called Grapes, and Grapes is called Strawberry, then the king of fruit is _______ ?

(a) Mango (b) Apple (c) Orange (d) Grapes

(Olympiad)

12. If Foot is called Hand, Hand is called Nose and Nose is called Eyes. Then, we breathe through _______ ?

(a) Eyes (b) Foot (c) Hands (d) Nose

13. If Mango is called Banana, Banana is called Coconut and Coconut is called Muskmelon, then which fruit contains water inside it?

(a) Mango (b) Banana (c) Muskmelon (d) Coconut

14. If Singing is called Dancing, Dancing is called Walking, Walking is called Tapping, then what does a singer do?

(a) Breaking (b) Walking (c) Tapping (d) Dancing

15. If Nobita is Shizuka, Shizuka is Zaiko and Zaiko is Gian, then who is the friend of Doraemon?

(a) Zaiko (b) Nobita (c) Shizuka (d) Gian

16. If Tom is Guffy, Guffy is Donald and Donald is Pooh, then who is the friend of Jerry?

(a) Pooh (b) Guffy (c) Jerry (d) Donald

17. If the code for MONKEY is YEKNOM then write the code for BUTTERFLY?

(a) YLFRETTUB (b) YBLUTETRF

(c) FYLTTERUB (d) RTTLEBULFY

18. If Rose is Lotus, Lotus is Lily and Lily is Tulip, then which flower blosooms in water ?

(a) Lily (b) Tulip (c) Rose (d) Jasmine

19. The rain is called cloud, cloud is called sky, sky is called sun, then who gives us rain?

(a) Rain (b) Cloud (c) Sky (d) Sun

20. If Dog is called Cat, Cat is called Mouse, Mouse is called Goat and Goat is called Elephant then, which is the smallest animal?

(a) Goat (b) Mouse (c) Cat (d) Elephant

21. If black is blue, blue is red, red is yellow, and yellow is orange, then what would be the colour of the sky?

(a) Red (b) Blue (c) Yellow (d) Black

22. If Sofa is called Shower, Shower is called Knife, Knife is called Tree, then what do we use for cutting vegetables?

(a) Shower (b) Tree (c) Sofa (d) Knife

23. If Circle is called Square and Square is called Triangle, Triangle is called as Rectangle which of these is used to form a Sphere?

(a) Square (b) Opaque (c) Triangle (d) Rectangle

24. If Orange is called Green, Green is called Black, and Black is called white, then what is the colour of our hair?

(a) Purple (b) White (c) Pink (d) Green

25. If Hand is called as Leg, Leg is called as Stomach, Stomach is called as Eyes, then Thumb is a part of _______ ?

(a) Stomach (b) Hand (c) Eyes (d) Leg

26. If the Sun is called as Planet, Planet is called as Moon and Moon is called as Earth, then what do we see at night?

(a) Sun (b) Earth (c) Moon (d) Planet

27. If Wrist is called Neck, Neck is called Wrist, Wrist is called Ankle, and Ankle is called Nose, then we wear watch around _______ ?

(a) Neck (b) Ankle (c) Ear (d) Toes

28. If Mobile phone is called Hand bag, Hand bag is called Vaccum Cleaner and Vaccum Cleaner is called purse. Then what do we use for talking to people?

(a) Hand bag (b) Vaccum Cleaner
(c) Purse (d) Mobile

29. If Book shelf is called as Table, Table is called as Mirror, Mirror is called as Washing Machine, and Washing Machine is called as Air Conditioner; then what do we use for washing clothes?

(a) Air Conditioner (b) Book Shelf
(c) Table (d) Mirror

30. If FLOWER is written as REWOLF, then 82674 will be written as __________.

(a) 48627 (b) 82674 (c) 46782 (d) 47628

(Olympiad)

LEVEL-2

Direction (Qs. 1-4): Given below some alphabets with their respective codes in certain numbers. Based upon these codes choose the correct code for the words given below.

CODES :

M	H	T	I	A	E	D	O	N
5	2	3	9	6	8	7	4	1

1. Write the correct code for MATH?

   (a) 9561 (b) 1692 (c) 5632 (d) 2659

2. Write the correct code for TIME?

   (a) 9658 (b) 3958 (c) 9235 (d) 6792

3. Write the code for DATE?

   (a) 2562 (b) 7638 (c) 9238 (d) 6541

4. Write the code for NOTE?

   (a) 1438 (b) 6924 (c) 8951 (d) 4364

5. Below given some Alphabets with their respective codes

S	F	T	I	A	R	H	N	O
3	5	2	9	6	1	7	8	4

   Now write the word STARFISH using their code. Which will be the correct code.

   (a) 36452719 (b) 32615937 (c) 96543126 (d) 39462521

6. Given below some numbers with their codes in Alphabets. Look at them carefully.

1	5	2	9	6	8	3	7
A	C	D	B	O	P	R	M

Now based upon the above coding what will be code of multiplication of B and R.

(a) 18 (b) 12 (c) 24 (d) 27

Directions (Qs. 7-12): Given below some tables of digits and Alphabets with their respective codes assigned to them. Carefully check each one of them and answer the questions.

7.

Letters	T	M	A	C	E	P	O	N
Codes	2	9	5	6	4	3	1	7

Write down the code for ACCEPT

(a) 293346 (b) 566432 (c) 695241 (d) 126957

8.

Letters	T	U	M	O	E	B	A	R	L
Codes	5	3	4	7	8	2	6	9	1

Write down the code for UMBRELLA.

(a) 34298116 (b) 61192437 (c) 76321194 (d) 45221398

9.

Letters	E	T	P	O	S	Y	M	N	C
Codes	3	9	2	5	6	8	4	7	1

Write down the code for ECOSYSTEM

(a) 259383694 (b) 315686934 (c) 439282391 (d) 569212947

10.

Letters	B	T	E	U	Y	R	O	F	L
Codes	6	9	2	1	5	4	3	7	8

Using the codes given above for each Alphabets. Write down the number code for the word BUTTERFLY.

(a) 8214496736 (b) 12995738 (c) 519928764 (d) 619924785

11. Using the codes given below, write down code for E S T I M A T E.

E	N	M	A	I	T	O	S
3	7	2	9	4	5	6	1

(a) 73245922 (b) 31542953 (c) 41252924 (d) 36292564

12. Write down the code for 215389.

Numbers	8	2	6	9	1	5	3	7
Codes	P	N	S	Q	R	B	O	L

(a) PNSQRB (b) QPOBRN (c) NRBOPQ (d) BRQSNP

13. If the code for HAPPY is 29881 and BRICK is 37946, then write down the code that justifies PRAY?

(a) 6938 (b) 8394 (c) 1978 (d) 8791

14. If ENGLISH is written as FOHMJTI, then how will TUESDAY be written in that code?

(a) YADSEUT (b) TUFTDAY (c) TUEYADS (d) UVFTEBZ

15. If we write CROCODILE as 296265347, then what is the code for LORD?

(a) 4695 (b) 5926 (c) 4397 (d) 5967

16. If we write ATTACK as CVVCEM, then how do you write AUGUST?

(a) NVVCEC (b) CWIWUV (c) VCVCNE (d) VCVECN

17. If TERMINATOR in certain code is written as 2569734286 then how do you write MONITOR?

(a) 9293687 (b) 8296378 (c) 9837286 (d) 6873925

18. If JUNE can be written as ITMD then, how can JULY be written as?

(a) ZMVK (b) KVMZ (c) XKTI (d) ITKX

19. If in a certain code, MANGO is written as OGNAM, then how will APPLE be written in that code?

(a) BQQMF (b) FMQQB (c) ELPPA (d) ZOOKD

20. If CHAIR is written as 39675 and NOSE is written as 2148, then how do you code RAIN?

(a) 5672 (b) 8675 (c) 5867 (d) 7658

21. If LESSON is written as 543321 and GARDEN as 867941, then how do you write DRAGON?

(a) 216897 (b) 867912 (c) 976821 (d) 129768

22. If BIHAR is written as 68745 and PUNE is written as 2139 then how do you write RAIPUR?

(a) 415854 (b) 548215 (c) 582415 (d) 552814

23. If SEVEN is written as 68482 and EIGHT is written as 87531, then how do you write NINE?

(a) 2728 (b) 6627 (c) 2766 (d) 2276

24. If STOVE is written as QRPST, then how do you write VOTES?

(a) SRPQT (b) TPQRS (c) SQPTR (d) SPRTQ

25. If 675 is written as 492 and 572 is written as 291, then how do you write 726?

(a) 941 (b) 914 (c) 361 (d) 352

26.

Sign	○△	△□	○●	△●
Codes	A 9	9 C	A D	9 D

From the above mentioned table write the code for the sign?

○△□●

(a) A9CD (b) AC9D (c) DCA9 (d) A9AD

27. If LOTUS is written as 76592 and MONEY is written 46813 then write down the code for TUNNEL?

(a) 762695 (b) 762139 (c) 598817 (d) 798515

28. If we assign some codes to certain alphabets as below

A → %, B → #, C → *, L → □ K → △, E → ○, M → □. So how would you write the code for LAKE?

(a) □ % △ ○ (b) ○ % △ □ (c) □ # ○ % (d) ◇ # ○ %

29. If we write DICTIONARY as 3954927610 then how do you write NATION?

(a) 792647 (b) 764927 (c) 726947 (d) 772469

30. In a certain code, – * @ + > is written as ÷ $ < ? =, then how is @ + > – * written in that code?

(a) = ? < $ ÷ (b) < ? = ÷ $ (c) $ ÷ = ? > (d) * – > + ?

Answers and Explanations

Level-1

1. **(d)** The sun rises in the East, but here, the code for East is South. So, the correct answer is (d).

2. **(d)** We drink tea/coffee in a cup, but here, the code for cup is spoon. So, correct answer is (d).

3. **(c)** We use eraser for erasing a drawing done by Pencil but here the code for Eraser is sharpener.

4. **(b)** Lion lives in a Den but the code for Lion is Eagle. So, the correct answer is (b).

5. **(c)** ⌂ would be written as 5 because it has 5 sides.

6. **(d)** Fish live only in water but the code for Fish is Frog. So, the correct answer is (d).

7. **(b)** In Holi we play the game of colours, but here the code for holi is colour. So, the correct answer is (b).

8. **(b)** The race is won by lion as the code for tortoise is lion.

9. **(d)** The last colour Indian flag is green and the colour code for green is 5.

10. **(a)** We get milk from cow but here the code for cow is kitten. So, the correct answer is (a).

11. **(c)** As we know that the king of fruits is Mango but here, the code for Mango is Orange. So, the correct option is (c).

12. **(a)** We breathe through our nose, but here, the code for nose is eyes. So, the correct answer is (a).

13. **(c)** Coconut has water inside it but here, the code for coconut is muskmelon. So, the correct answer is (c).

14. **(d)** Singing is done by singer but here the code for singing is Dancing. So, the answer is (d).

15. **(c)** Doraemon is friend of Nobita, but here, the code for Nobita is Shizuka. So, the correct answer is (c).

16. **(b)** Tom is the friend of Jerry, but here, Tom is coded as Guffy. So, the correct answer is (b).

17. **(a)** As,

$$\text{MONKEY} \xrightarrow{\text{Reversed}} \text{YEKNOM}$$

Similarly,

$$\text{BUTTERFLY} \xrightarrow{\text{Reversed}} \text{YLFRETTUB}$$

So, the correct answer is (a).

18. **(a)** Lotus blosooms in water and here the code for lotus is lily. So, the correct answer is (a).

19. **(c)** Cloud gives us Rain but here the code for Cloud is sky. So, the correct answer is (c).

20. **(a)** Mouse is the smallest animal but here, the code for Mouse is Goat. So, the correct answer is (a).

21. **(a)** As we know that the colour of sky is blue, but here, the code for blue is red. So, the correct answer is (a).

22. **(b)** We generally use Knife for cutting vegetables but here the code for Knife is Tree.

23. **(a)** Circle is used to form sphere. But here, the code for Circle is Square. So, the correct answer is (a).

24. **(b)** The colour of our hair is Black but here, the colour code for black is White. So, the correct answer is (b).

25. **(d)** Thumb is a part of Hand. But here, the code for Hand is Leg. So, the correct answer is (d).

26. **(b)** We see Moon at night. But here, the code for Moon is Earth. So, the correct answer is (b).

27. **(b)** We wear watch around our wrist. But here, the code for wrist is ankle. So, the correct answer is (b).

28. **(a)** We use Mobile phone for talking to people and here the code for Mobile phone is Hand bag. So, the correct answer is (a).

29. **(a)** We use Washing machine to wash our clothes. But here, the code for Washing machine is Air Conditioner. So, the correct answer is (a).

30. **(d)** As,

$$\text{FLOWER} \xrightarrow{\text{Reversed}} \text{REWOLF}$$

Similarly,

$$82674 \xrightarrow{\text{Reversed}} 47628$$

Level-2

1. **(c)** The code for MATH is 5632.
2. **(b)** The code for TIME is 3958.
3. **(b)** The code for DATE is 7638.
4. **(a)** The code for NOTE is 1438.
5. **(b)** The correct code for STAR-FISH will be 32615937.
6. **(d)** The code for B is 9 and code for R is 3.

   $\therefore B \times R = 9 \times 3 = 27$

7. **(b)** The code for

A	C	C	E	P	T
↓	↓	↓	↓	↓	↓
5	6	6	4	3	2

8. (a) The code for

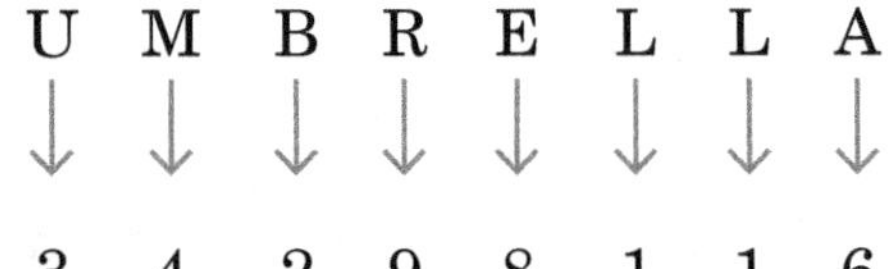

9. **(b)** The code for

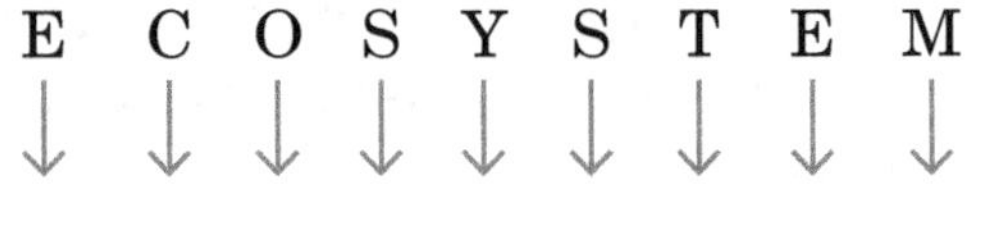

10. **(d)** The code for

B	U	T	T	E	R	F	L	Y
6	1	9	9	2	4	7	8	5

11. **(b)** The code for

E	S	T	I	M	A	T	E
↓	↓	↓	↓	↓	↓	↓	↓
3	1	5	4	2	9	5	3

12. **(c)** The code for 215389 is NRBOPQ.

13. **(d)**

Letters	H	A	P	Y	B	R	I	C	K
Codes	2	9	8	1	3	7	9	4	6

So, the code for PRAY is 8791.

14. **(d)** As,

E	N	G	L	I	S	H
+1 ↓	+1 ↓	+1 ↓	+1 ↓	+1 ↓	+1 ↓	+1 ↓
F	O	H	M	J	T	I

Similarly,

T	U	E	S	D	A	Y
+1 ↓	+1 ↓	+1 ↓	+1 ↓	+1 ↓	+1 ↓	+1 ↓
U	V	F	T	E	B	Z

So, the correct answer is (d).

15. **(a)** C (R) O C (O) (D) I (L) E ⟶ L O R D

2 (9) 6 2 (6) (5) 3 (4) 7   4 6 9 5

16. **(b)** As,

A	T	T	A	C	K
+2 ↓	+2 ↓	+2 ↓	+2 ↓	+2 ↓	+2 ↓
C	V	V	C	E	M

Similarly,

A	U	G	U	S	T
+2 ↓	+2 ↓	+2 ↓	+2 ↓	+2 ↓	+2 ↓
C	W	I	W	U	V

17. (c)

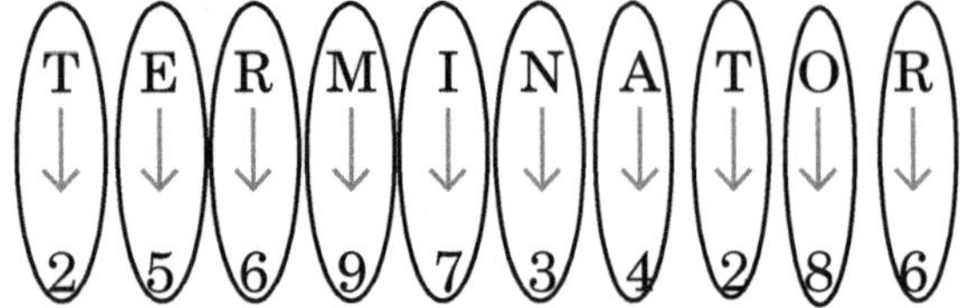

The code for

M	O	N	I	T	O	R
↓	↓	↓	↓	↓	↓	↓
9	8	3	7	2	8	6

18. (d) As,

J	U	N	E
↓ −1	↓ −1	↓ −1	↓ −1
I	T	M	D

Similarly,

J	U	L	Y
↓ −1	↓ −1	↓ −1	↓ −1
I	T	K	X

19. (c) As, MANGO $\xrightarrow{\text{Reversed}}$ OGNAM

Similarly, APPLE $\xrightarrow{\text{Reversed}}$ ELPPA

20. (a)

Letters	C	H	A	I	R	N	O	S	E
Codes	3	9	6	7	5	2	1	4	8

So, the code for RAIN is 5672.

21. (c)

Letters	L	E	S	O	N	G	A	R	D
Codes	5	4	3	2	1	8	6	7	9

So, the code for DRAGON is 976821.

22. (b)

Letters	B	I	H	A	R	P	U	N	E
Codes	6	8	7	4	5	2	1	3	9

The code for RAIPUR is 548215.

23. (a)

Letters	S	V	N	E	I	G	H	T
Codes	6	4	2	8	7	5	3	1

So, the code for NINE is 2728.

24. (d)

S	T	O	V	E
Q	R	P	S	T

⟶

V	O	T	E	S
S	P	R	T	Q

25. (b)

Letters	6	7	5	2
Codes	4	9	2	1

So, the code for 726 is 914.

26. (a) A9CD is the correct code.

27. (c)

Letters	L	O	T	U	S	M	N	E	Y
Codes	7	6	5	9	2	4	8	1	3

So, the code for TUNNEL is 598817.

28. (a) □ % △ ○ is the correct code.

29. (b)

Letters	D	I	C	T	I	O	N	A	R	Y
Codes	3	9	5	4	9	2	7	6	1	0

So, the code for NATION is 764927.

30. **(b)** As,

–	*	@	+	>
↓	↓	↓	↓	↓
÷	$	<	?	=

So, by direct code method, we get

@	+	>	–	*
↓	↓	↓	↓	↓
<	?	=	÷	$

Hence, the correct answer is (b).

CHAPTER 7

SPATIAL UNDERSTANDING

OBJECTIVES

- Students will understand their location and the location of an object in relation to their bodies.
- They will come to learn concepts such as direction, distance and location.
- Spatial awareness helps us understand, interact and appreciate the places we live.
- Students will be able to keep up to date with their surroundings and make sense of their cities.

INTRODUCTION

Spatial understanding is an organised knowledge of objects including oneself in a given space. Spatial understanding also involves understanding of these objects when there is a change of position and form.

Questions asked in this chapter are based on following topics.

Inside / Outside, Above / Below, Top / Bottom, Far / Near, On / Under, Thick / Thin and Few More

Examples:

1. Number of balls inside the net is ____________.

(a) 7 (b) 6 (c) 5 (d) 2

Ans. (a) Number of balls inside the net is 7.

2. Number of apples outside the box is ___________.

(a) 2 (b) 8 (c) 3 (d) 4

Ans. (c) Number of apples outside the box is 3

3. How many flowers are outside the vase?

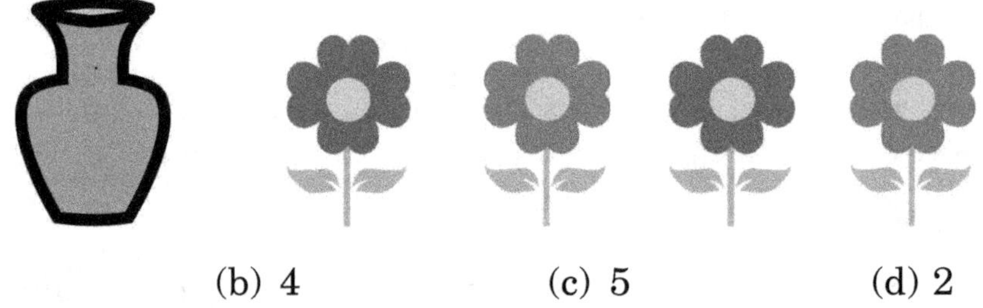

(a) 3 (b) 4 (c) 5 (d) 2

Ans. (b) 4 flowers are outside the vase.

Direction (Examples 4 and 5): Observe the picture carefully and answer the following questions.

1. How many children are there inside the bus?

(a) 2 (b) 3 (c) 1 (d) 4

Ans. (d) There are 4 children inside the bus.

2. How many children are standing outside the bus?

(a) 5 (b) 7 (c) 3 (d) 0

Ans. (a) There are 5 children standing outside the bus.

LEVEL-1

Directions (Qs. 1 & 2) : Sheryl, Pinky, Nancy, Richa, Shruti are going on a picnic with their teacher Miss Liza. All are standing in the queue and waiting for the bus. Now answer the following questions.

1. ________________ is standing nearest to Ms. Liza.

   (a) Nancy (b) Pinky (c) Sheryl (d) Richa

2. ________________ is standing in the last.

   (a) Sheryl (b) Pinky (c) Nancy (d) Richa

Direction (Qs. 3 & 4) : Study the picture and answer the following questions.

3. How many people are still buying things in the super market?

   (a) 6 (b) 2 (c) 1 (d) 5

4. How many people are standing at the cash counter for billing?

(a) 3 (b) 5 (c) 2 (d) 7

Direction (Qs. 5 & 6) : Rita washed her clothes and now she is hanging them in the garden for drying. Now answer the following questions.

5. How many clothes are hanging on the rope?

(a) 5 (b) 8 (c) 4 (d) 2

6. How many clothes are left in the tub?

(a) 1 (b) 4 (c) 6 (d) 5

Direction (Qs. 7-9): Observe the given picture and answer the following questions.

7. How many birds are sitting on the tree?

(a) 10 (b) 2 (c) 1 (d) 5

8. How many birds are flying?

(a) 1 (b) 8 (c) 5 (d) 4

9. How many birds are playing on the sand?

(a) 4 (b) 3 (c) 8 (d) 0

Direction (Qs. 10 & 11): Observe the picture of a village and answer the following questions.

10. How many cows are standing in the village?

(a) 2 (b) 3 (c) 4 (d) 1

11. How many women are sitting there?

(a) 5 (b) 4 (c) 3 (d) 2

Direction (Qs. 12 & 13): Observe the pictures of different flowers and answer the following questions.

12. How many yellow coloured flowers in the picture?

(a) 3 (b) 2 (c) 4 (d) 5

13. How many blue and purple coloured flowers in the picture?

(a) 2, 3 (b) 1, 3 (c) 3, 4 (d) 4, 2

Direction (Qs. 14 & 15): Observe the given picture and answer the following questions.

14. How many fishes are there in the river?

(a) 5 (b) 9 (c) 7 (d) 10

15. How many octopus are there in the river?

(a) 7 (b) 1 (c) 6 (d) 2

Direction (Qs. 16 & 17): Observe the picture and give answer for the following questions.

16. What is the position of book "P"?

(a) Last in queue

(b) Middle

(c) First in queue

(d) Second Last in queue

17. What is the position of book "S"?

(a) Last in queue

(b) Middle

(c) First in queue

(d) Second Last in queue

Direction (Q. 18): Observe the picture and answer the following questions.

18. How many fruits are there on the ground?

(a) 5 (b) 4 (c) 8 (d) 0

19. How many eggs are there in the nest?

(a) 4 (b) 8 (c) 7 (d) 15

Direction (Qs. 20-24): Study the pictures and answer the following questions.

20. Who is sitting right to the John?

(a) Puja (b) Rita (c) John (d) Sheru

21. Who is sitting first behind the John?

(a) Rita (b) Puja (c) Sheru (d) John

22. Who is sitting at the last seat of the car?

(a) Todo (b) Sheru (c) Rita (d) Puja

23. Who is sitting with Sheru in the middle seat?

(a) Rita (b) Puja (c) John (d) Todo

24. How many people are sitting in the car.

(a) 5 (b) 4 (c) 3 (d) 2

Direction (Qs. 25 & 26): Observe the pictures and give answer for the following questions.

25. How many children are playing on the swings?

    (a) 2 (b) 3 (c) 4 (d) 1

26. How many children are playing in the park?

    (a) 4 (b) 3 (c) 5 (d) 9

27. How many people are there under the umbrella?

    (a) 2 (b) 3 (c) 5 (d) 4

28. How many people (including animal) are sitting on the magical flying carpet?

(a) 3 (b) 5 (c) 2 (d) 7

29. Study the picture and answer the following questions.

Piglet is sitting ____________ the Pooh and Tigger?

(a) In front (b) Behind (c) Between (d) Above

Direction (Qs. 30 & 31): See the picture and answer the following questions.

30. Who is sitting nearest to the Principal's room?

    (a) Ashi (b) Ashish (c) Tom (d) None

31. Who is sitting farthest to the Principal's room?

    (a) Tom (b) Ashish (c) Ashi (d) None

LEVEL-2

1. Observe the picture and choose the correct statement.

(a) Bag is behind the books.

(b) Two notebooks and two apples are under the table.

(c) Scale is behind the crayons.

(d) Bag is under the table.

Direction (Qs. 2 & 3): Observe the figure of birthday party and answer the following questions.

2. How many cupcakes and candies are on the table?

(a) 4 ,5 (b) 5 ,6 (c) 3 ,6 (d) 6 ,4

3. How many kids wear birthday cap?

(a) 4 (b) 6 (c) 5 (d) 3

4. How many girls and boys are there in the given picture ?

(a) 4,3 (b) 3,4 (c) 4,5 (d) 4,4

Direction (Qs. 5 & 6): See the picture and answer the following questions.

5. How many fruits are there on the ground?

(a) 5 (b) 4 (c) 7 (d) 3

6. How many fruits are there on the tree?

(a) 10 (b) 16 (c) 14 (d) 18

Direction (Qs. 7 & 8): Study the picture and answer the following questions.

7. Which runner is standing at the finish line?

   (a) Runner 47 (b) Runner 27 (c) Runner 32 (d) Runner 55

8. Which runner is at the second position?

   (a) Runner 47 (b) Runner 27 (c) Runner 32 (d) Runner 55

Direction (Qs. 9 & 10): Observe the pictures and answer the following questions.

9. Blocks are ______________ the cake.

   (a) After (b) Before (c) Over (d) Across

10. Balloons are ______________ the cake.

    (a) After (b) Before (c) Over (d) Across

Direction (Qs. 11 & 12): See the picture carefully and answer the following questions.

11. Who is nearest to the house?

(a) Rohan (b) Piyush (c) Both (d) None

12. Who is farthest from the house?

(a) Rohan (b) Piyush (c) Both (d) None

Direction (Qs. 13 & 14): See the picture and answer the following questions.

13. How many tomatoes are in the basket?

(a) 8 (b) 9 (c) 5 (d) 0

14. How many tomatoes are outside the basket?

(a) 4 (b) 5 (c) 3 (d) 0

Direction (Qs. 15 & 16): See the picture and answer the following questions.

15. The boy is sitting ______________ the cage.

(a) Inside (b) Outside (c) Under (d) On

16. The bird is sitting ______________ the cage.

(a) Inside (b) Outside (c) Under (d) On

Direction (Qs. 17 & 18): Observe the picture and answer the given questions.

Picture 1 Picture 2

17. In picture – 1, the girl is standing ____________ the black-board.

    (a) Between (b) In front of (c) Behind (d) On

18. In picture – 2, the girl is standing ____________ the black-board.

    (a) Between (b) In front of (c) Behind (d) On

19. The box is ____________ the ball.

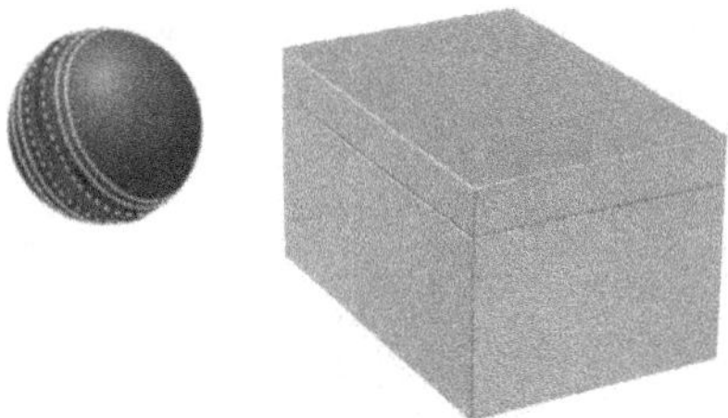

    (a) Next to (b) In front of (c) Behind (d) On

Direction(Q. 20): Observe the picture and answer the given question.

20. The kite is ____________ the girl.

    (a) Below (b) Above (c) Between (d) Over

21. Our nose is ____________ the two eyes.

(a) Below (b) Above (c) Between (d) Across

22. Cat is sitting ____________ the Christmas tree.

(a) Behind (b) Above (c) On (d) In Front of

Direction (Q. 23): Study the picture and answer the question.

23. A cat is sitting ____________ the umbrella.

(a) Above (b) Below (c) On (d) Under

24. An aeroplane is flying ____________ the sky.

(a) In (b) On (c) Over (d) Above

25. What is the position of the blue colour book?

(a) Top (b) Bottom (c) Middle (d) Below

Answers and Explanation

Level-1

1. **(c)** Sheryl is standing nearest to Ms. Liza
2. **(d)** Richa is standing last in the queue.
3. **(b)** 2 people are still buying things in the super market.
4. **(c)** 2 people are standing at the cash counter.
5. **(a)** 5 number of clothes are hanging on the rope.
6. **(d)** 5 number of clothes are left in the tub.
7. **(c)** Only 1 bird is sitting on the tree.
8. **(a)** Only 1 bird is flying.
9. **(b)** 3 birds are playing on the sand.
10. **(a)** Only two cows are standing in the village.
11. **(d)** Only two women are sitting.
12. **(c)** There are 4 yellow coloured flowers in the picture
13. **(b)** There are one blue and three purple coloured flowers in the picture.
14. **(c)** There are 7 fishes in the river.
15. **(b)** There are only one octopus in the river.
16. **(c)** First in queue
17. **(a)** Last in queue
18. **(b)** 4 (2 mangoes and 2 apples) are there on the ground.
19. **(a)** 4 eggs are there in the nest.
20. **(b)** Rita is sitting to the right of John.
21. **(c)** Sheru is sitting just behind the John.
22. **(a)** Todo is sitting at the last seat of the car.
23. **(b)** Puja is sitting with Sheru in the middle seat.
24. **(c)** 3 people are sitting in the car.
25. **(d)** Only one child is playing on the swings.
26. **(a)** 4 children are playing in the park.
27. **(b)** 3 people are there under the umbrella.
28. **(a)** 3 People are sitting on the magical flying carpet.
29. **(c)** Piglet is sitting between the Pooh and Tigger.
30. **(c)** Tom is sitting nearest to the Principal's room.
31. **(c)** Ashi is sitting farthest to the Principal's room.

Level-2

1. **(d)** Bag is under the table is the correct statement.
2. **(b)** There are 5 cup cakes and 6 candies on the table.
3. **(c)** 5 kids wear birthday cap.
4. **(d)** 4 boys and 4 girls are there in the given picture.
5. **(b)** 4 fruits are there on the ground.
6. **(b)** 16 fruits are there on the tree.
7. **(c)** Runner 32 is standing at the finish line.
8. **(a)** Runner 47 is at the second position.
9. **(b)** Blocks are before the cake.
10. **(a)** Balloons are after the cake.
11. **(b)** Piyush is nearest to the house.
12. **(a)** Rohan is farthest from the house.
13. **(c)** 5 tomatoes are in the basket.
14. **(b)** 5 tomatoes are outside the basket.
15. **(b)** The boy is sitting outside the cage.
16. **(a)** The bird is sitting inside the cage.
17. **(b)** The girl is standing in front of the black-board.
18. **(c)** The girl is standing behind the black-board.
19. **(a)** The box is next to the ball.
20. **(b)** The kite is above the girl.
21. **(c)** Our nose is between the two eyes.
22. **(d)** Cat is sitting in front of the Christmas tree.
23. **(d)** A cat is sitting under the umbrella.
24. **(a)** An aeroplane is flying in the sky.
25. **(c)** The blue colour book is in the middle.

CHAPTER

8

GEOMETRICAL SHAPES

OBJECTIVES

- Students will know the properties of different 2D and 3D shapes.
- Students will recognise difference between 2D and 3D shapes.
- Students will learn how to move a shape around, enlarge it, rotate it without it being changed in shape.

INTRODUCTION

Geometry is all about shapes and their properties. Geometrical shapes consists of points, lines, planes, square etc.

SHAPES AND THEIR NAMES

2D Geometrical Shapes	3D Geometrical Shapes
1. = Rectangle	= Cube
2. = Square	= Cuboid
3. = Circle	= Sphere
4. = Oval	= Cone
5. = Triangle	= Cylinder

LINES

Slanting Lines = / \

Vertical Lines = |

Horizontal Lines = ——

Curved Lines = ~

All slanting, vertical and horizontal lines are straight lines.

Examples:

Type-1: Identify Shapes

1. Which one of the following is a square?

   (a) ▭ (b) □ (c) △ (d) ○

Ans. (b)

Explanation:

A square has four equal sides.

Type-2: Count Sides

2. How many corners does this shape have?

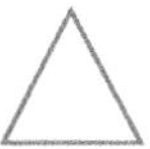

   (a) 4 (b) 2 (c) 5 (d) 3

Ans. (d)

Explanation:

A triangle has three sides.

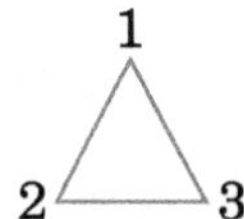

Type-3: Similar Shapes

3. Which shape is similar to the group of three given below?

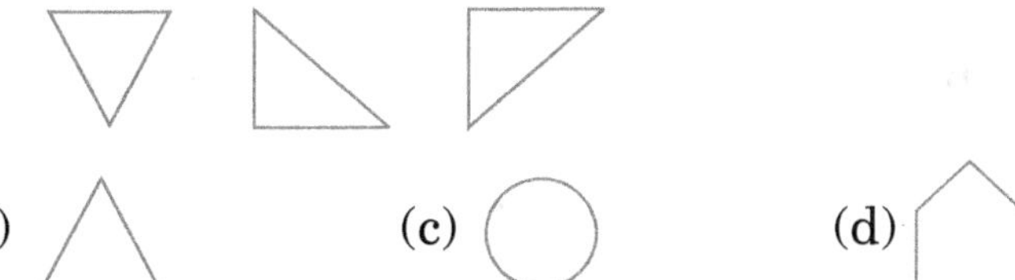

(a) (b) (c) (d)

Ans. (b)

Explanation:

Option (b) is similar to the group of three figures. So, option (b) is the correct answer.

Type-4: Hidden Shapes

4. In which of the following figures is the shape hidden?

Ans. (c)

Explanation:

Option (c) has the exact hidden shape.

1. How many straight lines are there in the figure given below?

(a) 3 (b) 4 (c) 5 (d) 6

2. Count the number of squares in the following figure.

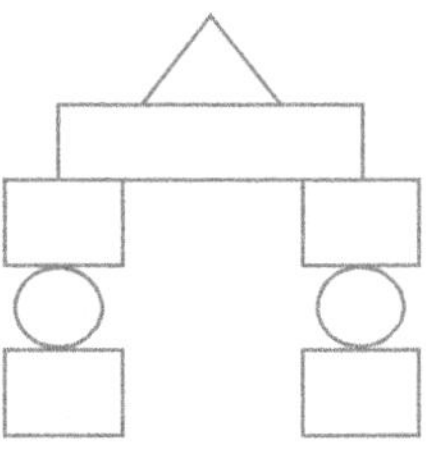

(a) 5 (b) 4 (c) 3 (d) 6

3. Which of the following figures contains exactly four circles?

(a) 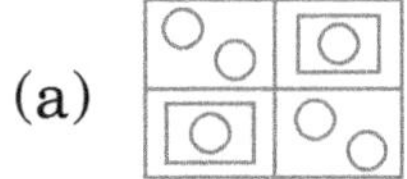 (b)  (c) 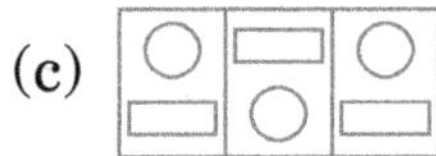 (d) 

4. Match the shapes with their names.

A. 

1. Circle

B.

2. Triangle

C.

3. Rectangle

D.

4. Square

(a) A-2, B-4, C-1, D-3 (b) A-1, B-2, C-3, D-4

(c) A-4, B-3, C-2, D-1 (d) A-3, B-2, C-4, D-1

5. Dice is an example of ______________ shape.

(a) Square (b) Circle (c) Cube (d) Rectangle

6. What shape will you get if you trace around a cricket ball?

(a) Triangle (b) Square (c) Oval (d) Circle

7. The figure is made up of ______________ circles.

(a) 4 (b) 7 (c) 8 (d) 10

8. The figure is made up of ______________ triangles.

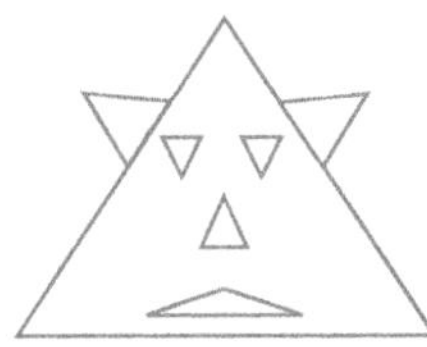

(a) 8 (b) 7 (c) 9 (d) 10

9. How many solid/3D shapes are there in the picture?

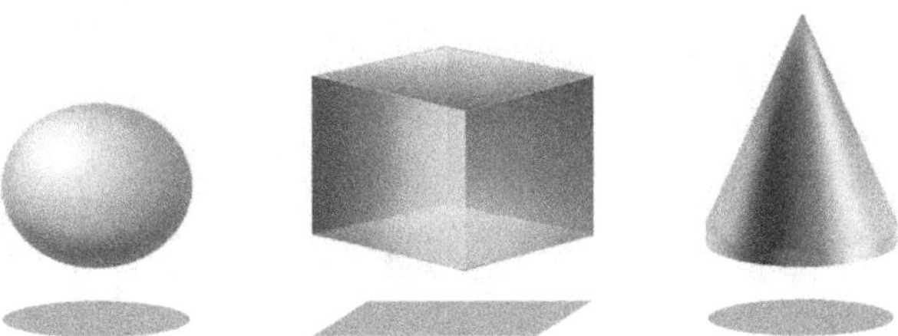

(a) 10 (b) 7 (c) 5 (d) 3

10. How many circles are there in the given picture?

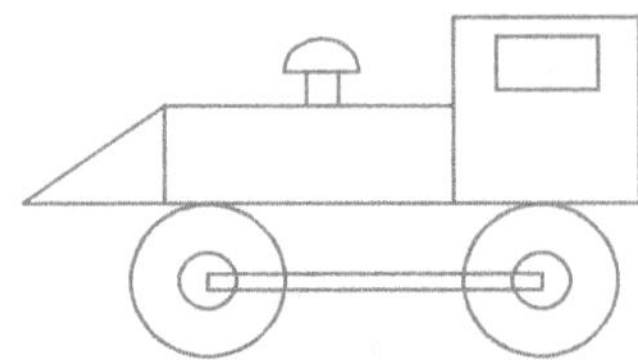

(a) 0 (b) 5 (c) 4 (d) 10

11. How many circles are there in the given figure?

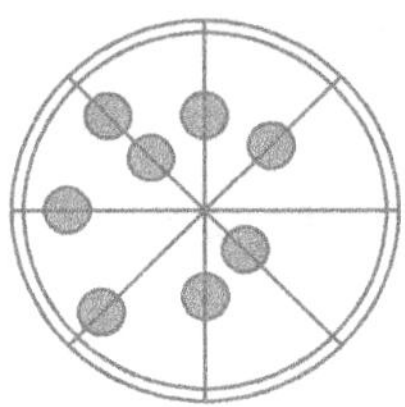

(a) 6 (b) 12 (c) 8 (d) 10

12. How many squares are there in the given picture?

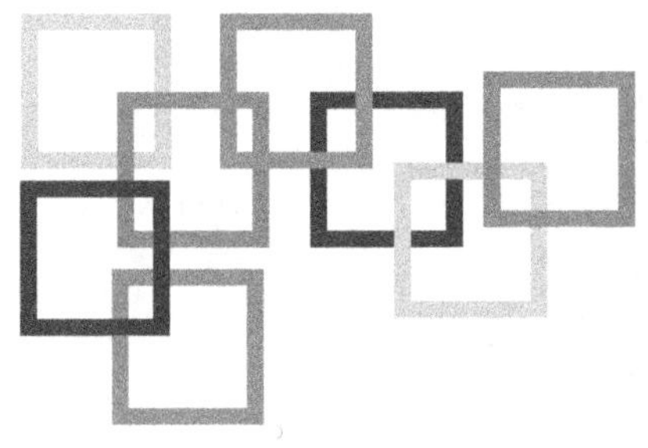

(a) 8 (b) 7 (c) 6 (d) 10

Direction (Qs. 13-15) : Study the picture and answer the following questions.

13. Alisha has a ______________ shape in her hand.

(a) Circle (b) Square (c) Triangle (d) Rectangle.

14. Johnny has a ______________ shape in his hand.

(a) Circle (b) Square (c) Triangle (d) Rectangle

15. How many squares are there in the above figure?

(a) 7 (b) 8 (c) 6 (d) 0

16. How many triangles are there in this abstract?

(a) 15 (b) 13 (c) 20 (d) 25

17. These shapes are known as ______________ shapes.

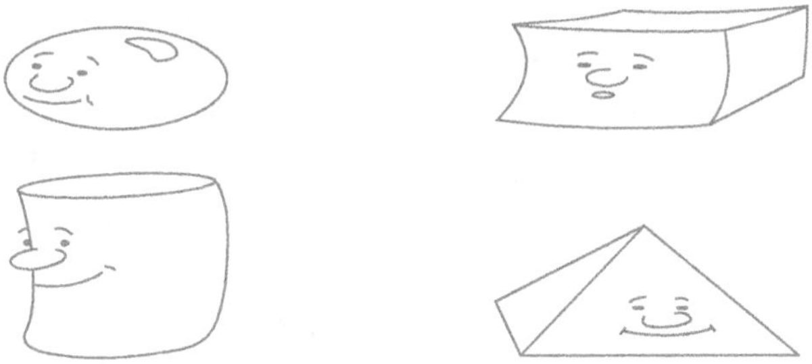

(a) Flat shapes (b) Solid shapes (c) Both (a) and (b) (d) 2D shapes

18. Which solid shape is used to draw the shape (X)?

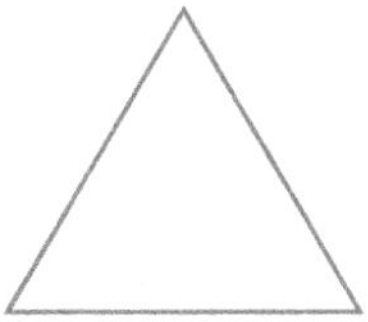

(X)

(a)  (b)  (c)  (d)

19. Identify the shape of a bin as given below.

(a) Sphere (b) Cone (c) Cylindrical (d) Cuboids

20. How many numbers of shapes are there in this picture?

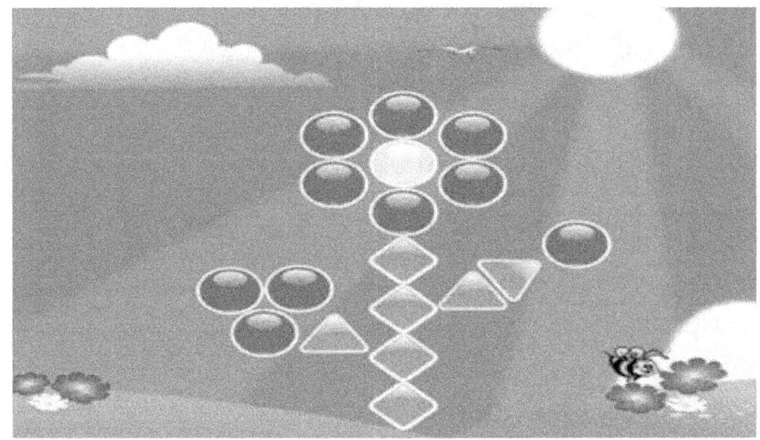

(a) 18 (b) 16 (c) 20 (d) 15

21. There are ____________ cylinders in the figure.

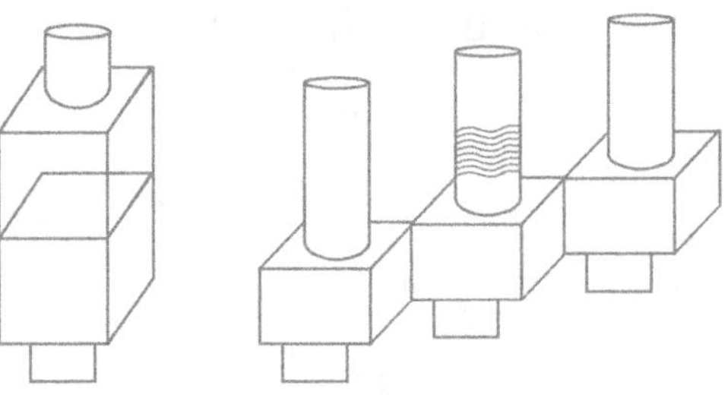

(a) 5 (b) 7 (c) 4 (d) 2

Direction (Qs. 22-24): Look at the figure carefully and answer the following questions.

22. How many circles are there in the figure?

(a) 10 (b) 20 (c) 30 (d) 40

23. Total number of triangles in the figure are ______________.

(a) 15 (b) 13 (c) 20 (d) 25

24. Total number of squares in the figure are ______________.

(a) 10 (b) 2 (c) 6 (d) 7

25. Which solid shape can be obtained by using triangle?

(a) 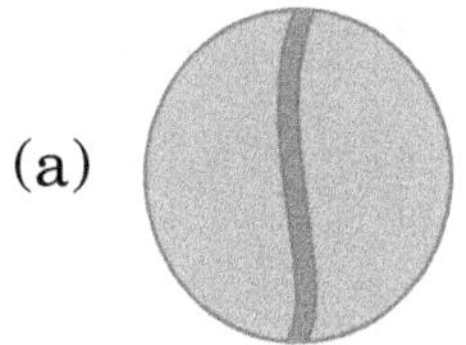

(b) 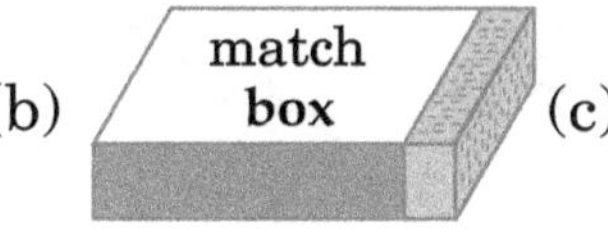

(c) 

(d) 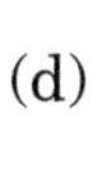 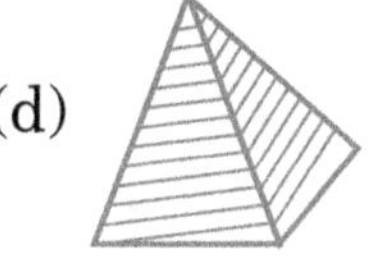

26. I have 6 square faces. A dice or a sugarcube looks like me. Who am I?

(a)

(b) 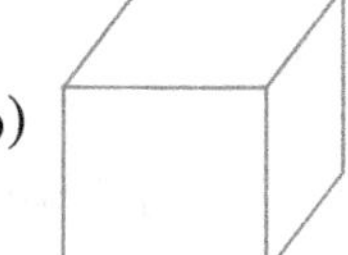

(c) 

(d)

27. This figure is made up of ____________ triangles.

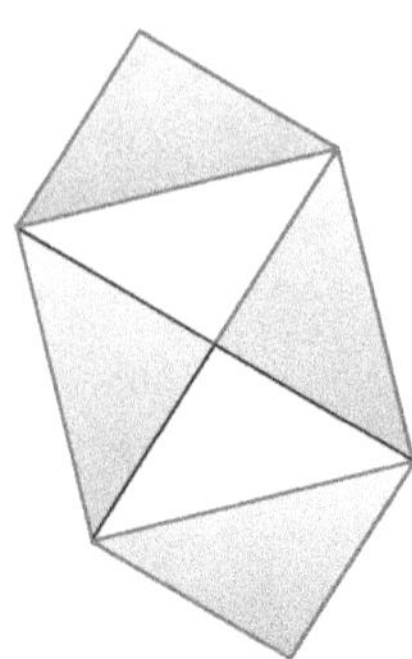

(a) 8 (b) 6 (c) 9 (d) 10

28. How many rectangles are there in the given figure?

(a) 9 (b) 8 (c) 10 (d) 11

29. How many circles, triangles and rectangles in the given crown?

(a) 13, 9, 6 (b) 12, 6, 8 (c) 14, 6, 6 (d) 13, 6, 8

30. In rectangle pair of ____________ are equal.

(a) Same sides (b) Opposite sides

(c) Insides (d) Outsides

1. Find the number of circles in the given figure.

(a) 7 (b) 8 (c) 6 (d) 10

2. How many curved lines are there in the given figure?

(a) 12 (b) 10 (c) 8 (d) 15

3. How many triangles are there in the given figure?

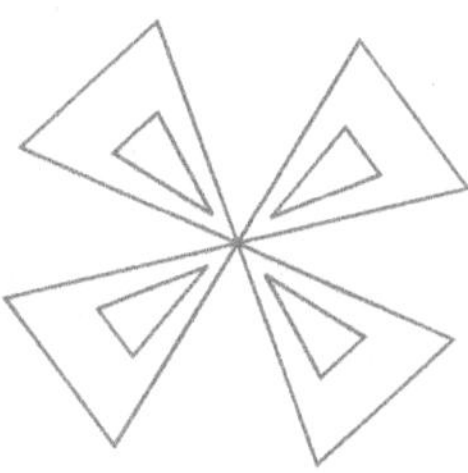

(a) 5 (b) 2 (c) 3 (d) 8

4. Name the shape of the shaded face.

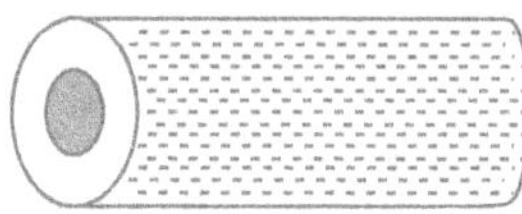

(a) Triangle (b) Circle (c) Square (d) Rectangle

Direction (Qs. 5-8): Look at the figure and answer the following questions.

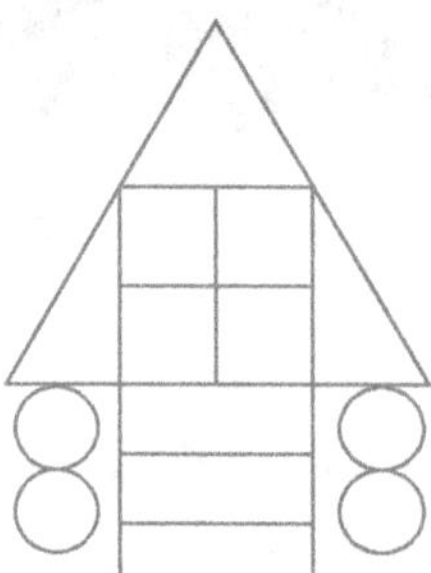

5. There are ____________ circles in the given figure.

   (a) 5 (b) 3 (c) 4 (d) 8

6. There are ____________ triangles in the figure.

   (a) 10 (b) 5 (c) 3 (d) 4

7. There are ____________ squares in the figure.

   (a) 6 (b) 7 (c) 5 (d) 8

8. How many rectangles are there in the figure below triangle?

   (a) 10 (b) 6 (c) 15 (d) 4

9. How many sides does a square has?

   (a) 5 (b) 6 (c) 4 (d) 8

10. Rectangle has ____________ corners and ____________ sides.

   (a) 5, 5 (b) 4, 4 (c) 2, 4 (d) 5, 2

11. A sphere has ____________ face and ____________

   (a) Conical and 8 corners (b) Square and 4 corners

   (c) Triangular face and 6 corners (d) Circular and no corner.

12. How many triangles are there in the figure?

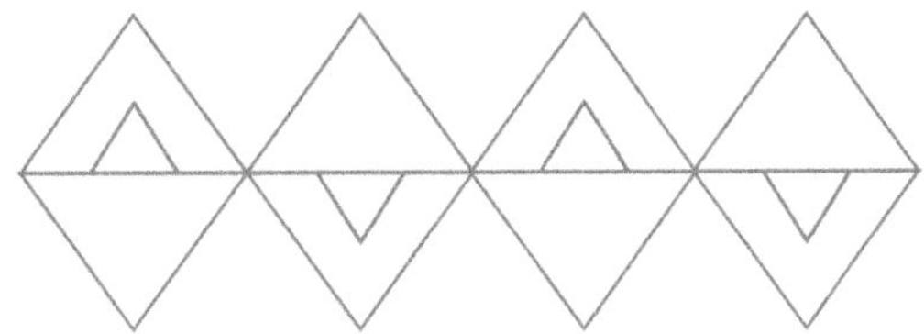

(a) 10 (b) 9 (c) 8 (d) 12

13. Match the shapes with their names.

(A) (1) Cylinder

(B) (2) Sphere

(C) (3) Pyramid

(a) A-3, B-1, C-2 (b) A-1, B-2, C-3

(c) A-2, B-3, C-1 (d) A-1, B-3, C-2

14. A cubiod has ____________ rectangular faces and ____________ sides.

(a) 8, 12 (b) 6, 12 (c) 10, 14 (d) 10, 15

15. A cone has two types of faces one is ____________ and second is ____________.

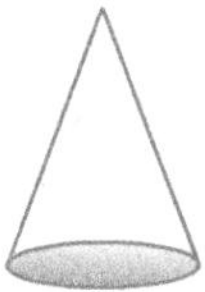

(a) Rectangular and circular (b) Circular and square

(c) Triangular and circular (d) Circular and cubical

16. A cube has ____________ sides and ____________ corners.

(a) 6, 12 (b) 12, 12 (c) 12, 8 (d) 10, 12

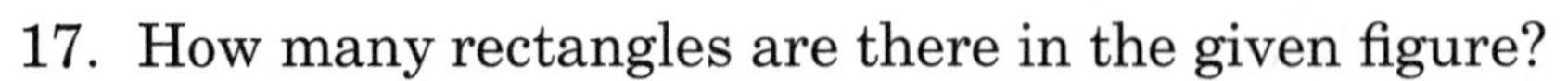

17. How many rectangles are there in the given figure?

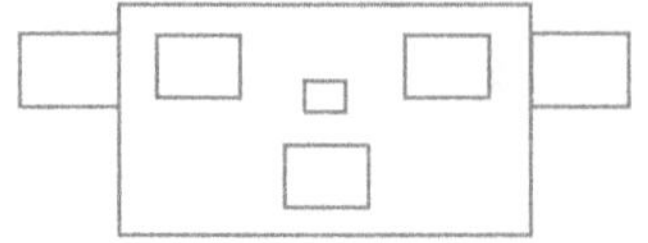

(a) 6 (b) 7 (c) 8 (d) 9

18. Count the number of slanting lines in the given figure?

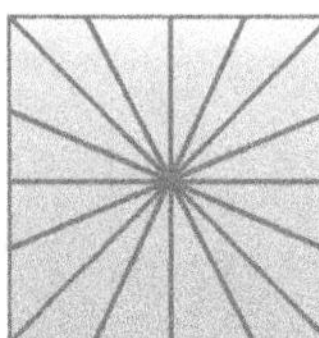

(a) 15 (b) 12 (c) 13 (d) 11

19. Count the number of straight lines in the given figure?

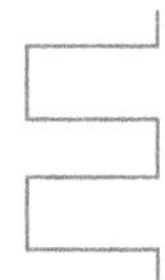

(a) 9 (b) 8 (c) 10 (d) 12

20. Find the number of cubes in the given figure?

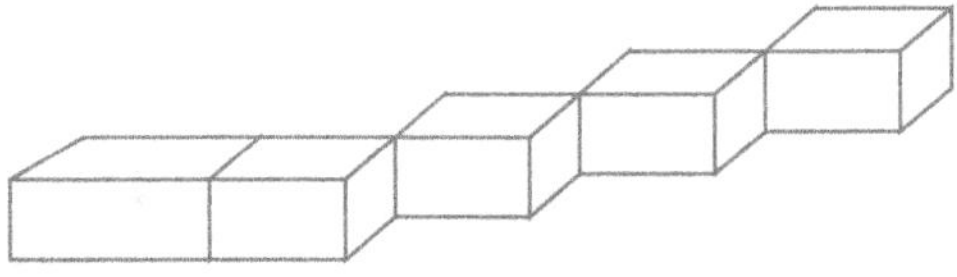

(a) 6 (b) 5 (c) 4 (d) 0

21. How many circles are there in the given necklace?

(a) 20 (b) 25 (c) 21 (d) 15

22. The given figure has __________ slanting lines.

(a) 12 (b) 11 (c) 10 (d) 14

(Olympiad)

23. Which combination of letters is NOT hidden in the logo?

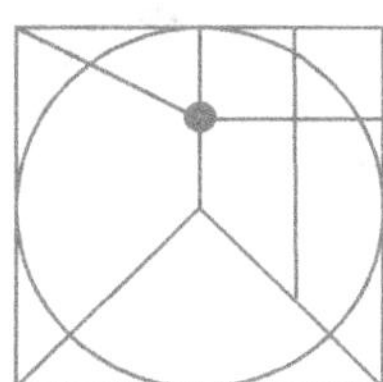

(a) IOF (b) VCL (c) EDS (d) HTI

(Olympiad)

24. There are ________ triangles, ________ circles and ________ squares respectively in the given figure.

(a) 11, 4, 2 (b) 12, 4, 3 (c) 13, 5, 2 (d) 12, 6, 2

(Olympiad)

25. There are ________ number of sleeping lines, ________ numbers of slanting lines and ________ number of standing lines in the given figure.

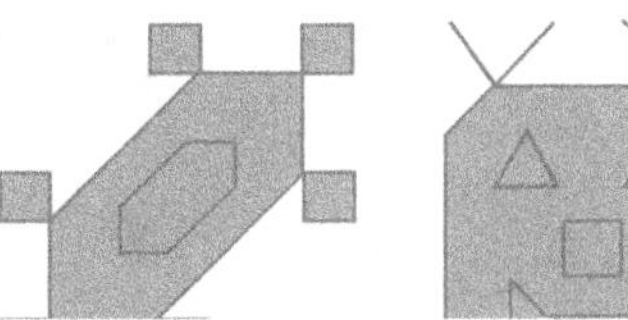

(a) 22, 16, 20 (b) 23, 14, 19 (c) 20, 16, 18 (d) 18, 16, 20

(Olympiad)

26. There are ______ squares and ______ circles.

(a) 2, 25 (b) 3, 23 (c) 1, 24 (d) 2, 24

(Olympiad)

27. ____________ is shaded with red and _______ is shaded with blue in the given figure.

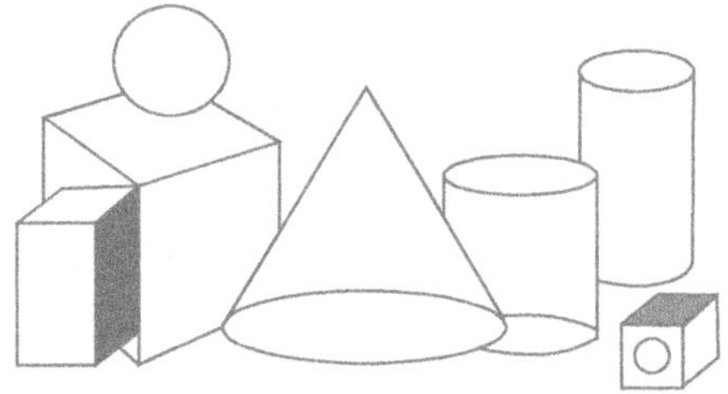

(a) Square and Circle (b) Rectangle and Square

(c) Circle and Rectangle (d) Triangle and Circle

(Olympiad)

28. There are _______ squares and _____ circles in the given figure.

(a) 7, 18 (b) 10, 18 (c) 6, 20 (d) 8, 17

(Olympiad)

29. Latika has collected 6 equal sized squares and 1 rectangle for her maths project. Identify the solids she formed with the collected material.

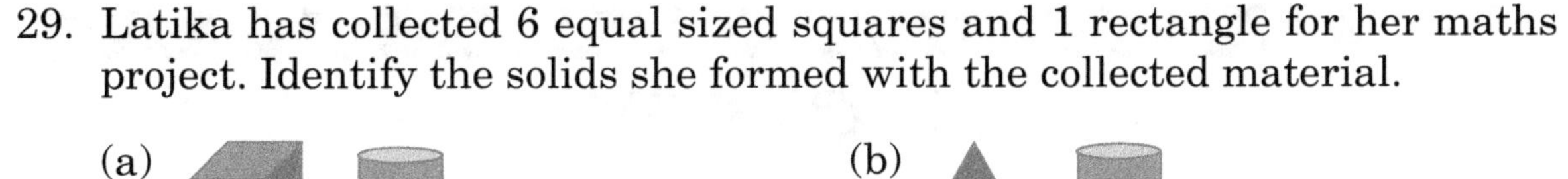

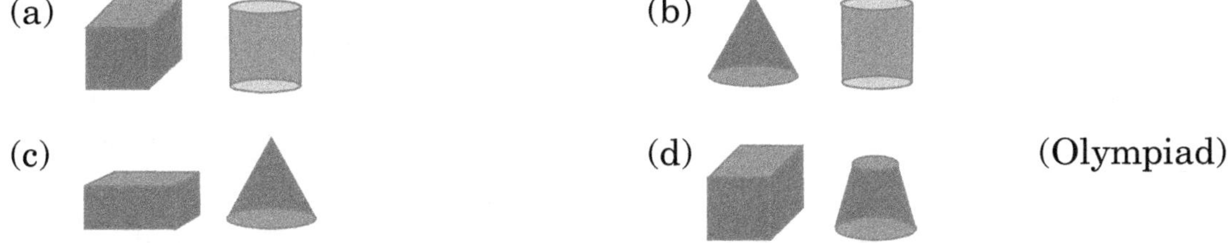

(a) (b) (c) (d)

(Olympiad)

30. How many triangles and squares respectively are there in the given figures?

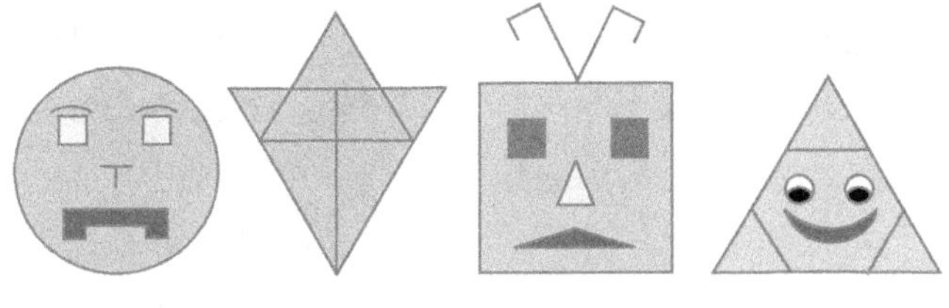

(a) 18, 6 (b) 14, 5 (c) 15, 4 (d) 16, 5

(Olympiad)

31. How many squares and standing lines respectively are there in the given figure?

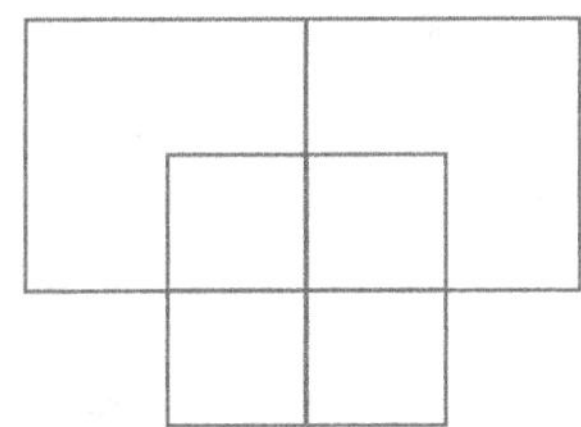

(a) 8, 11 (b) 7, 5 (c) 8, 9 (d) 5, 9

(Olympiad)

32. How many shapes have the number of sides greater than 3?

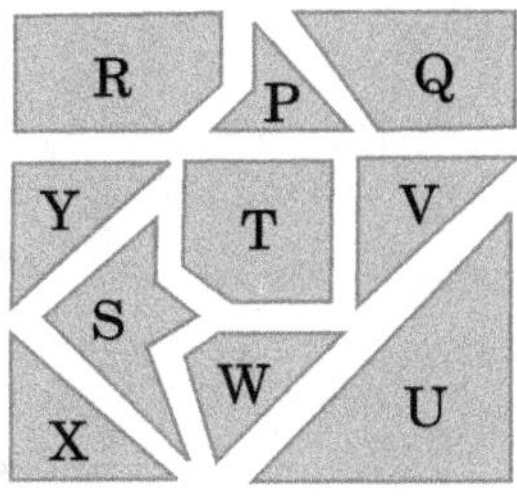

(a) 4 (b) 3 (c) 2 (d) 6

(Olympiad)

Answers and Explanations

Level-1

1. **(c)** Number of lines can be counted as

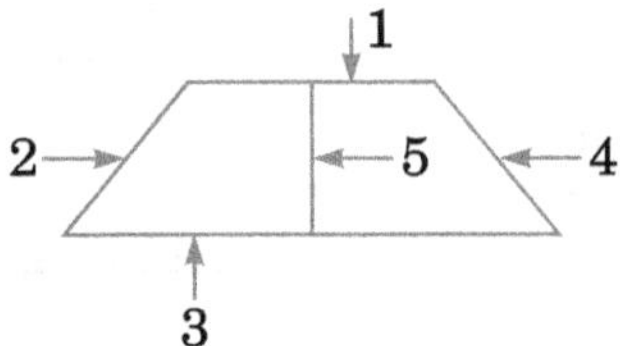

So, there are 5 straight lines in the above figure.

2. **(b)** No. of squares can be counted as

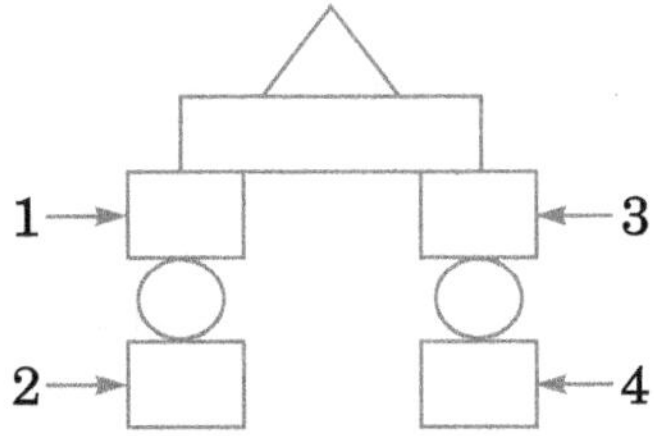

So, there are 4 squares in the above figure.

3. **(b)** In option (b), there are exactly four circles.

4. **(a)** A-2, B-4, C-1, D-3

5. **(c)** Dice is an example of cube shape.

6. **(d)** If we trace around a cricket ball we will get a circle shape.

7. **(a)** Number of circles can be counted as

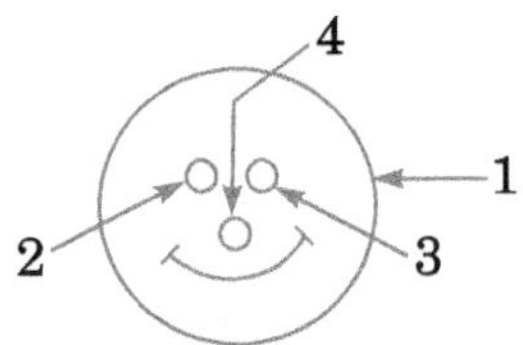

So, there are 4 circles in the above figure.

8. **(b)** Number of triangles can be counted as

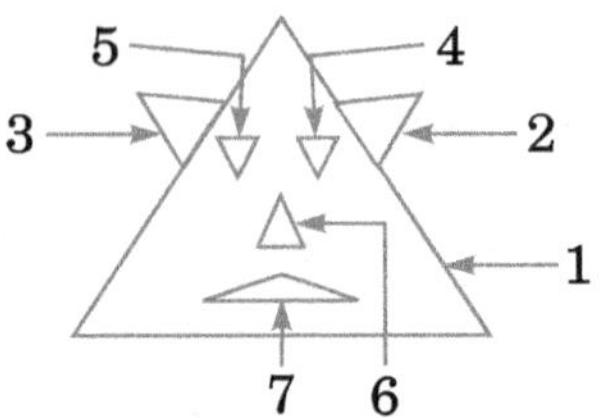

So, there are 7 triangles in the above figure.

9. **(d)** There are 3 solid/3D shapes in the picture.

10. **(c)** Number of circles can be counted as

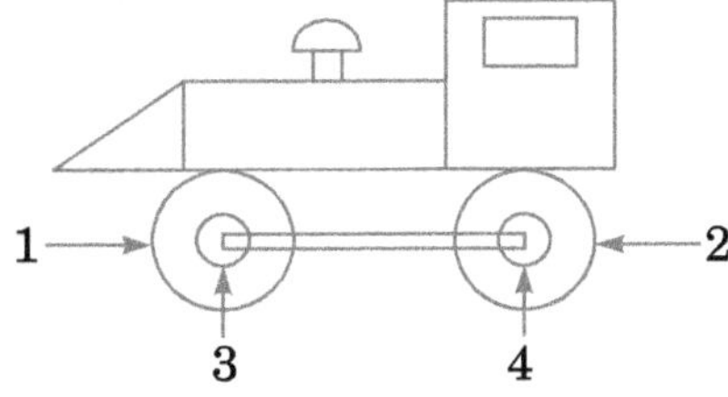

So, there are 4 circles in the above figure.

11. **(c)** Number of circles can be counted as

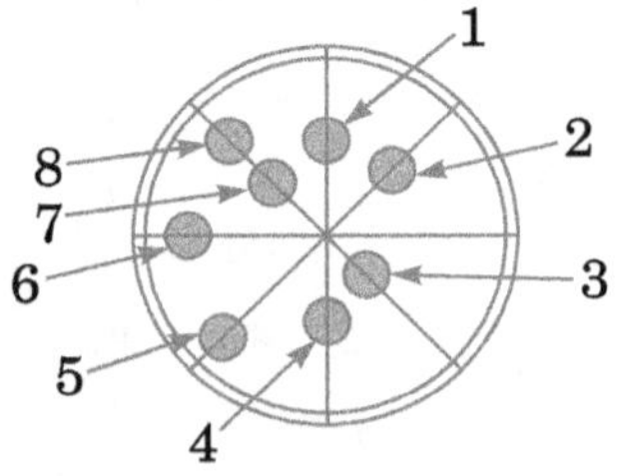

So, there are 8 circles in the above figure.

12. **(a)** Number of squares can be counted as:

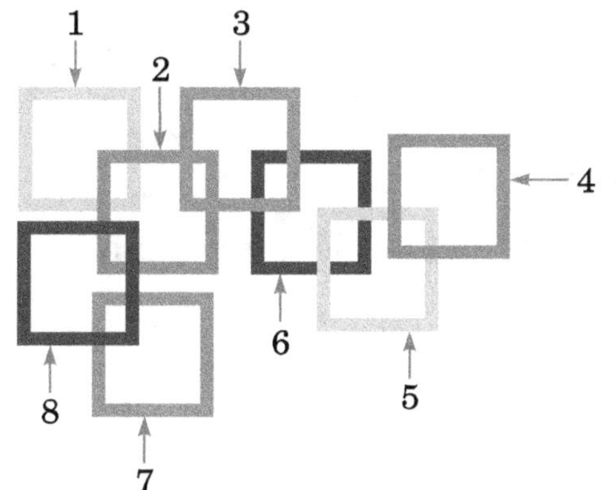

So, there are 8 squares in the above figure.

13. **(c)** Alisha has a triangle shape in her hand

14. **(b)** Johnny has a square shape in his hand.

15. **(c)** There are 6 squares in the given figure.

16. **(b)** There are 13 triangles in the given abstract.

17. **(b)** Solid shapes

18. **(a)** In option (a) [triangle figure] is used to draw the shape (X).

19. **(c)** The shape of a bin is Cylindrical shape.

20. **(a)** There are 18 number of shapes in the given picture.

21. **(c)** There are 4 cylinders in the figure.

22. **(a)** There are 10 circles in the figure.

23. **(b)** There are 13 triangles in the figure.

24. **(c)** There are 6 squares in the figure.

25. **(d)** Option (d) is correct answer.

26. **(b)** 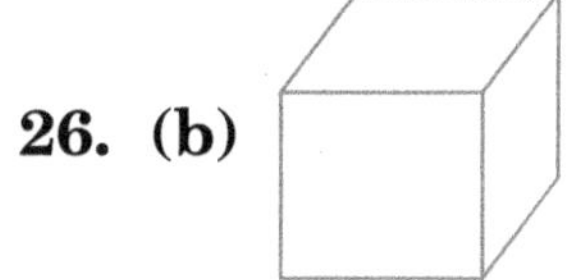

27. **(d)** 10

28. **(c)** 10

29. **(c)** There are 14 circles, 6 triangles and 6 squares in the crown.

30. **(b)** Opposite side

Level-2

1. **(c)** There are 6 circles in the figure.

2. **(a)** 12 curved lines in the given figure.

3. **(d)** 8 triangles in the given figure.

4. **(b)** Circle

5. **(c)** 4

6. **(d)** 4

7. **(c)** 5

8. **(b)** 6

9. **(c)** 4 sides

10. **(b)** Rectangle has 4 corners and 4 sides.

11. **(d)** Circular face and no corner.

12. **(d)** 12

13. **(a)** A-3, B-1, C-2

14. **(b)** 6 rectangular faces and 12 sides.

15. **(c)** Triangular and circular

16. **(c)** 12 sides and 8 corners.

17. **(b)** 7

18. **(b)** 12

19. **(a)** 9

20. **(b)** 5

21. **(c)** 21

22. **(c)** 10

23. **(c)** EDS

24. **(c)** 13, 5, 2

25. **(a)** 22, 16, 20

26. **(d)** 2, 24

27. **(b)** Rectangle and Square

28. **(d)** 8, 17

29. **(a)**

30. **(d)** 16, 5

31. **(b)** 7, 5

32. **(d)** 6

EMBEDDED FIGURE

OBJECTIVES

- Students will learn to manipulate their mental image of an object in order to reach a certain conclusion.
- They will constitute a noticeable feature of something.

INTRODUCTION

Embedded figure is a part of a non-verbal reasoning and it is used to evaluate cognitive skills in children.

Definition

Embedded figure means to find out the hidden figure/shape in a given figure.

Examples:

1. Identify the figure in which following figure (X) is embedded/hidden?

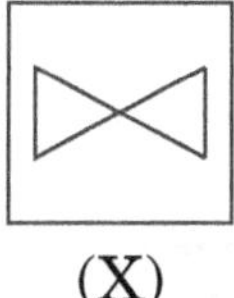

(X)

(a) 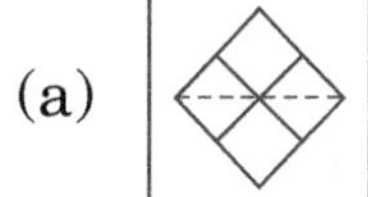 (b) 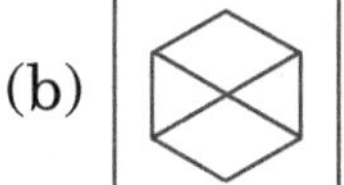 (c) 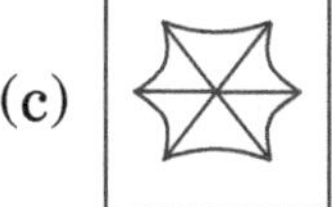 (d) 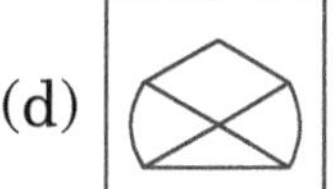

Ans. (b) The given figure (X) is embedded in figure (b)

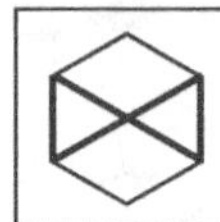

So, option (b) is correct.

2. Observe the figure carefully and answer the question based on it.

Which shape is embedded in the above figure?

Ans. (d) Shape given in option (d) is embedded/hidden in the figure as shown below.

So, option (d) is correct.

3. Which of the following parts is embedded in the given figure (X)?

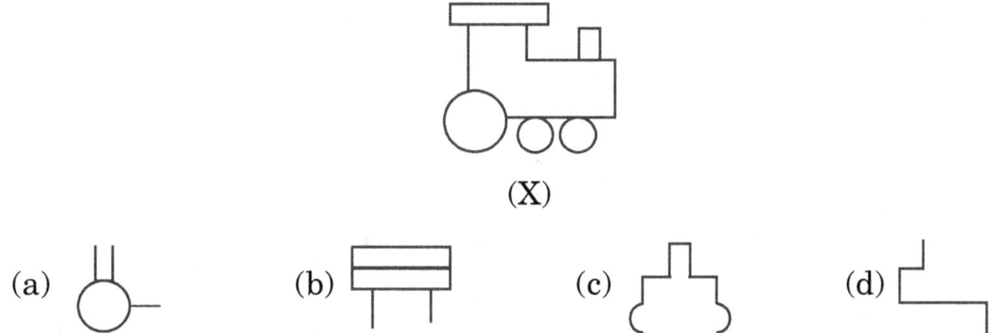

Ans. (d) Shape given in option (d) is embedded in the given figure as shown below.

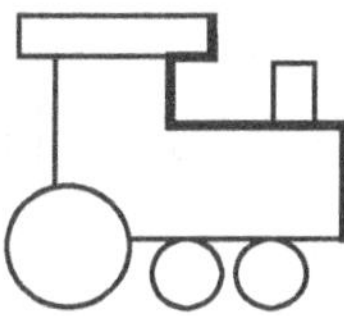

So, option (d) is correct.

4. Helly drew four different teddies as shown below. Identify the teddy in which of the following figure (X) is embedded.

Ans. (c) The given figure (X) is embedded in teddy (c) as shown below.

So, option (c) is correct.

5. In which of the following figures, the given shape (X) is embedded?

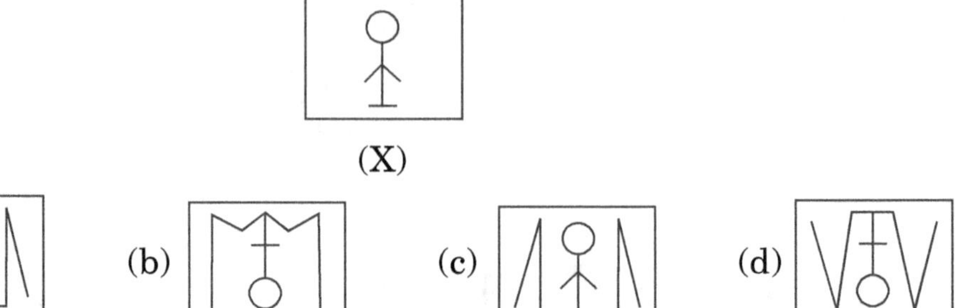

Ans. (c) The given figure (X) is embedded in option figure (c) as shown below

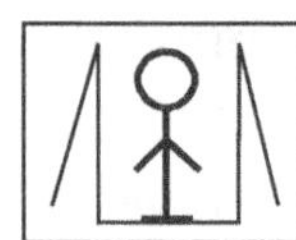

Example 6. In which of the following figures the given figure (X) is embedded?

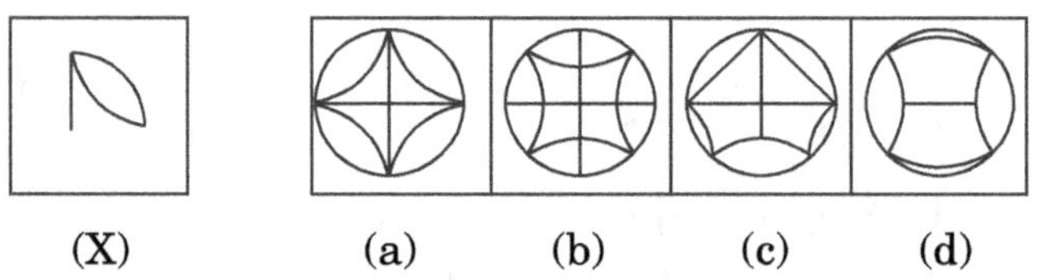

Ans. (a) The given figure (X) is embedded in option figure (a) as shown below:

LEVEL-1

1. In which of the following figures, the given shape (Y) is embedded?

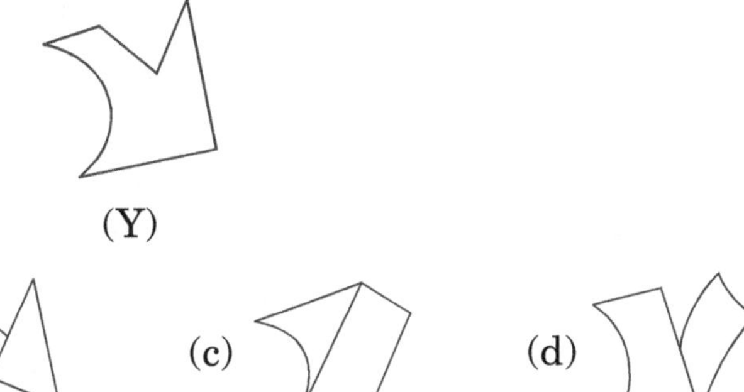

(Y)

(a) (b) (c) (d)

2. Which of the following figures is embedded in figure (M).

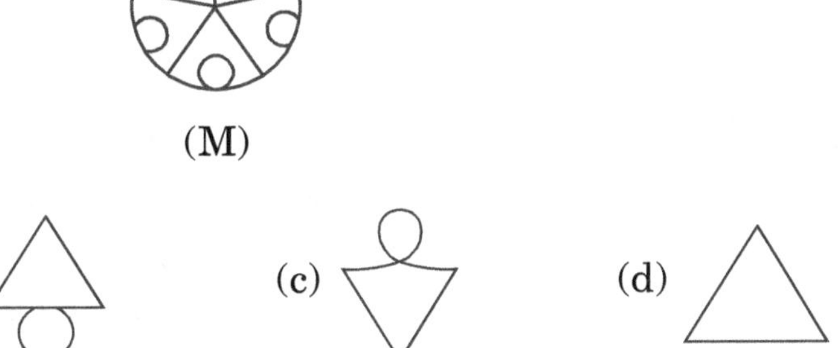

(M)

(a) (b) (c) (d)

3. In which of the following figures the shape (X) is embedded.

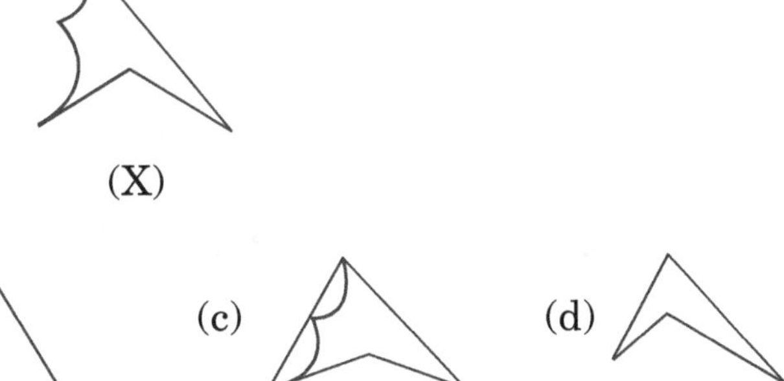

(X)

(a) (b) (c) (d)

4. Which of the following shapes is embedded in the figure (X).

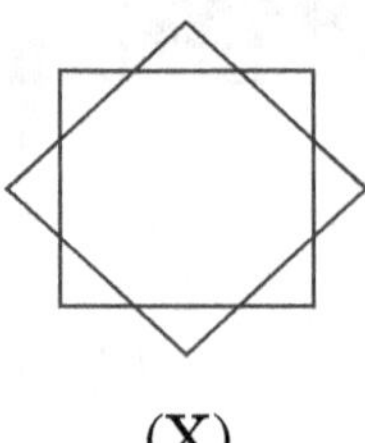

(X)

(a) 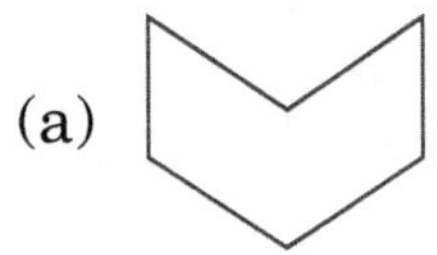 (b)  (c)  (d) 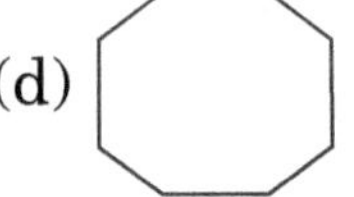

5. In which of the following figures, the shape (O) is embedded.

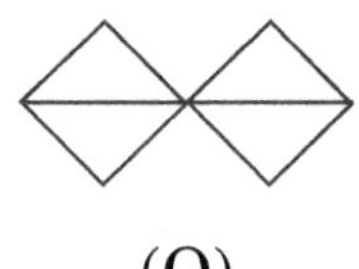

(O)

(a) (b) 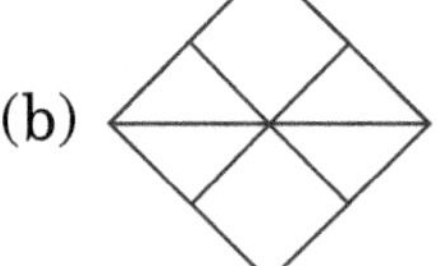 (c) 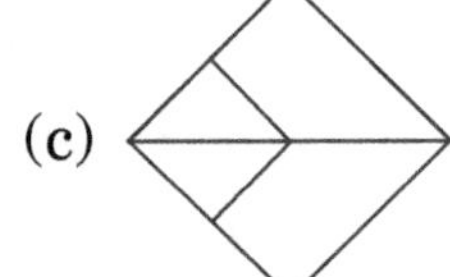 (d) 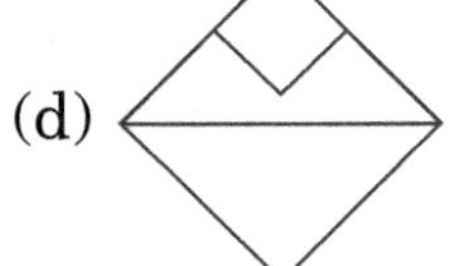

6. Identify the shape which is hidden in figure (X).

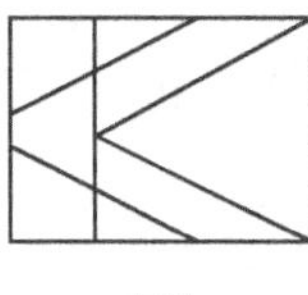

(X)

(a) D (b) J (c) M (d) K

7. Select the figure in which the given figure (D) is hidden.

(D)

8. Select the figure which is hidden in the given figure (X)?

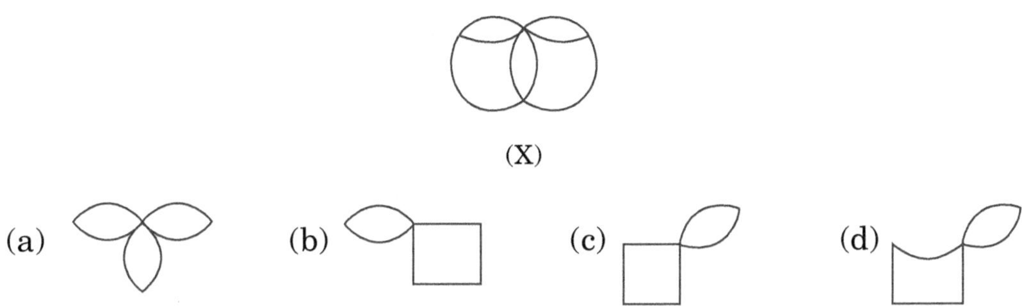

9. Among the 4 figures given in the options, which figure the shape L belongs to?

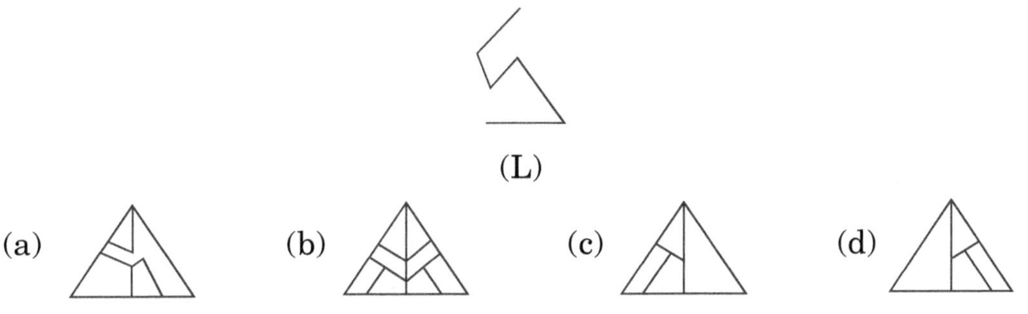

10. Identify the figure in which the given figure (Y) is hidden?

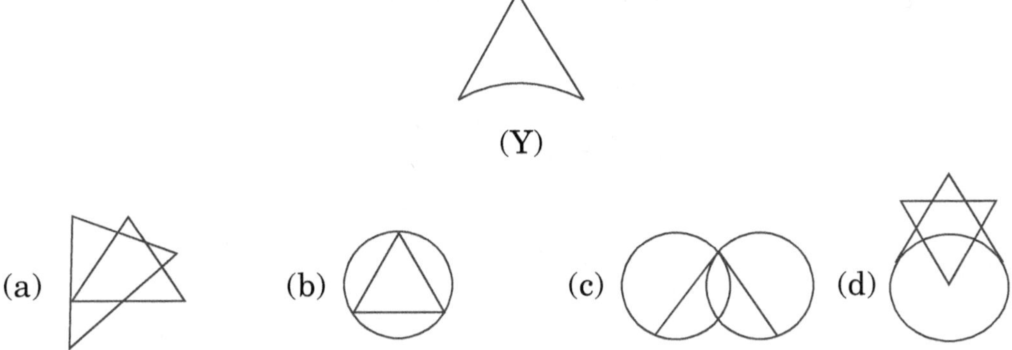

11. Which of the following shapes is embedded in the given figure (X)?

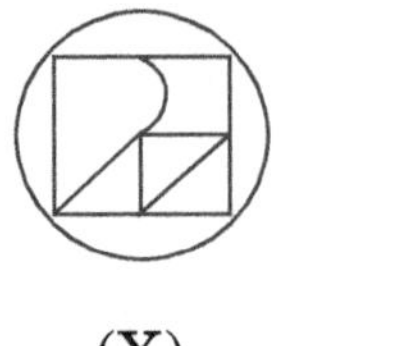

(X)

(a) 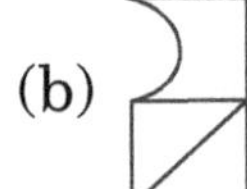 (b) 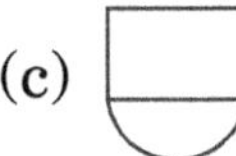 (c) (d) 

12. Kimi draws a figure as shown below:

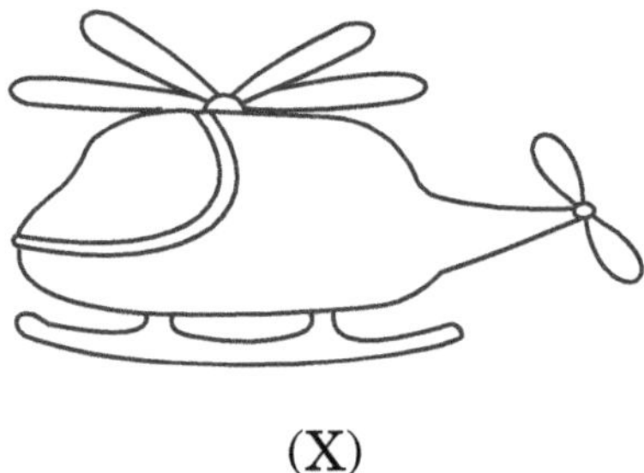

(X)

Identify the figure which is hidden in the figure (X).

(a)  (b) 

(c)  (d) 

13. Observe the picture carefully and answer the question based on it.

Which shape is hidden in the above figure.

(a)  (b)  (c)  (d) 

14. Identify the figure in which following figure (M) is hidden.

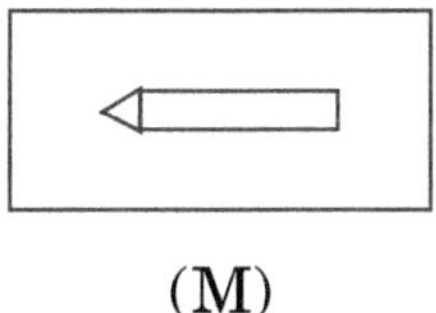

(M)

(a) 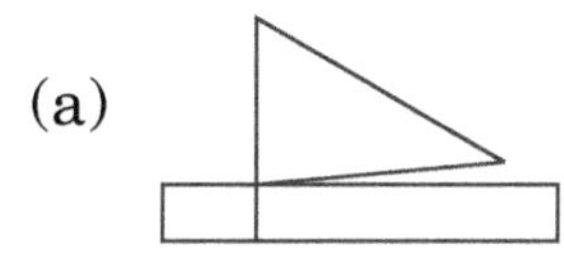 (b) 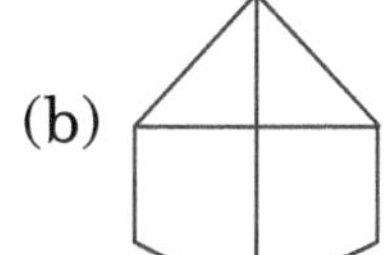 (c) 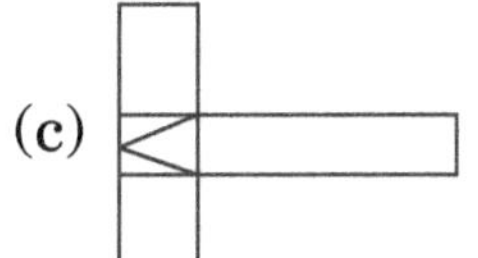 (d) 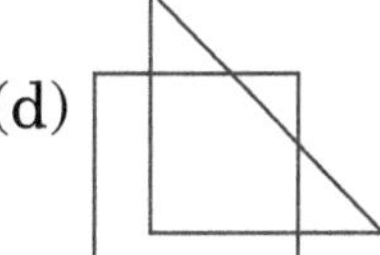

15. Which of the following shapes is embedded in the given cube?

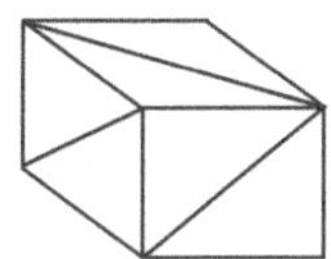

(a) 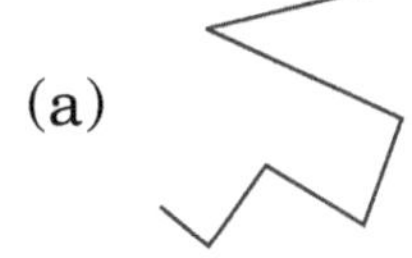 (b)  (c)  (d) 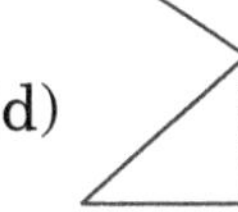

16. Choose the figure in which the given figure (X) is embedded.

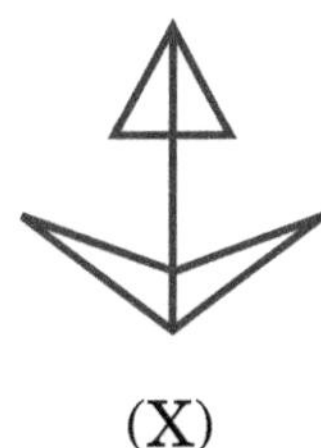

(X)

(a) 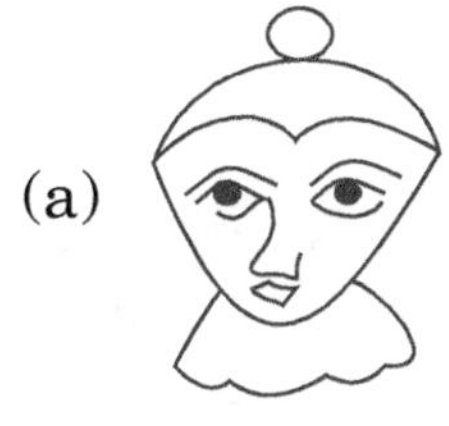 (b)  (c)  (d) 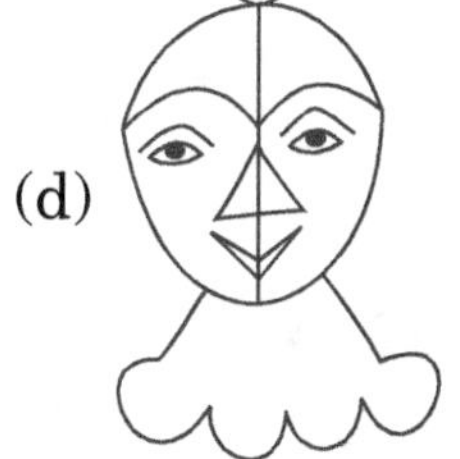

17. Find out the figure in which the given pattern 'M' is embedded.

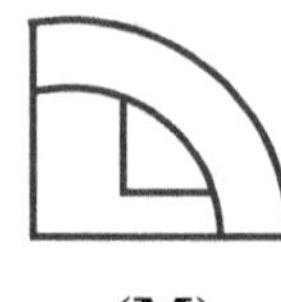

(M)

(a) 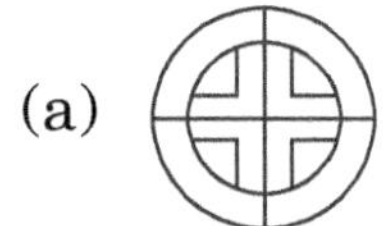 (b) 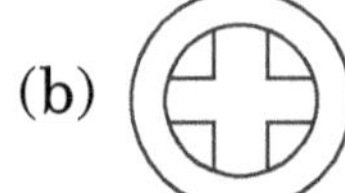 (c)  (d) 

18. Find the figure in which the given figure (X) is embedded.

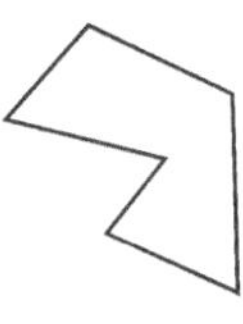

(X)

(a) 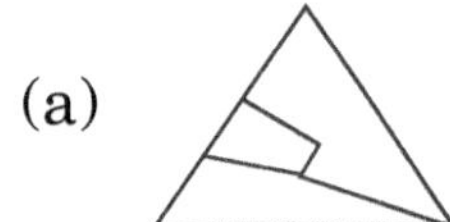 (b) (c)  (d)

19. Which of the following figures is embedded in figure (X)?

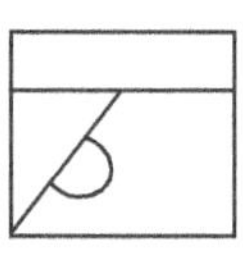

(X)

(a) 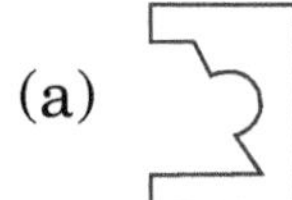 (b) (c) 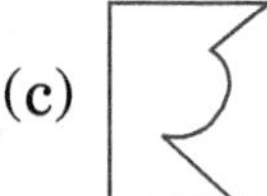 (d)

20. Which of the following parts is hidden in the given figure?

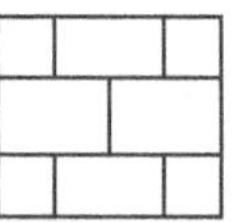

(a) 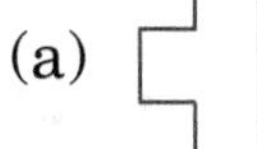 (b)  (c) 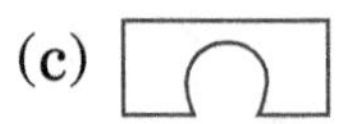 (d) 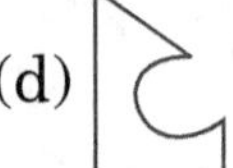

21. In which figure the given shape (Y) is embedded?

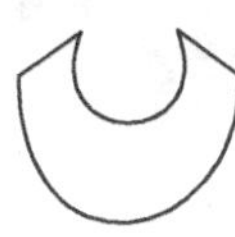

(Y)

(a)  (b) 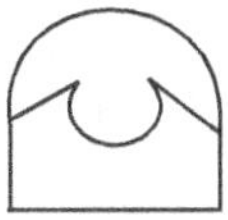 (c) 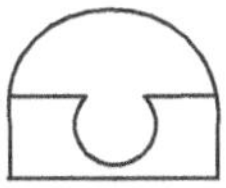 (d)

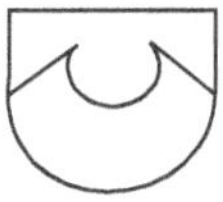

LEVEL-2

1. Elly draws a figure as shown below.

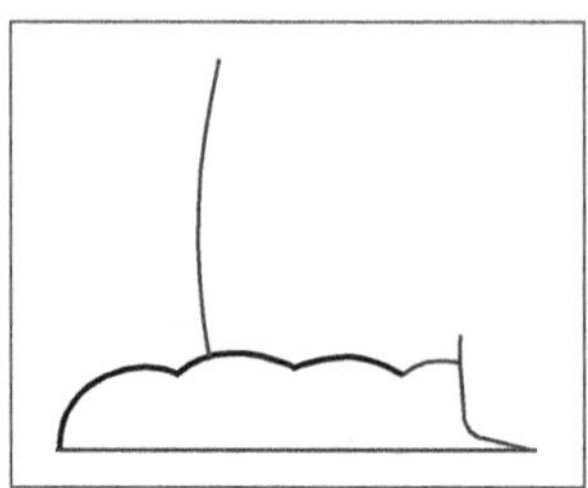

Identify the figure in which the above figure is embedded.

(a)  (b) 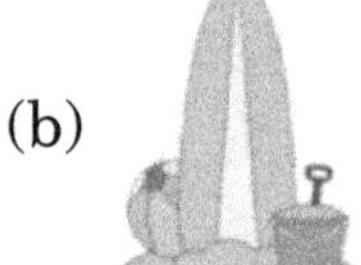 (c) 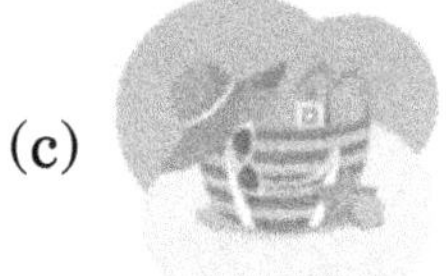 (d) 

2. Find the given shape is embedded in which figure from the given options.

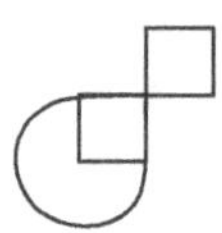

(a) 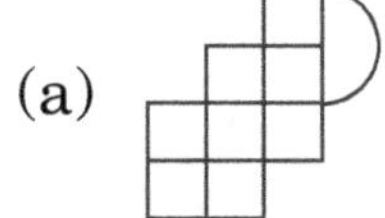 (b) 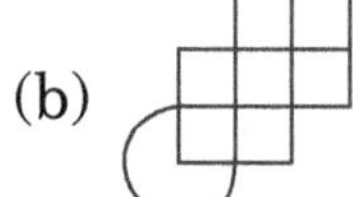 (c) 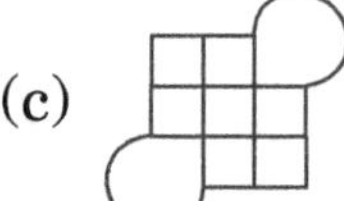 (d) 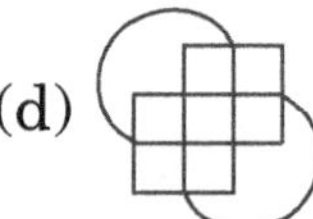

3. Find out which of the following parts is exactly embedded in the figure given below?

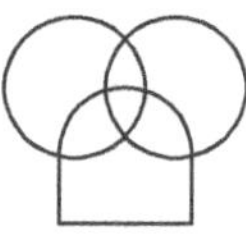

(a)  (b) 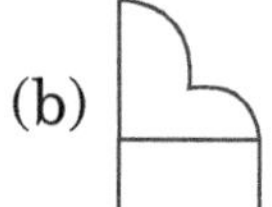 (c) 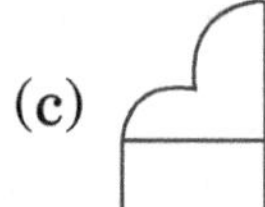 (d) 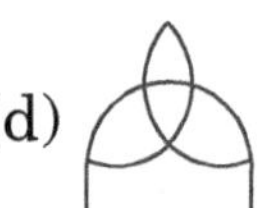

4. Shape (X) belongs to which figure?

(X)

(a) 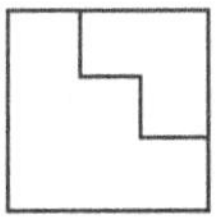 (b) 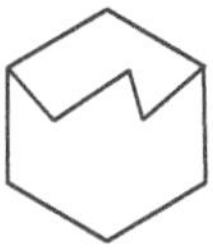 (c) 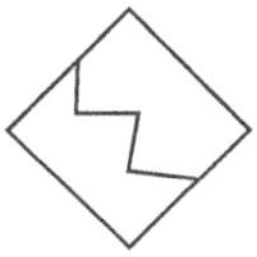 (d)

5. Which shape is embedded in the following figure (M)?

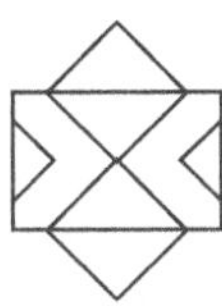

(M)

(a) 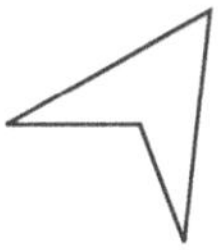 (b) 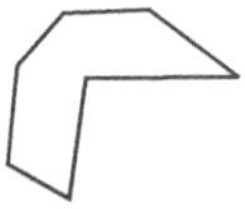 (c)  (d)

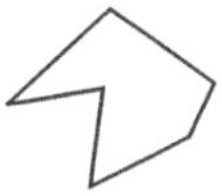

6. Which shape belongs to the following figure (X)?

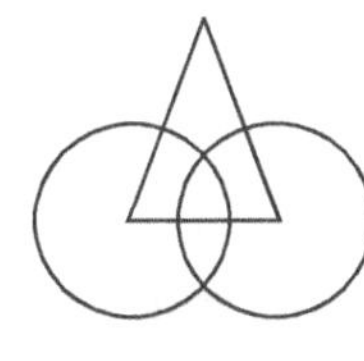

(X)

(a) 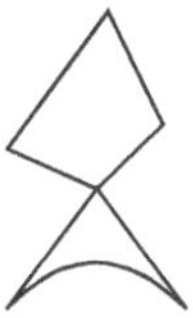 (b)  (c) 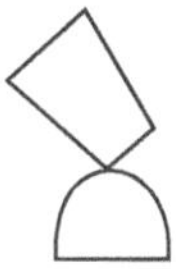 (d)

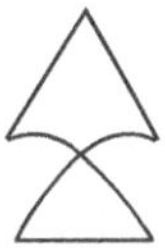

7. In which figure the given shape (A) is embedded?

(A)

(a) 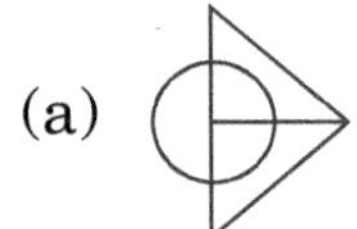 (b) 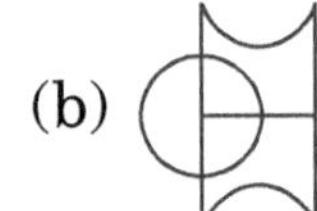 (c) 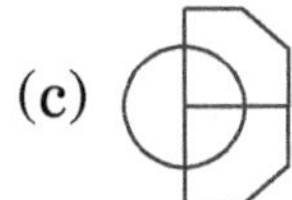 (d) 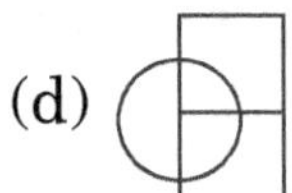

8. Find the figure in which the given figure (X) is embedded.

(X)

(a) 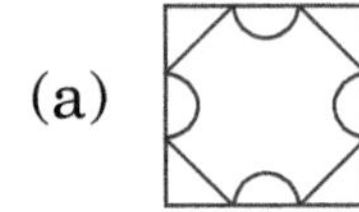 (b)  (c) 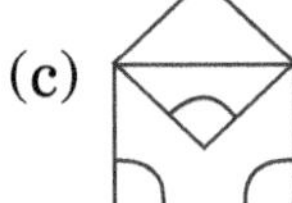 (d) 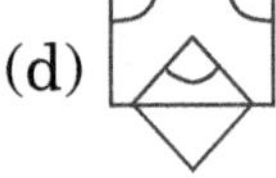

9. Which shape is embedded in the given figure (Y)?

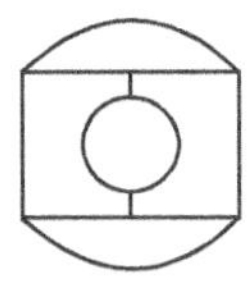

(Y)

(a)  (b) (c) 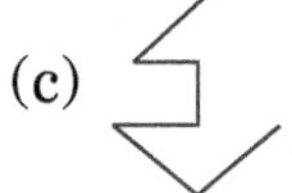 (d)

10. In which of the following figure in the given figure (L) is embedded?

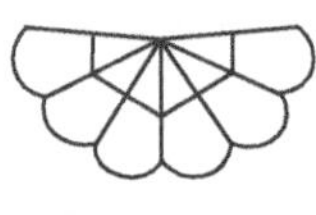

(L)

(a)  (b)  (c) 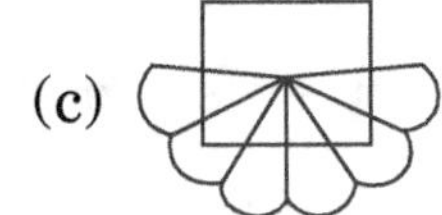 (d) 

11. Find out the shape embedded in the given shape (N).

(N)

(a)  (b)  (c)  (d) 

12. In which figure the given shape (M) is embedded?

(M)

(a) 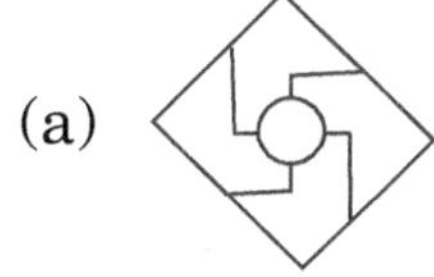 (b) (c) 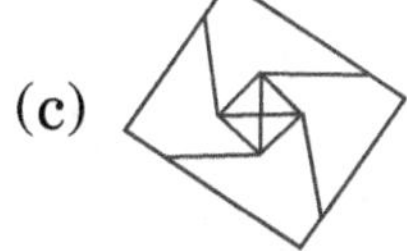 (d)

13. Among the shapes given in the options, which shape is exactly embedded in the given figure.

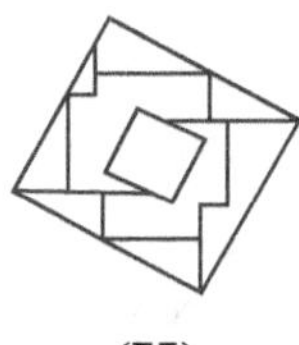

(X)

(a)  (b) 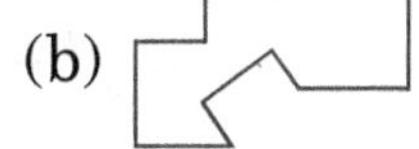 (c)  (d) 

14. Find out which number is embedded in the following figure (X).

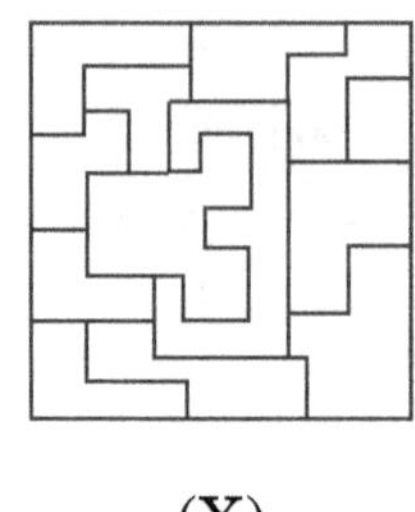

(X)

(a) (b) 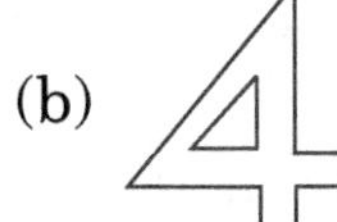 (c) 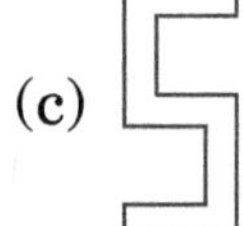 (d) 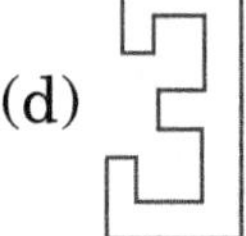

15. In which figure the given shape (X) is embedded?

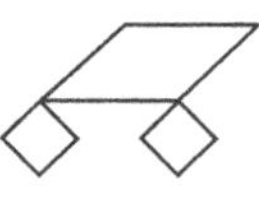

(X)

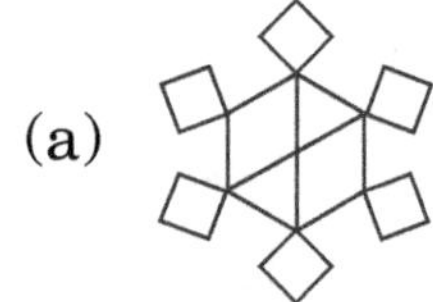 (b) (c) 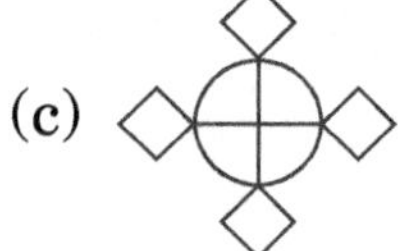 (d)

16. In which figure the given shape (Y) is embedded?

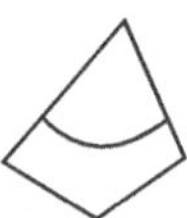

(Y)

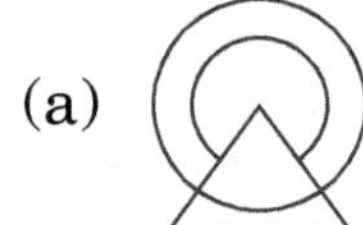 (b) (c)  (d) 

Direction (Qs. 17 & 18): Observe the picture carefully and answer the questions based on it.

17. Which picture is hidden in the above picture?

(a) 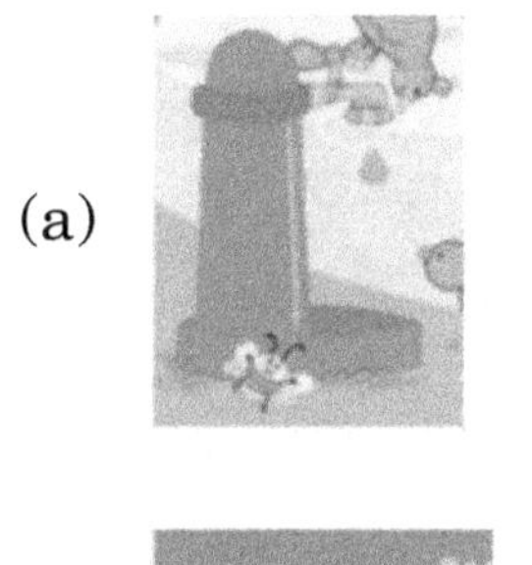

(b) 

(c) 

(d) 

18. How many of the pictures below are hidden in the above picture?

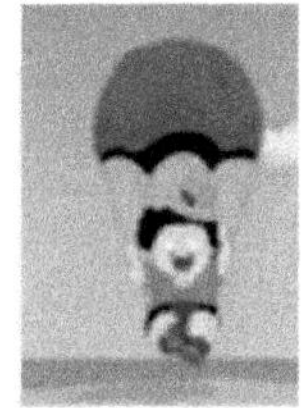    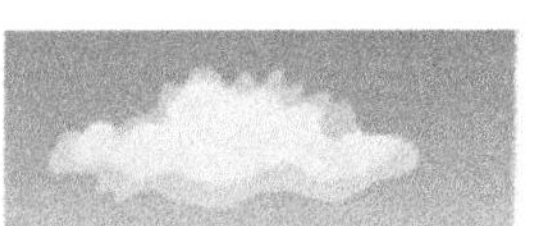

(a) 5 (b) 4 (c) 2 (d) 3

19. Find out the shape which is embedded in the given figure (X).

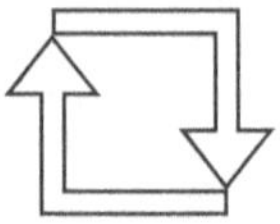

(X)

(a)  (b) 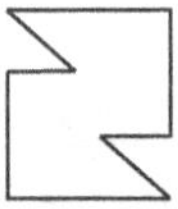 (c)  (d)

20. In which figure the given figure (X) is embedded?

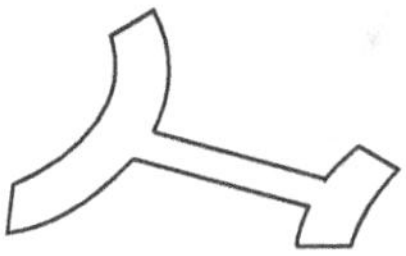

(X)

(a)  (b)  (c) 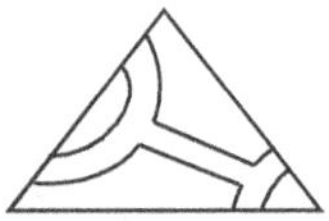 (d)

21. Find out the embedded shape in the given figure (X).

(X)

(a)  (b)  (c) 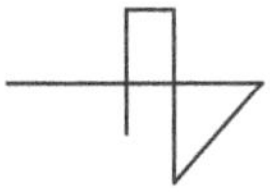 (d)

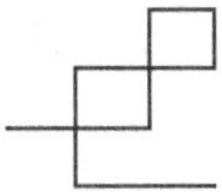

22. In which figure the shape (Y) is embedded?

(Y)

(a) 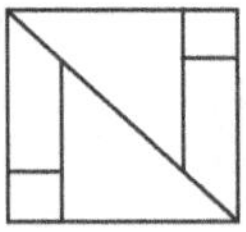 (b)  (c)  (d)

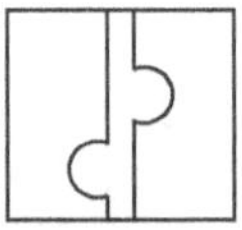

23. In the following shape, which shape is hidden in the given image (M).

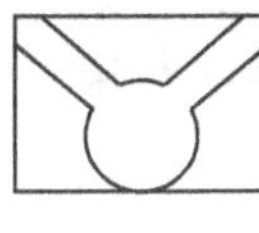

(M)

(a)  (b) 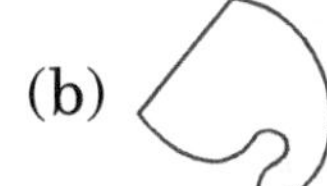 (c)  (d) 

24. Identify the shape exactly embedded in Figure (X).

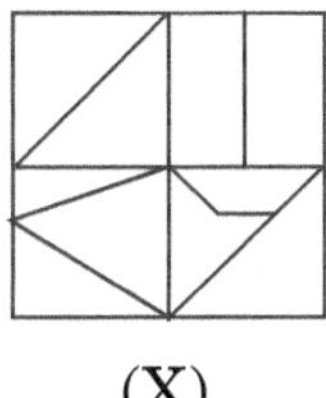

(X)

(a) 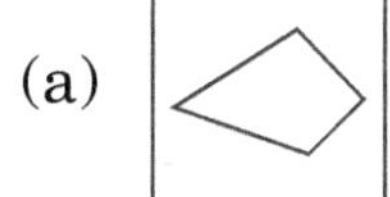 (b) 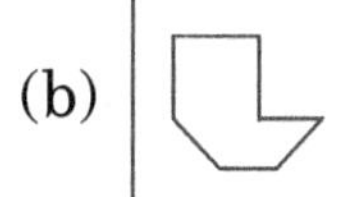 (c) 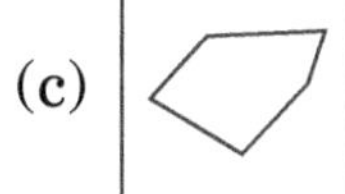 (d) 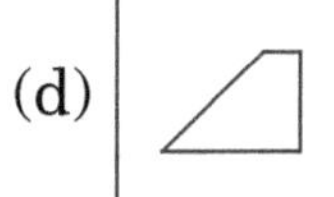

(Olympiad)

25. In which figure the shape (X) is embedded?

Shape (X)

(a) 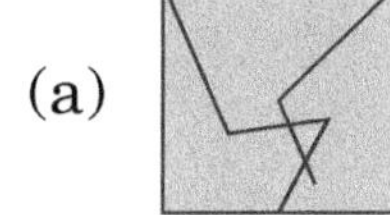 (b) 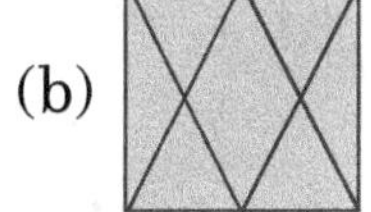 (c) 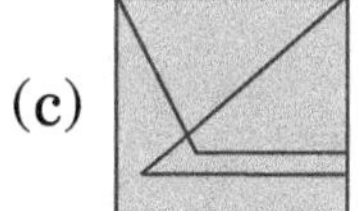 (d) 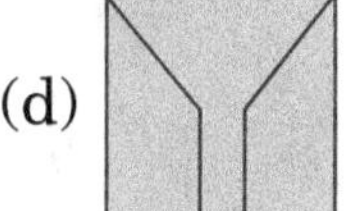

(Olympiad)

Answers and Explanations

Level-1

1. **(b)** 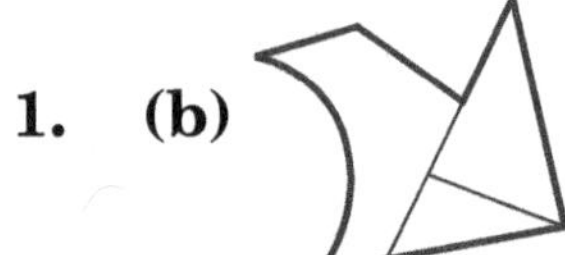

2. **(a)**

3. **(c)** 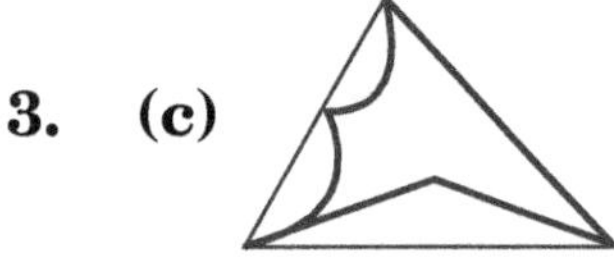

4. **(d)**

5. **(b)** 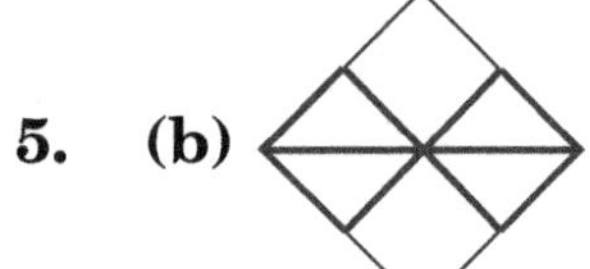

6. **(d)**

7. **(c)** 

8. **(a)**

9. **(b)**

10. **(d)** 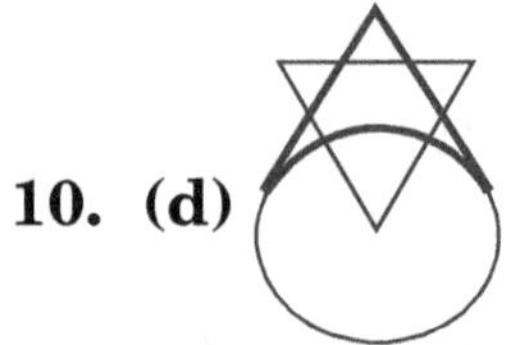

11. **(b)** 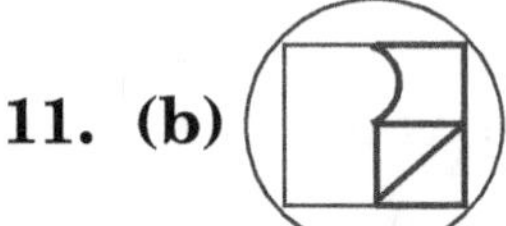

12. **(c)** 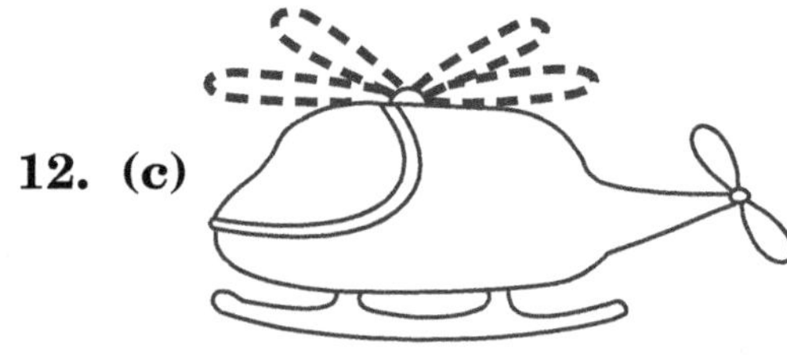

13. **(b)** 

14. **(c)** 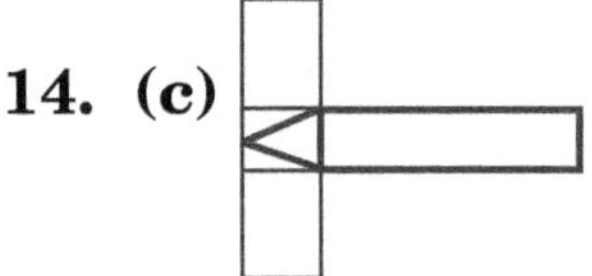

15. **(d)**

16. **(d)** 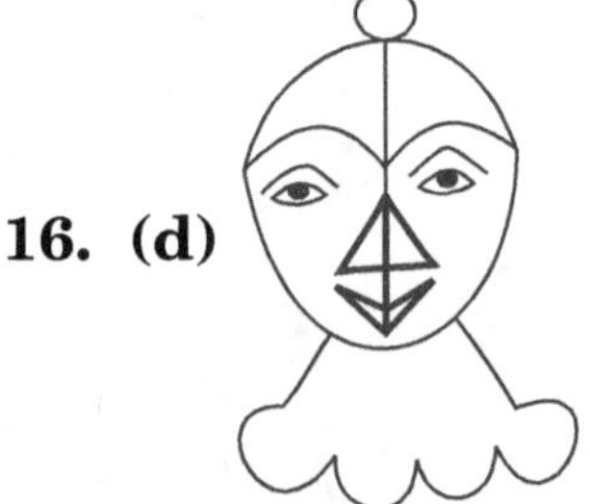

17. **(a)** 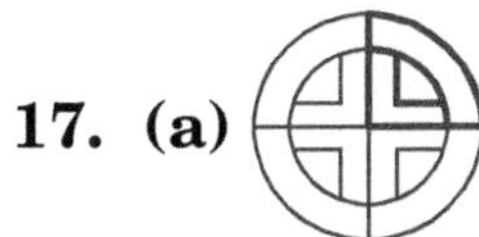

18. **(d)** 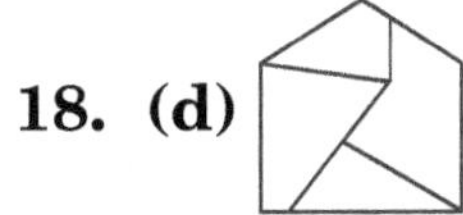

19. **(b)** 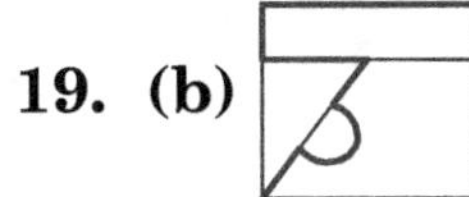

20. **(a)** 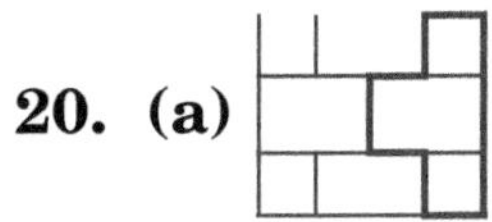

21. **(d)** 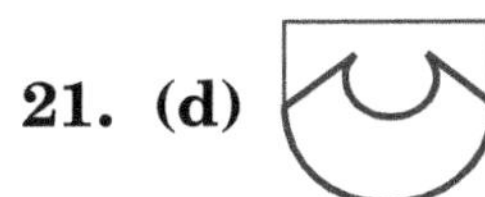

Level-2

1. **(b)** 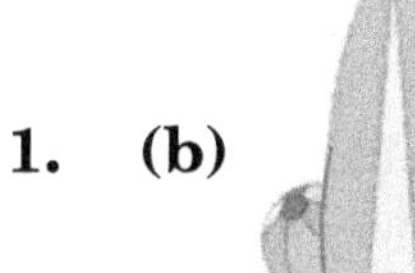

2. **(b)** 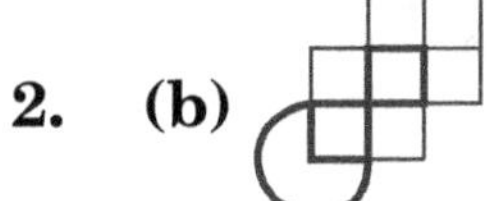

3. **(d)**

4. **(b)**

5. **(c)**

6. **(d)**

7. **(b)**

8. (c) 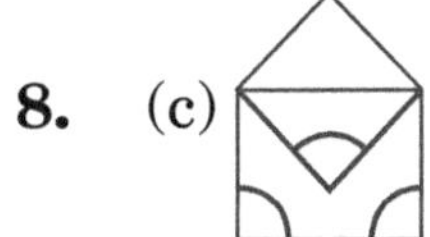

9. (b) 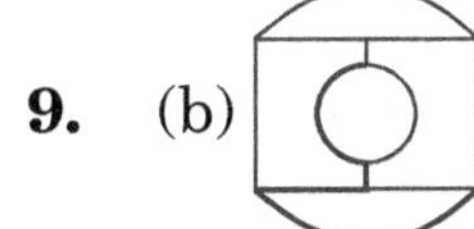

10. (d) 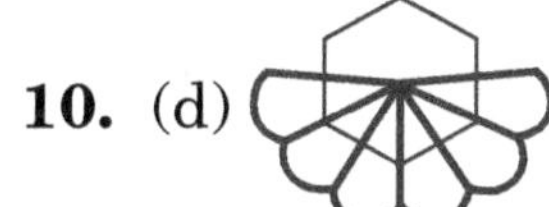

11. (c) 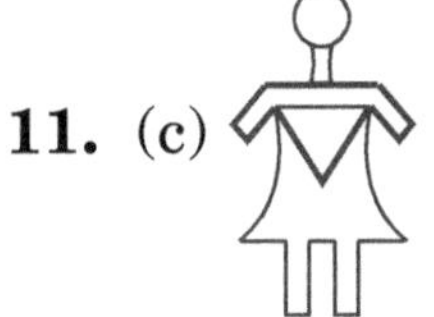

12. (a) 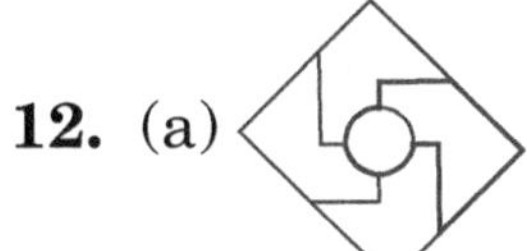

13. (b) 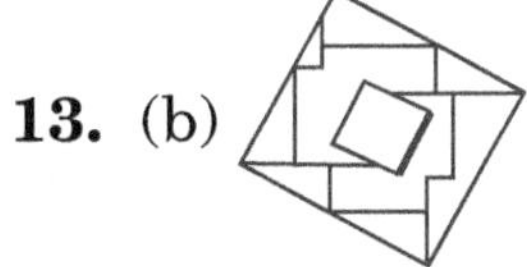

14. (d) 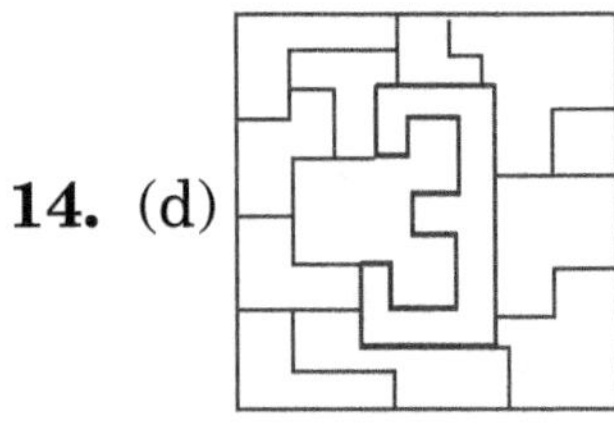

15. (a) 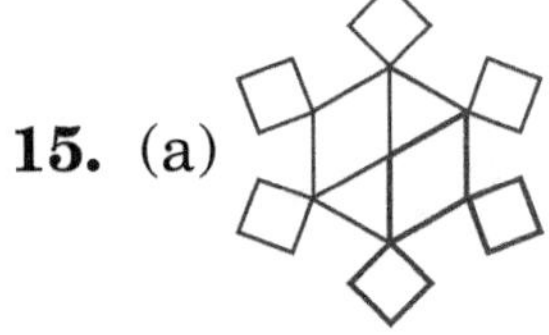

16. (d) 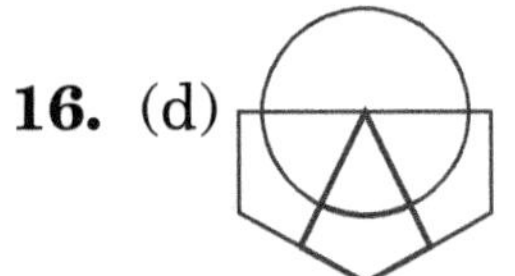

17. **(c)** Picture given in option (c) is hidden in the given picture.

18. **(b)** Four pictures are hidden in the given picture.

19. **(b)** 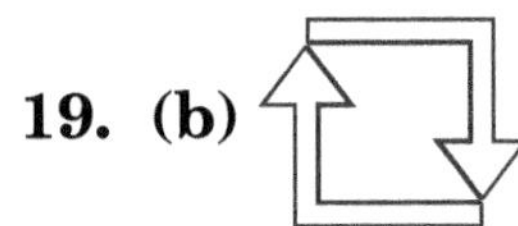

20. **(c)** 

21. **(b)** 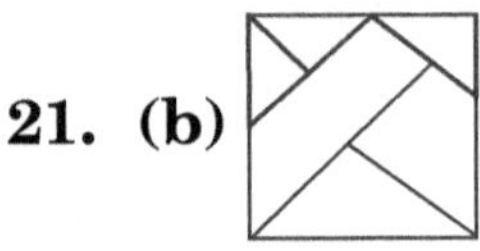

22. **(b)** 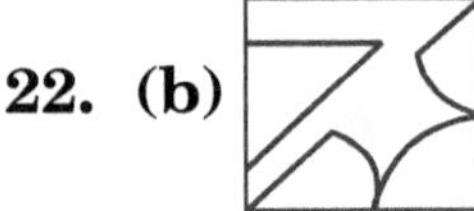

23. **(a)** 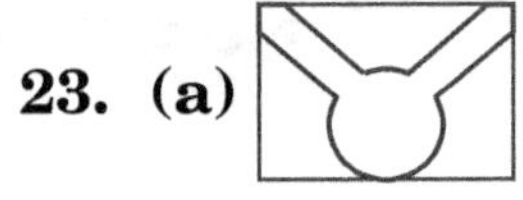

24. **(b)** 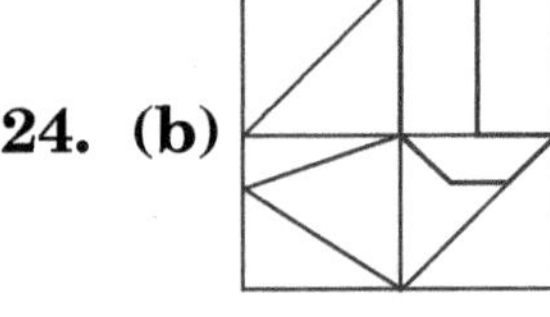

25. **(b)** 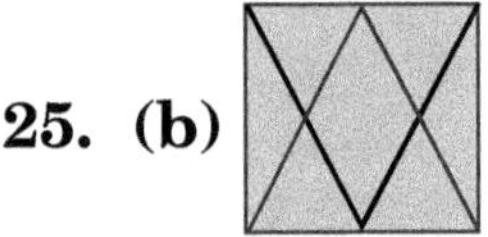

ESTIMATION

OBJECTIVES

- Students will involve in estimating real-life quantities such as distance, areas and volumes.
- Estimation allows students to make judgements about how much time, money, food..... they will need.
- In estimation, students use their mathematical reasoning which ultimately saves time and money.

INTRODUCTION

Estimation is a rough calculation of the value, number, quantity, or extent of something.

Examples:

1. How many sweets are in the box? Estimate.

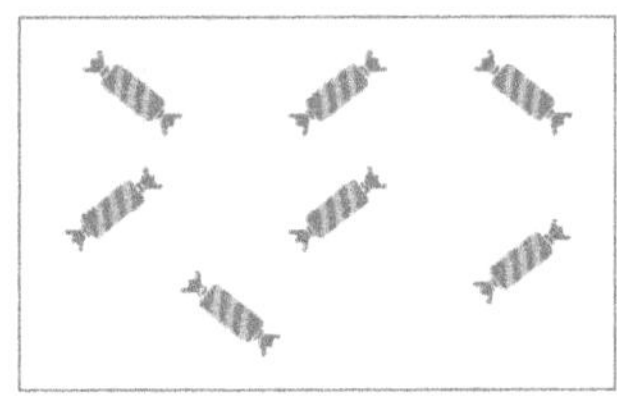

(a) 6 (b) 7 (c) 8 (d) 9

Ans. (b) There are 7 sweets in the box

2. Reha went to the zoo and saw some Giraffes and Alligators. She made a picture graph of the animals at the zoo:

Alligators							
Giraffes							

Which animal did she see fewer of ?

(a) Alligators (b) Giraffes (c) Both (d) None of them

Ans. (b) Count the number of each animal in the graph. She saw 7 Alligators and 3 Giraffes. So, she saw fewer Giraffes.

3. Which bus is the shortest among the following?

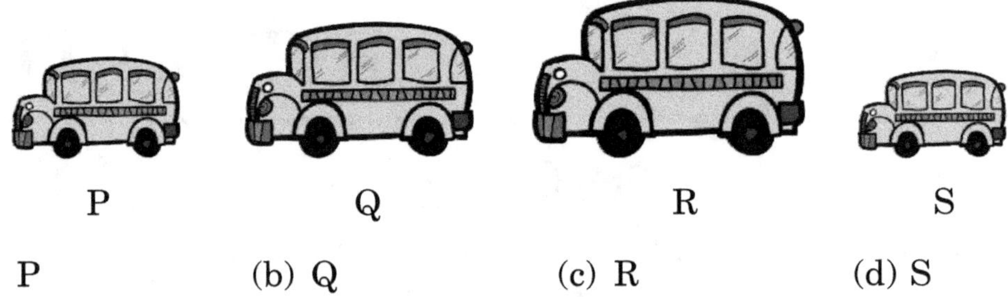

P Q R S

(a) P (b) Q (c) R (d) S

Ans. (d) Bus S is shortest among them.

4. Which tower is taller than B?

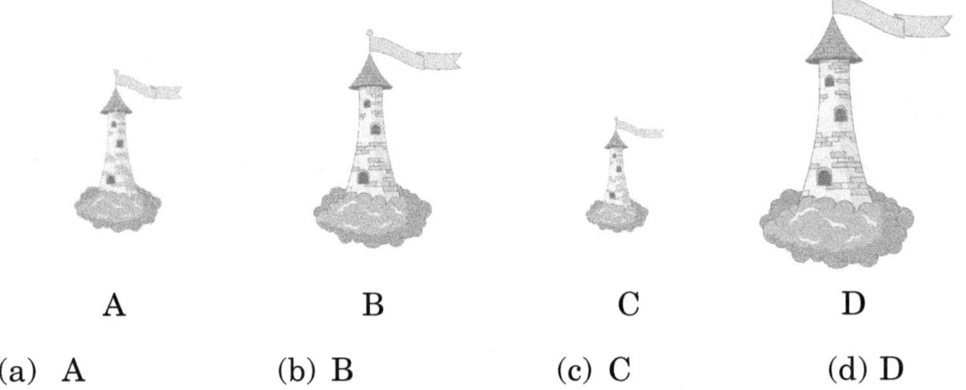

A B C D

(a) A (b) B (c) C (d) D

Ans. (d) Tower D is taller than B.

5. Estimate the weight of a rubber?

(a) 2 g (b) 2 kg (c) 200 g (d) 5 kg

Ans. (a) The estimated weight of a rubber is 2 g.

LEVEL-1

1. Who is the tallest and shortest among them?

(a) Ricky and Ria
(b) John and Miley
(c) John and Ria
(d) Ricky and Ray

2. Look at the time in the clock. What will be the time after 1 hour and 30 minutes?

(a) 3 : 30 (b) 6 : 30 (c) 4 : 30 (d) 5 : 30

3. Estimate the sum by rounding off the number to the nearest hundred first and then the question.

$$\begin{array}{r} 510 \\ +\ 378 \\ \hline \end{array} \longrightarrow \begin{array}{r} 500 \\ +\ 400 \\ \hline ? \\ \hline \end{array}$$

(a) 500 (b) 200 (c) 900 (d) 1000

4. Estimate the sum by rounding off the number to nearest tens place and then calculate the answer of the question?

$$\begin{array}{r} 521 \\ -\ 318 \\ \hline \end{array} \quad \longrightarrow \quad \begin{array}{r} 520 \\ -\ 320 \\ \hline ? \\ \hline \end{array}$$

(a) 200 (b) 300 (c) 400 (d) 500

5. Which addition problem has a sum of about 70?

(a) 11 + 11 (b) 59 + 12 (c) 13 + 28 (d) 44 + 47

6. What is 25 rounded off to the nearest ten?

(a) 20 (b) 30 (c) 40 (d) 26

7. What is 12 rounded off to the nearest ten?

(a) 20 (b) 15 (c) 10 (d) 8

8. Choose the wrong statement:

(A) If you add 0 to a number, you get the same number. ☐

(B) If you subtract 0 from a number, you get the same number. ☐

(C) If you multiply a number by 0, you get the same number. ☐

(D) All are correct. ☐

(a) (B) (b) (A) (c) (D) (d) (C)

9. At 4 : 30, the minute hand is at

(a) 12 (b) 4 (c) 5 (d) 6

10. In the given addition problem, the missing digit is _____________?

$$\begin{array}{r} 3\ \ 9\ \ 5 \\ +\ 2\ \square\ \ 7 \\ \hline 6\ \ 4\ \ 2 \\ \hline \end{array}$$

(a) 3 (b) 4 (c) 5 (d) 6

11. Mona is 6 years old and her friend Nitu is 8 years old. Estimate the sum of their ages after 2 years?

(a) 14 years (b) 16 years (c) 24 years (d) 18 years

12. If Aruna saves ₹. 10 each day, how much will she save in a week?

(a) ₹ 48 (b) ₹ 56 (c) ₹ 70 (d) ₹ 90

13. The month whose name begins with "N" is the ____________ month of the year. It has ____________ days in a month.

(a) Seventh, 31 (b) Eleventh, 30 (c) Ninth, 30 (d) Eight, 31

14. Which one of these can you buy with just ₹100?

(a) Sports shoes (b) CD player

(c) Bicycle (d) Bag of toffees

15. Which tree is taller than S but shorter than Q?

P Q R S

(a) P (b) S (c) Q (d) R

16. Which statement will make this equation complete?

20 __________ 15

(a) is greater than (b) is less than

(c) is equal to (d) None of these

17. Which one of the following is heaviest among them?

(a) Leaf (b) Hammer (c) Book (d) Plate

18. Which one of the following is more in number than others?

(a) ★★★ ★★★ ★★ (b) (c) (d)

19. What is the approximate price range of a normal sharpener?

(a) ₹. 5-10 (b) ₹. 7-12 (c) ₹. 3-5 (d) ₹. 8-11

20. John had 32 toffees. He gave 4 toffees to each of his friends and no toffee is left behind. Estimate John's number of friends?

(a) 12 (b) 15 (c) 8 (d) 28

21. A lift can carry a weight of 150 kg. The weights of four men P, Q, R, S are given. Which combination can travel by the lift?

P – 96 kg; Q – 73 kg; R – 69 kg; S – 84 kg

(a) P and Q (b) Q and R (c) P and S (d) None of them

22. Fill in the blank with the appropriate number.

5 tens	4 ones	–	2 tens	=	?

(a) 50 (b) 34 (c) 44 (d) 70

23. Estimate 5 meters into centimeters?

5 metres = ___?___

(a) 700 cm (b) 300 cm (c) 500 cm (d) 1400 cm

24. Raina had 6 m of golden ribbon. Her mother bought 25 m 75 cm of green ribbon. Estimate the total length of the ribbon altogether?

(a) 21 m 75 cm (b) 31 m 75 cm (c) 41 m 75 cm (d) 80 m 25 cm

25. Nisha drinks 10 glasses of limewater using glass Q in a day. Pooja drinks 10 glasses of lime water using glass P in a day. Who drinks more lime water in a day?

P

Q

(a) Nisha (b) Pooja (c) Both (d) None of these

26. Estimate 4300 m to kilometres?

4300 m = ?

(a) 5 km 300 m (b) 7 km 200 m (c) 4 km 300 m (d) 2 km 700 m

27. Which book is thicker than all?

P Q R S

(a) P (b) S (c) Q (d) R

28. We estimate the mass in ____________ ?

(a) kilograms (b) grams

(c) kilometers (d) Both (a) and (b)

29. Mohan bought 10 kg 250 g of potato, 7 kg 500 g of onion and 2 kg 400 gm of tomato. Estimate the total weight of the vegetables?

(a) 20 kg 150 gm (b) 50 kg 500 gm

(c) 70 kg 300 gm (d) 40 kg 250 gm

30. Kelly asked her friends what they had for breakfast. She made a tally chart of the results:

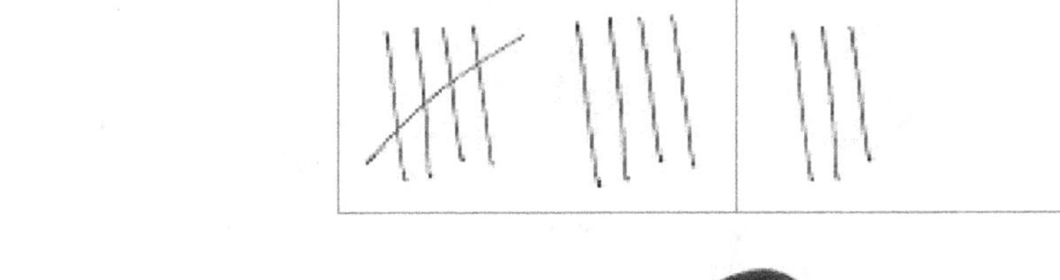

How many friends had doughnuts for breakfast.

(a) 8 (b) 3 (c) 4 (d) 11

LEVEL-2

1. Soumya wants to buy the heaviest fruit from the fruit stall. Which fruit will she buy?

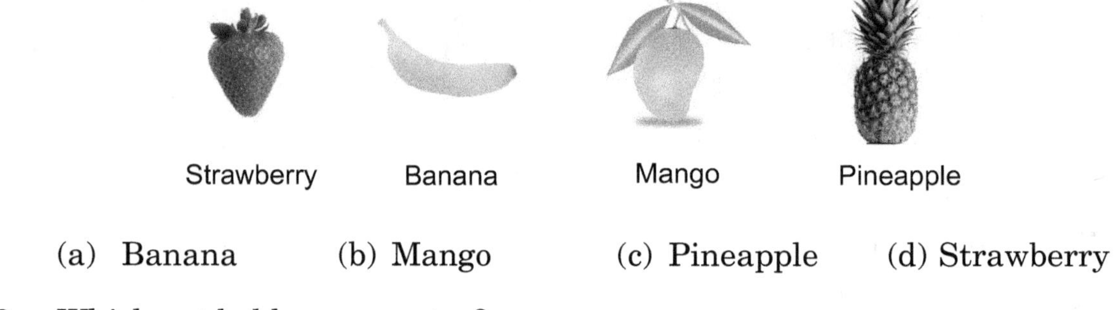

(a) Banana (b) Mango (c) Pineapple (d) Strawberry

2. Which pot holds more water?

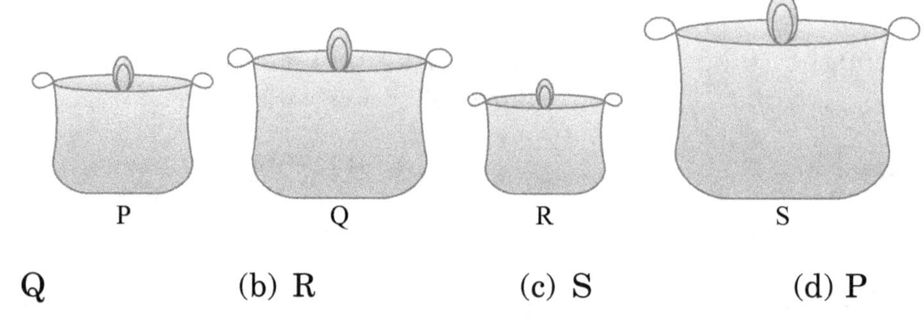

(a) Q (b) R (c) S (d) P

3. Which Cartoon character is taller than Jerry but shorter than Donald?

(a) Tweety (b) Micky (c) Pikachu (d) Shinchan

Direction (Qs. 4-9): Look at the picture and select the correct option that gives the correct estimation of length, weight or capacity.

4. Amount of coffee in a Cup.

(a) 50 mL (b) 50 cm (c) 50 gm (d) None of these

5. Weight of the Laptop.

(a) 2 L (b) 2 m (c) 2 kg (d) None of these

6. Length of a Saree.

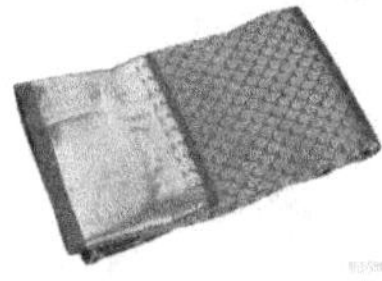

(a) 5 m (b) 5 km (c) 5 L (d) 5 cm

7. Weight of a Watermelon.

(a) 300 g (b) 300 mL (c) 3 kg (d) 3.5 L

8. Quantity of water in a Bottle.

(a) 5 kg (b) 500 mL (c) 5 km (d) 5 gm

9. Length of a Syringe.

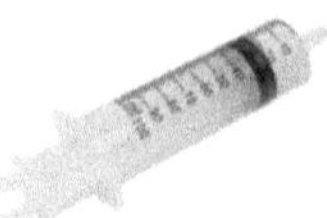

(a) 10 gm (b) 8 cm (c) 10 mL (d) 5 km

10. Which of the following is the lightest among all?

(a)  (b)  (c)  (d) 

11. If 2 cups of water = , so 3 glasses are equal to __________?

(a)  (b) 

(c)  (d) 

12. Rohan is shorter than __________ and __________

(a) Meeta and John (b) John and Radha

(c) Meeta and Radha (d) None of these.

13. Misha has some bags of rice. The total weight of all the bags of rice is 35 kg. The weight of each bag is 7 kg. Estimate the number of bags does Misha have?

(a) 2 (b) 7 (c) 5 (d) 4

14. Mohit, Mohan, Ram and Sunny leave their respective homes at 7:30 a.m. for the school. Mohit reaches school at 7:45 a.m. Mohan reaches at 7:40 a.m. Ram reaches at 7:50 a.m. and Sunny reaches at 7:39 a.m. Who reaches earliest to the school and who reaches last respectively?

(a) Sunny and Ram (b) Mohit and Mohan
(c) Sunny and Mohit (d) Mohan and Ram

15. It takes 6 cups of water to fill up the kettle. It takes 3 cups of water to fill up the teapot. How many teapots of water are needed to fill up the kettle?
(a) 6 (b) 2 (c) 5 (d) 4

16. If there are 10 sweets in one jars. Then how many sweets will be there in 3 similar jars?
(a) 24 (b) 36 (c) 30 (d) 22

17. There were 136 marbles in a box. Siya put 26 more marbles in the same box. Estimate the number of marbles in the box?
(a) 166 (b) 156 (c) 152 (d) 162

Direction (Qs. 18-21): See the picture and answer the following questions. Here are the weight of 3 students.

Radha = 30 kg   Rahul = 20 kg   Rohit = 40 kg

18. The lightest student is __________?
(a) Radha (b) Rahul (c) Rohit (d) None of these

19. The heaviest student is __________?
(a) Rahul (b) Radha (c) Rohit (d) None of these

20. Radha is heavier than __________.
(a) Rohit (b) Rahul (c) Both (d) None of these

21. Rahul is __________ than Rohit and Radha.
(a) Heavier (b) Lighter
(c) Both (a) and (c) (d) None of these

Direction (Qs. 22-24): Estimate the weight of the given objects.

22. Estimate the weight of an Egg.

(a) 39 kg (b) 39 gm (c) 39 mL (d) 39 km

23. Estimate the weight of a Cherry.

(a) 7 g (b) 7 kg (c) 8 kg (d) 10 kg

24. Estimate the weight of a Television.

(a) 15 g (b) 20 gm (c) 10 gm (d) 15 kg

Direction (Qs. 25-28): The name of different objects are given below. Find out and write whether their weights will be expressed in grams or kilograms?

25. TOOTHPASTE Toothpaste __________?

(a) Grams (b) Kilograms

(c) Both (d) None of these

26. OREO Small pack of biscuit __________?

(a) kilogram (b) grams

(c) both (a) and (b) (d) None of these

27. Pumpkin __________?

(a) kg (b) g

(c) both (a) and (b) (d) None of these

28. Jackfruit __________?

(a) g (b) kg

(c) both (a) and (b) (d) None of these

29. Which of the following objects holds more liquid?

(a) Glass (b) Bottle (c) Cup (d) Tank

30. Look at the bottle filled with certain quantity of milk. Now, answer the following question.

Which bottle contains the most milk?

(a) Q (b) P (c) R (d) None of these

Answers and Explanations

Level-1

1. **(b)** John is the tallest and Miley is the shortest among them.
2. **(c)** The time will be 4 : 30 after 1 hour and 30 minutes.

   1 hour = 60 minutes

   Right now the time is = 3 'o' clock.

   After 1 hour the time will be = 4 'o' clock

   Then add 30 minutes more in it. So, the time will be 4 : 30.
3. **(c)** 900
4. **(a)** 200
5. **(b)** 59 + 12

   Round the figure to the nearest tens

59	⟶	60
+ 12	⟶	+ 10
		70

6. **(b)** 30
7. **(c)** 10
8. **(d)** C
9. **(d)** 6

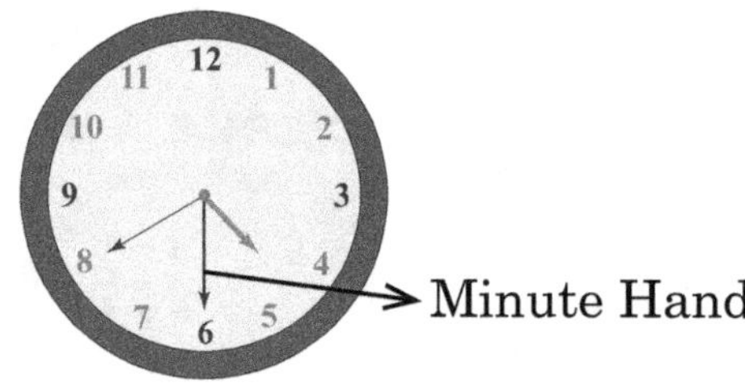

10 **(b)** 4

$$\begin{array}{r} {}^{1}\,{}^{1}\quad \\ 3\;9\;5 \\ +\,2\;\boxed{4}\;7 \\ \hline 6\;4\;2 \\ \hline \end{array}$$

11. **(d)** 18 years

   Present age of Mona = 6 years

   After 2 years her age will be

   = 6 + 2 years

   = 8 years

   Present age of Nitu = 8 years

   After 2 years her age will be

   = 8 + 2 years

   = 10 years

   Estimated sum of their ages is

   = 10 + 8 = 18 years
12. **(c)** ₹ 70

   Each day Aruna saves = ₹ 10

   In seven days she will save

   = 10 × 7

   = ₹ 70
13. **(b)** Eleventh, 30
14. **(d)** Bag of toffees can be bought with just ₹ 100.
15. **(a)** P is taller than S but shorter than Q.
16. **(a)** 20 __>__ 15, 20 is greater than 15.
17. **(b)** Hammer

18. **(a)** Stars are more than other items ★★★ ★★★ ★★ = 8.

19. **(c)** The approximate price range of a normal sharpener is ₹. 3-5.

20. **(c)** 8

Total number of toffees = 32

He gave 4 each to his friends.

Number of friends John have

= 32 ÷ 4

= 8

21. **(b)** Q and R

Q = 73

R = 69

73 + 69 = 142 kg

142 kg is below than 150 kg so both Q and R can travel in the lift easily.

22. **(b)** 34

	Tens	Ones
	5	4
−	2	0
	3	4

23. **(c)** 500 cm

1 m = 100 cm

5 m = 5 × 100 = 500 cm.

24. **(b)** 31 m 75 cm

		M	CM	
Raina has	=	6	00	ribbon
Raina's mother bought	= +	25	75	ribbon
Total length of ribbon		31	75	

31 m 75 cm

25. **(b)** Pooja drinks more lime water in a day.

26. **(c)** 4300 m = 4300 ÷ 1000

= 4 km 300 m

27. **(b)** Book S is thicker than all.

28. **(d)** We estimate the masses of the objects in kilograms and grams.

29. **(a)**

	kg	g
	①①	
Potato	1 0	250
Onion	+ 7	500
Tomato	2	400
	2 0 kg	150 gm

30. **(b)** 3 friends had doughnuts for breakfast.

Level-2

1. **(c)** Pineapple is the heaviest fruit among them. So, she will buy Pineapple.
2. **(c)** Pot S holds more water.
3. **(c)** Pikachu is taller than Jerry but shorter than Donald.
4. **(a)** 50 mL
5. **(c)** 2 kg
6. **(a)** 5 metres
7. **(c)** 3 kg
8. **(b)** 500 mL
9. **(b)** 8 cm
10. **(a)** Feather
11. **(d)**
12. **(a)** Meeta and John
13. **(c)**

    Total weight of rice bags = 35 kg

    Weight of each bag = 7 kg

    Number of bags Misha have

    = 35 ÷ 7 = 5

    Total Number of bags she has

    = 5 bags
14. **(a)**

    Sunny reaches school the earliest at 7:39 a.m.

    Ram reaches school last at 7:50 a.m.
15. **(b)**

    It takes 3 cups of water to fill up teapot.

    2 teapots contain 3 cups of water each.

    2 teapots (3 + 3) = 6 (Kettle)
16. **(c)**

    Number of sweets in 1 jar = 10

    Number of sweets in 3 jars

    = 10 × 3 = 30
17. **(d)**

		①
Total number of marbles	=	136
Number of marbles Siya put in the box	=	+ 26
Estimation of total number of marbles		162

18. **(b)** Rahul = 20 kg
19. **(c)** Rohit = 40 kg
20. **(b)** Rahul = 20 kg
21. **(b)** Lighter
22. **(b)** 39 gm
23. **(a)** 7 g
24. **(d)** 15 kg
25. **(a)** Grams
26. **(b)** Grams
27. **(a)** kg
28. **(b)** kg
29. **(d)** Tank
30. **(b)** Bottle P contains 3 liters of milk.

CHAPTER 11

PROBLEM SOLVING

OBJECTIVES

- Students will identify different problem solving styles and methods.
- They will apply methods to specific problems.
- A problem-solving approach can be used to encourage students to make generalization about rules and concepts.
- It develops students' confidence in their own ability to think mathematically.

INTRODUCTION

Problem solving is a process of working through details of a problem to reach a solution.

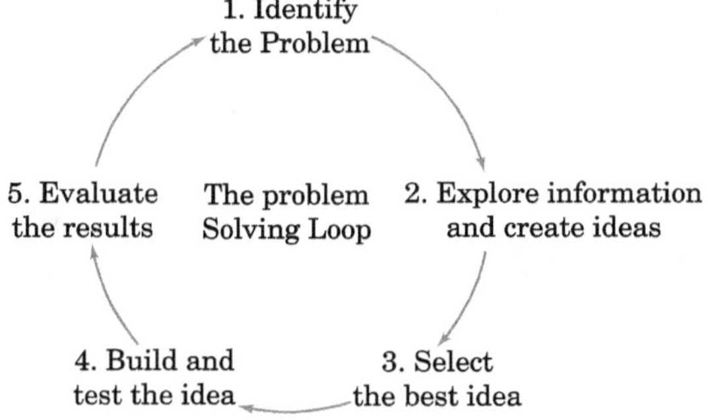

- Students will learn the use of one piece of information in the problem.
- They will organise the given information.

Examples:

1. Rihana plucks 5 flowers in her garden. The 1st flower is pink. The 2nd flower is white. The 3rd flower is pink. If this pattern continues, what colour is the 5th flower?

   (a) White (b) Pink (c) Red (d) Yellow

Ans. (b) The pattern is as follows:

1st flower	2nd flower	3rd flower	4th flower	5th flower
Pink	White	Pink	White	Pink

So, the colour of the 5th flower is Pink.

2. There are 2 bikes and 2 cars in a parking lot. How many wheels do they have in all?

(a) 16 (b) 8 (c) 24 (d) 12

Ans. (d)

Explanation

A bike has 2 wheels.

2 bikes have 2 + 2 = 4 wheels

A car has 4 wheels

2 cars have = 4 + 4 = 8 wheels

Total wheels = 4 + 8 = 12

3. Misha went to the grocery store. She bought 18 packs of cookies and 12 packs of noodles. How many packs of groceries did she buy in all?

(a) 12 (b) 26 (c) 30 (d) 18

Ans. (c)

18 + 12 = 30

So, she bought 30 packs of groceries in all.

4. Jay had 14 marbles in his collection. He lost 6 marbles. How many marbles does he have now?

(a) 20 (b) 14 (c) 6 (d) 8

Ans. (d)

14 – 6 = 8

He now has 8 marbles

5. • Lina said, "My number is the same as the number of fingers on my two hands."

- Mohit said, "My number is 4 less than Lina's."

What is Mohit's number?

(a) 5 (b) 6 (c) 7 (d) 10

Ans. (b)

Lina's number = Fingers in two hands = 10

Mohit's number = 10 – 4 = 6

LEVEL-1

1. Mohan starts his science exam practice from 1st December 20**. If he practises for 15 days then his practice finishes on _______?

December – 20**						
S	M	T	W	T	F	Saturday
				1	2	3
4	5	6	7	8	9	10
11	12	13	14	15	16	17
18	19	20	21	22	23	24
25	26	27	28	29	30	31

(a) Friday (b) Thursday (c) Saturday (d) Wednesday

2. Mrs. Meena gave drinks to the people coming to the fair. She gave 75 drinks. There were 12 people who did not get drinks. How many peoples were in the fair?

(a) 80 (b) 87 (c) 90 (d) 100

3. John sold 76 hot dogs with mustard. He sold 64 hot dogs with redish.

How many hot dogs were sold by John altogether?

(a) 120 (b) 160 (c) 140 (d) 98

4. Mrs. Khurana's biggest tomato was 20 pounds.

Mrs. Malik's biggest tomato was 14 pounds.

Mrs. Sharma's biggest tomato's weight was 3 pounds lighter than Mrs. Khurana's.

Whose tomato was lightest?

(a) Mrs. Khurana (b) Mrs. Malik

(c) Mrs. Sharma (d) None of these

5. Read the given information carefully and answer the following question.

I. Rishi and Jimmy like playing Hockey.

II. Kushal and Jimmy like to playing Badminton.

Who likes playing both the games?

(a) Jimmy (b) Rishi

(c) Kushal (d) Either Kushal or Rishi

6. Twelve children are on the ride. Five more get on and two get off.

How many children are now on the ride?

(a) 15 (b) 20 (c) 10 (d) 12

7. Cost of Drinks in the fair is ₹ 1.00 each.

How many drinks can Mr. John buy for ₹ 10/-?

(a) 5 (b) 10 (c) 8 (d) 15

8. A clown blew up 80 balloons and sold 50 balloons. He was left with _______ balloons?

(a) 30 (b) 25 (c) 20 (d) 40

Direction (Qs. 9 & 10): Study the given information and answer the following questions carefully. There are three friends namely A, B and C. Each of them likes different colours viz. Blue, Yellow, and Green.

- B does not like yellow and green.
- A likes yellow colour.

9. Who likes green colour?

(a) B (b) C

(c) A (d) Cannot be determined

10. Who does not like blue and green colour?

(a) B (b) A (c) C (d) None of these

11. Jenny ate 5 apple custards and 6 strawberry custards. Her Grandpa ate only apple custard. How many custards did Jenny eat?

(a) 12 (b) 13 (c) 14 (d) 11

12. There are three cities, A, B and C.

- A is not a hill station.
- B and C are not historical places.
- B and C are alike.

Which city is a historical place?

(a) A (b) B

(c) C (d) Cannot be determined.

13. In the school carnival Kiran is working at the popcorn stand. She started the day with 22 bags of popcorn. At noon she had 11 bags left. Now she is left with _______ bags?

(a) 15 (b) 20 (c) 11 (d) 25

14. Shivani and Ria are good at English. Kavya is good at Maths. Shivani and Kavya are good at Science. Who is good at English and Science?

(a) Ria (b) Kavya (c) Shivani (d) None of these

15. Shalu saw 6 chocolates at the chocolate shop. The 1st chocolate was Dairy Milk. The 2nd chocolate was Kit-Kat. The 3rd chocolate was Dairy Milk. If this pattern continues, what chocolate was the 6th chocolate?

(a) Snickers (b) Munch (c) Dairy Milk (d) Kit-Kat

16. The cost of a ticket for bumper car ride is ₹ 50. Radha buys 3 tickets. How much do the tickets cost in all?

(a) 120 (b) 130 (c) 140 (d) 150

17. Fifteen people picked a card from the deck in the magical show. Four people put their cards back. How many people did not put their cards back?

(a) 15 + 4 (b) 15 – 4 (c) 27 – 13 (d) 30 + 15

18. Aayat is taller than Shreya and Shreya is taller than Pulkit and Pulkit is taller than Ronit. Who is shortest among them?

(a) Shreya (b) Ronit (c) Pulkit (d) Aayat

19. The clown show at the circus is the most popular show. There are 10 clown shows today. Each show uses two helpers from the audience. How many helpers will be used in all at today's clown show?

(a) 5 (b) 10 (c) 15 (d) 20

Direction (Qs. 20 & 21): Read the following information carefully and answer the questions based on it.

Gopal is shorter than Ashok but taller than Kunal. Naveen is shorter than Kunal.

20. Who is tallest?

(a) Gopal (b) Ashok (c) Kunal (d) Naveen

21. Who is shortest?

(a) Gopal (b) Ashok (c) Kunal (d) Naveen

22. A bee has 6 legs. How many legs do 6 bees have?

(a) 12 (b) 36 (c) 18 (d) 24

23. Hitesh is older than Jaya. Amit is older than Hitesh.

Which one of the following statements is correct?

(a) Jaya is the oldest (b) Hitesh is the youngest

(c) Hitesh is younger than Amit (d) Amit is the youngest

24. In a school, A and B were teaching Hindi and English. C and B were teaching English and Maths. Who among the teachers was teaching English, Hindi and Maths?

(a) B (b) C (c) A (d) None

25. Tina read 20 pages of her Novel yesterday. Today, She read 7 pages. What is the total number of pages did she read?

(a) 27 (b) 13 (c) 7 (d) 20

Direction (Qs. 26 & 27): Study the given information carefully and answer the questions.

The following picture illustrates the schedule of Laveena's foods. She starts with Pasta at 9:00 am and rotates the wheel by one step in clockwise direction to find the food for the next hour

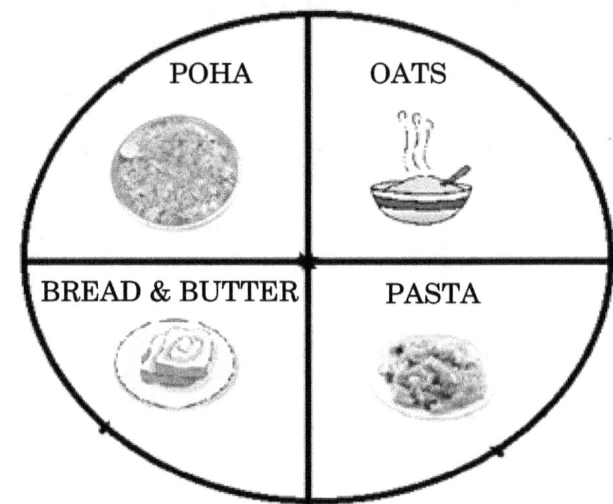

26. What will she eat after 2 hours?

(a) Bread and Butter (b) Oats

(c) Poha (d) Pasta

27. What will she eat at 12:00 noon?

(a) Poha (b) Oats

(c) Bread and Butter (d) Pasta

28. Megan has 12 seashells. How many more seashells does she need to find to have 24 seashells in her collection?

(a) 12 (b) 36 (c) 24 (d) 16

Direction (Qs. 29 & 30): Some friends were sitting on a rectangular table in a café to celebrate Shorya's birthday. Answer the following questions based on the picture shown.

29. Who is seated opposite to Riya?

    (a) Chinu (b) Rihan (c) Kavya (d) Golu

30. How many friends were there to celebrate Shorya's birthday?

    (a) 7 (b) 6 (c) 8 (d) 10

LEVEL-2

Direction (Qs. 1 & 2): Study the information carefully and answer the following questions.

Raj, Dev, Manav and Juhi competed in the long jump. Their jump lengths were 9 feet, 10 feet, 11 feet and 12 feet. Juhi jumped the farthest. Dev jumped an even number of feet. Manav jumped farther than Raj.

1. Who jumped at the least distance?

   (a) Raj (b) Dev (c) Manav (d) Juhi

2. Who jumped at the third place, if boys are arranged in ascending order on the basis of their jumps?

   (a) Raj (b) Dev (c) Manav (d) Juhi

3. Ahna lives in a building. There are two floors above and one floor below her floor. How many floors are there in the building?

   (a) 5 floors (b) 2 floors (c) 3 floors (d) 4 floors

4. Sunny asked Nancy to move 1 step away forward. If he is on the second step, where will she be after moving?

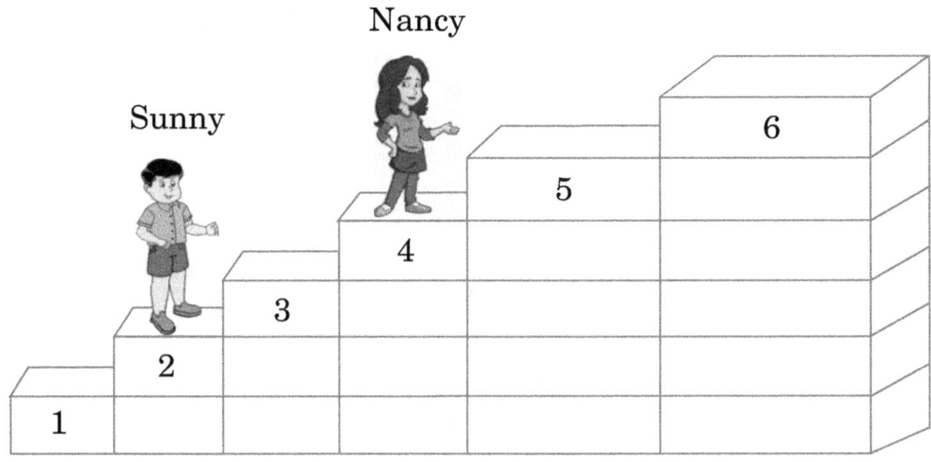

   (a) Third step (b) Fourth step (c) Sixth step (d) Fifth step

5. Five boys took part in a race. Shivam finished before Rishab but behind Adi. Kabir finished before Manan but behind Rishab. Who won the race?

   (a) Rishab (b) Manan (c) Adi (d) Kabir

Direction (Qs. 6-7): Study the given information carefully and answer the following questions.

Four boys, A, B, C and D are sitting around the corners of a rectangular table facing at the centre.

6. If A and C interchange their positions, who will be sitting right to the A?

   (a) B (b) D (c) A (d) C

7. Who is sitting left of B?

   (a) A (b) C (c) D (d) None of these

8. In a contest the first cow ate 10 bunches of grass. The second cow ate 13 bunches of grass. How many more bunches of grass were eaten by the second cow from the first one?

   (a) 3 (b) 5 (c) 2 (d) 7

9. Montu is a prize winning boy. He has 14 ribbons at home.

   He wins 4 more ribbons today. How many ribbons does Montu have in all?

   (a) 14 – 4 (b) 18 – 4 (c) 14 + 4 (d) 10 – 4

Direction (Qs. 10 & 11): Read the given information carefully and answer the following questions

Kush, Vaani and Ramesh each has a pet dog.

- Vaani's dog is smaller than Ramesh's dog.
- Ramesh's dog is neither the biggest nor the smallest.

10. Who has the biggest dog?

    (a) Kush (b) Vaani (c) Ramesh (d) None of these

11. Who has the smallest dog?

(a) Vaani (b) Kush (c) Ramesh (d) None of these

Direction (Qs. 12-14): Study the given information carefully and answer the following questions.

A. The girl's house has more than three windows.

B. The fireman's house has one less than three windows.

C. The doctor's house has one more window than the fireman's.

D. The boy's house does not have more than one window.

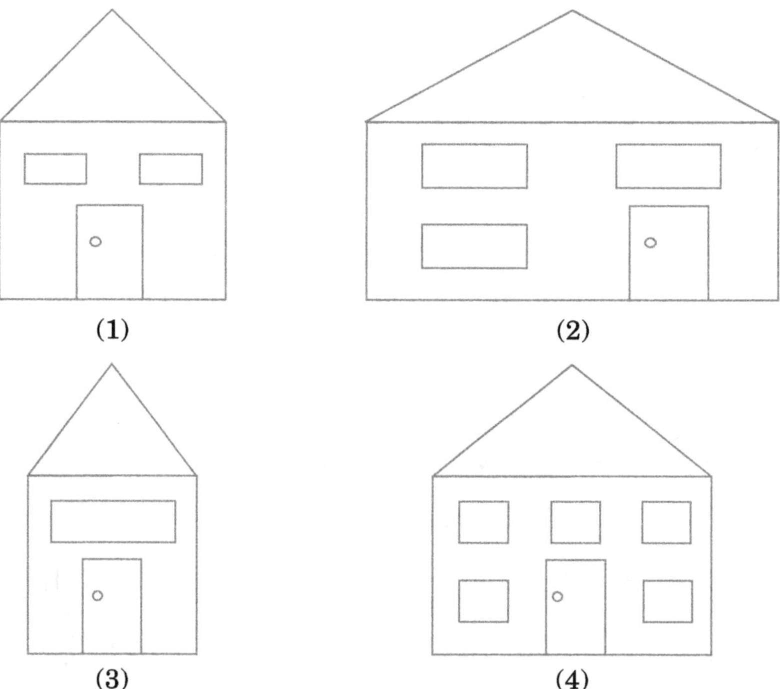

12. Whose house has only one window?

(a) The girl (b) The boy (c) The fireman (d) The doctor

13. How many windows does girl's house have?

(a) 1 (b) 2 (c) 3 (d) 5

14. Whose house has two windows?

(a) The girl (b) The boy (c) The fireman (d) The doctor

Direction (Qs. 15 & 16): Read the given clues and answer the following questions.

- There are five shelves. Each shelf has different toys.
- The boat is in the middle shelf.
- The skipping rope is in the top shelf.
- The ball is next to the boat.
- The teddy is in between the boat and the car.

15. Which toy is kept in between the skipping rope and the boat?

(a) Teddy (b) Ball (c) Boat (d) Skipping rope

16. Which toy is kept in shelf - 2 ?

(a) Teddy (b) Boat (c) Ball (d) Car

Direction (Qs. 17 & 18): Study the information carefully and answer the following questions.

- There are 50 children in a play school.
- There are total 3 groups.
- In group 2 there are a total of 20 children.
- In group 1 there are half as many children in group 2.
- Group 3 has the same number of children as in group 2.

17. How many children are there in group 1.

(a) 50 (b) 20 (c) 10 (d) 30

18. Which statement is correct?

(a) No group has the same number of children.

(b) Group 3 has the maximum number of children.

(c) Group 2 has double as many children in group 1.

(d) None of these

19. Taaz is older than Naaz. Naaz was seven 3 years ago. Saaz is 5 years old. Which one of the following statements is correct?

(a) Taaz is seven years old.

(b) Naaz is four years old.

(c) Saaz is half of Naaz's age.

(d) None of these

20. A, P and R sitting in a row. A and P are at the ends. Who is sitting in the middle?

(a) A (b) P (c) R (d) None

Direction (Qs. 21-25): Study the information carefully and answer the following questions.

A, B, C and D are sitting on a bench. A is sitting next to B, D is sitting next to C. C is on the third position from left.

21. Who is sitting at the right corner?

(a) A (b) B (c) C (d) D

22. Who is sitting at the second position from right?

(a) A (b) B (c) C (d) D

23. Which two persons are sitting in the middle?

(a) BA (b) BD (c) AC (d) AD

24. Who is sitting at the left corner?

(a) A (b) B (c) C (d) D

25. Who is sitting at the second place from left?

(a) A (b) B (c) C (d) D

26. Rai, Sai, Kavi and Raag swam in a race. Rai had the best time. Raag was not faster than Sai. Kavi came second. Which diagram below shows the correct order of the boys from fastest to slowest?

	Fastest			Slowest
(a)	Rai	Sai	Kavi	Raag
(b)	Rai	Kavi	Sai	Raag
(c)	Rai	Kavi	Raag	Sai
(d)	Raag	Kavi	Sai	Rai

27. Sheena had 20 balloons. 2 of them popped. She gave 2 balloons to her brother and 4 to her best friend. Now, she has _______ balloons?

(a) 18 (b) 12 (c) 15 (d) 20

28. A fast food place sells french fries, hot dogs and burgers. A packet of french fries costs more money than a hotdog but less than a burger. Which fast food costs the most?

(a) French Fries (b) Hot dogs

(c) Burgers (d) None of these

29. The students in the science club were collecting bugs for their bug collection. Zara caught 10 bugs and Rohit caught 8 bugs. Karan caught 18 bugs and Mehar caught 6 bugs. How many bugs did they have all together?

(a) 36 (b) 28 (c) 42 (d) 24

30. Liya wants to make 55 jumps over the jump rope. Shalini wants to make 20 jumps over the jump rope. Liya has only 25. How many more jumps does Liya need to make?

(a) 20 (b) 30 (c) 40 (d) 50

31. In a cricket match, Vijay scored 20 runs. Mohit scored 5 runs more than Vijay. Vicky scored the same number of runs as Vijay. Who scored the highest runs.

(a) Vijay (b) Mohit (c) Vicky (d) None

Answers and Explanations

Level-1

1. **(b)** Mohan's practice finishes on 15th December 20** and the day will be Thursday.

2. **(b)**

Number of people who got drinks	=	75
Number of people who did not get drinks	=	12
Total number of people in the fair	=	75 + 12 = 87

3. **(c)**

Number of Mustard hot dogs sold by John	=	76
Number of Radish hot dogs sold by John	=	64
Total hot dogs sold by John	=	76 + 64 = 140

4. **(b)**

Weight of Mrs. Khurana's tomato	=	20 pounds
Weight of Mrs. Malik's tomato	=	14 pounds
Weight of Mrs. Sharma's tomato	=	20 – 3 = 17 pounds

20 pounds > 17 pounds > 14 pounds

So, Mrs. Malik's tomato was 'lightest'.

5. **(a)** According to the given information,

Persons / Games	**Hockey**	**Badminton**
Rishi	√	
Jimmy	√	√
Kushal		√

So, from the above table it is clear that, Jimmy likes playing both the games.

6. (a)

Total number of children on the ride	=	12
Five more get on it	=	12 + 5 = 17
Number of children get off from the ride	=	2
Total number of children are now on the ride	=	17 – 2 = 15

7. (b)

Cost of each drink	=	₹ 1.00/-
Cost of 10 drinks	=	1 × 10 = 10/-

So, Mr. John can buy 10 drinks from ₹ 10/-.

8. (a)

Total number of balloons blew up by clown	=	80
Number of balloons sold	=	50
Total number of balloons left with clown	=	80 – 50 = 30

9. (b)

Person	Colour
A	Yellow
B	Blue
C	Green

It is clear from the above table that C likes green colour.

10. (b) A like yellow colour, so he does not like blue and green colour.

11. (d) Jenny ate = 5 + 6 = 11

So, Jenny ate 11 custards.

12. (a) B and C are hillstations.

So, A is a historical place.

13. (c)

She started the day with	=	22 bags
In afternoon she had	=	11 bags
Now she is left with	=	22 – 11 = 11 bags.

14. (c) According to the given information,

	English	Maths	Science
Shivani	√		√
Ria	√		
Kavya		√	√

So, only Shivani is good at English and Science.

15. (d) The pattern is as follows:

1st chocolate	2nd chocolate	3rd chocolate	4th chocolate	5th chocolate	6th chocolate
Dairy Milk	Kit-Kat	Dairy Milk	Kit-Kat	Dairy Milk	Kit-Kat

So, the 6th chocolate was Kit-Kat.

16. (d)

Cost of 1 ticket for bumper car ride = ₹ 50

Cost of 3 tickets car ride = 50×3 = ₹ 150

17. (b)

Number of people picked the card from the deck = 15

Number of people put their cards back = 4

Number of people did not put their cards back = $15 - 4$

So, $15 - 4$ people did not put their cards back.

18. (b) Aayat > Shreya > Pulkit > Ronit.

So, Ronit is shortest among them.

19. (d)

Number of shows today = 10

Each show uses 2 helpers from the audience = $10 \times 2 = 20$

So, 20 helpers will be used in all at today's clown show.

Solutions: (20 & 21)

Ashok > Gopal > Kunal > Naveen

20. (b) Ashok is tallest.

21. (d) Naveen is shortest.

22. (b) $6 \times 6 = 36$

The bees have 36 legs in all.

23. (c) Amit > Hitesh > Jaya

So, Hitesh is younger than Amit.

24. (a) According to the given information,

	Hindi	English	Maths
A	√	√	
B	√	√	√
C		√	√

So, it is clearly shown from the above table that, teacher B was teaching all the three subjects.

25. (a) 20 + 7 = 27

So, She read 27 pages.

26. (c) She will eat Poha after 2 hours.

27. (b) She will eat Oats at 12:00 noon.

28. (a) 24-12=12

So, Megan needs 12 more seashells.

29. (d) Golu is seated opposite to Riya.

30. (a) There were 7 friends to celebrate Shorya's birhtday.

Level-2

1. (a)

Raj	<	Dev	<	Manav	<	Juhi
(9 feet)		(10 feet)		(11 feet)		(12 feet)

So, Raj jumped at the least distance.

2. (c) Ascending Order:

Raj	<	Dev	<	Manav	<	Juhi
(9 feet)		(10 feet)		(11 feet)		(12 feet)

3. (d)

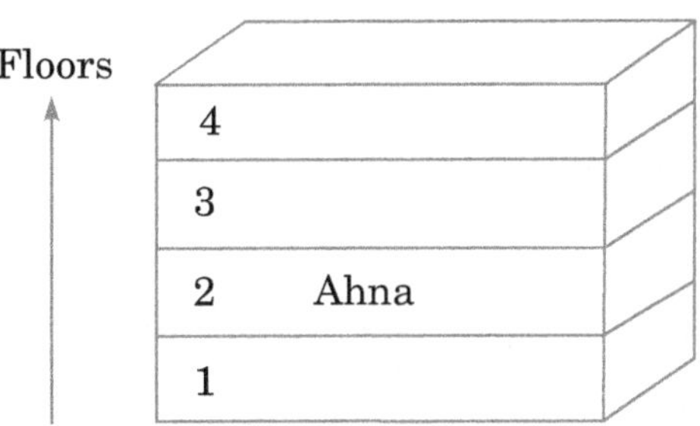

So, it is clear from the above figure that there are four floors in the building.

4. (d)

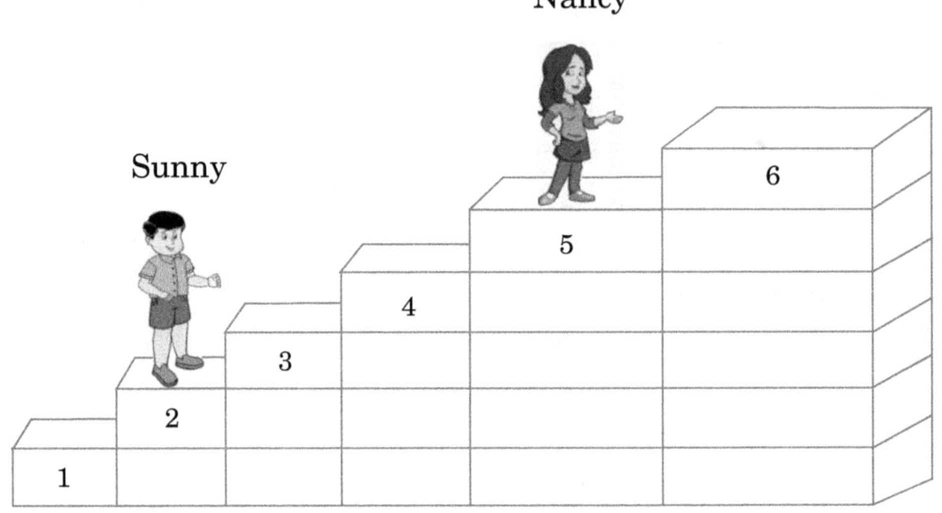

So, Nancy will be on 5th step.

5. **(c)** Adi > Shivam > Rishab > Kabir > Manan

So, Adi won the race.

6. **(b)** Sitting Arrangement after Interchanging

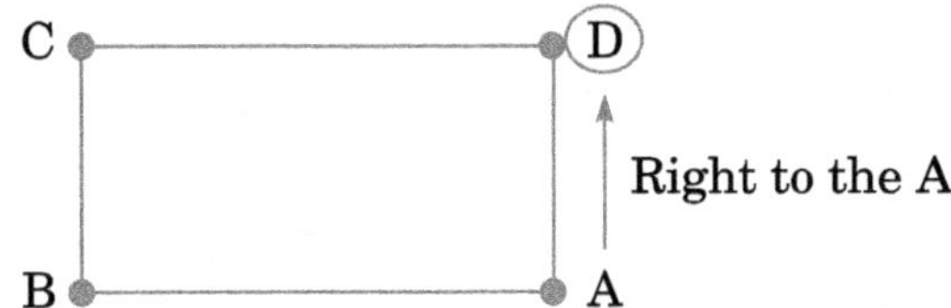

So, D is sitting right to the A.

7. **(a)**

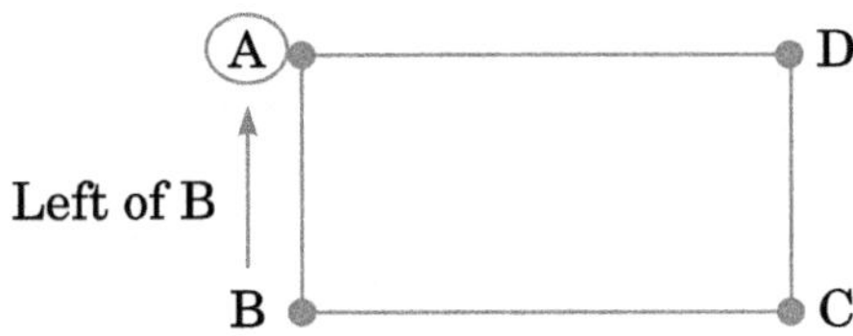

A is sitting left of B.

8. **(a)**

Total bunches of grass eaten by the first cow = 10

Total bunches of grass eaten by second cow = 13

Number of more bunches of grass eaten by the second cow from the first one = 13 – 10 = 3

3 more bunches of grass eaten by the second cow.

9. **(c)** 14 + 4

Solutions: (10 & 11):

Persons	Dog
 Kush	
 Vaani	
 Ramesh	

10. **(a)** Kush has the biggest dog.

11. **(a)** Vaani has the smallest dog.

12. **(b)** The boy's house has only one window.

13. **(d)** The girl's house has five windows.

14. **(c)** The fireman's house has two windows.

15. (b)

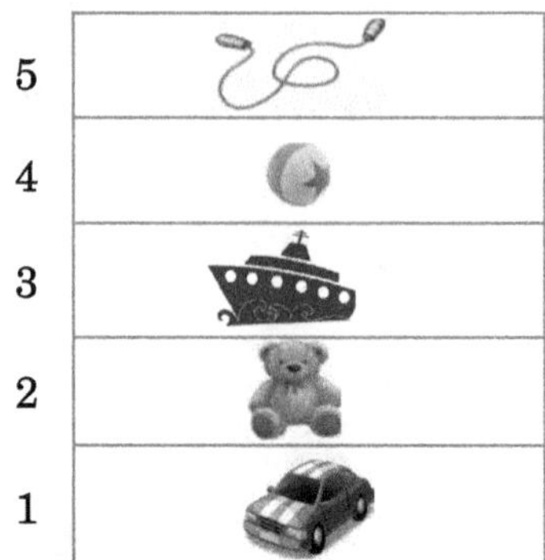

Ball is kept in between the skipping rope and the boat.

16. (a)

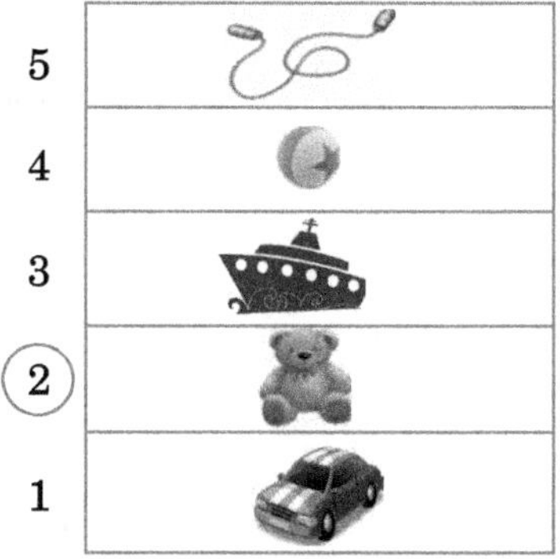

Teddy is kept in shelf 2.

17. (c) Number of children in group 2 = 20

Number of children in group 1 = half of 20 = 10

18. (c) Group 1 has = 10 children

Group 2 has = 20 children (10 + 10)

19. (c) Naaz's current age = 7 + 3 = 10

Saaz's age = half of 10 = 5

20. (c)

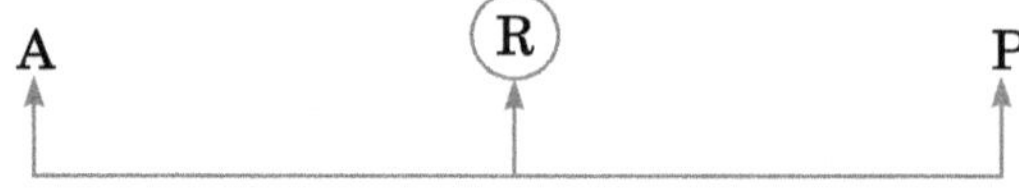

It is clearly shown from the above diagram that R is sitting in the middle.

Solutions: (21-25):

Sitting Arrangement

21. (d) D is sitting at the right corner.

22. (c) C is sitting at the second position from right.

23. (c) A C are sitting in the middle.

24. (b) B is sitting at the left corner.

25. (a) A is sitting at the second place form left.

26. (b) Correct Order of Boys from fastest to slowest:

Rai > Kavi > Sai > Raag.

27. (b)

Sheena had total 20 balloons.

Number of balloons popped	=	2
Number of balloons given to her brother	=	2
Number of balloons given to her best friend	=	4

Now, she has = 20 – (2 + 2 + 4)

= 20 – 8

= 12.

28. (c)

Burger > French Fries > Hot dog

So, Burger costs the most.

29. (c) 10 + 8 + 18 + 6 = 42

So, they have 42 bugs all together.

30. **(b)** 55 – 25 = 30

So, Liya needs 30 jumps to make

31. **(b)** Vijay and Vicky scored 20 runs

Mohit scored 5 runs more than Vijay i.e. 20 + 5 = 25 runs

So, Mohit scored the highest runs.

www.ingramcontent.com/pod-product-compliance
Lightning Source LLC
LaVergne TN
LVHW080847170826
845678LV00006B/1729

* 9 7 8 9 3 5 5 6 4 4 0 3 9 *